Intermediate Tropical Agriculture Series

D1745315

General Editor

Dr W. J. A. Payne

Consultant in tropical livestock production

Agricultural Economics and Marketing in the Tropics

2nd edition

J. C. Abbott Ph.D.

Formerly Agricultural Services Division, FAO, Rome

J. P. Makeham

Department of Agricultural Economics and Business Management
University of New England, Australia

Longman

Longman Scientific and Technical
Longman Group UK Limited,
Longman House, Burnt Mill, Harlow,
Essex CM20 2JE, England
and Associated Companies throughout the world

First published 1990

British Library Cataloguing in Publication Data

Abbott, J. C. (John Cave), *1919–*
    Agricultural economics and marketing in the tropics. –
    2nd ed – (Intermediate tropical agriculture series)
    1. Tropical regions. Agricultural industries.
    I. Title   II. Makeham, J. P.   III. Series 338.1'0913

ISBN 0-582-02903-1

Contents

Acknowledgements

Chapters 1, 2, 3 and 5 were written mainly by J. C. Abbott. J. A. Mollett kindly read the section on planning and H. Meliczek that on land tenure systems; each made valuable suggestions.

Chapter 4, on Farm management is, with minor modifications, the work of Professor J. P. Makeham. He also advised on the approach adopted in the text as a whole. J. E. Bessell kindly read Chapter 4 and made valuable suggestions for its organisation. C. Perch helped draft the section on estimating future prices.

When they made their contributions all of the above were working for the Food and Agriculture Organisation (FAO) of the United Nations. They have drawn freely upon its materials and sources. They gratefully acknowledge the assistance they have received from the Organisation and many colleagues on its staff. This does not mean that FAO necessarily subscribes to all the statements made in this text. For these the authors are personally responsible.

The Publisher is grateful to Dr Abbott for providing the photographs on pages 30, 51, 56, 58 and 84 and the Food and Agriculture Organisation for providing the photographs on pages 50, 52 and 53.

The Publisher would like to thank Anne Bolt for permission to reproduce the cover photograph.

Other titles in the Intermediate Tropical Agriculture Series

Already published:

H. T. B. Hall, *Diseases and Parasites of Livestock in the Tropics*, Second Edition
Describes the causes, symptoms, treatment and control of the main diseases of livestock in the Tropics.

C. N. Williams, W. Y. Chew and J. H. Rajaratnam, *Tree and Field Crops of the Wetter Regions of the Tropics*

Details are supplied of the botany, climatic and soil requirements, cultivation and management, harvesting and, where appropriate, processing of a large number of crops.

J. A. Eusebio, *Pig Production in the Tropics*
Covers all aspects of pig raising in tropical areas, including nutrition, housing, breeding and marketing, with relevant biological details.

M. E. Adams, *Agricultural Extension in Developing Countries*
Explains the background and practicalities of extension work in the developing world.

H. F. Heady and E. B. Heady, *Range and Wildlife Management in the Tropics*
Covers all aspects of rangeland from planting and maintenance to cultural considerations.

D. Y. Coy, *Accounting and Finance for Managers in Tropical Agriculture*
A useful guide to modern accounting practice for both students of agriculture and farm managers.

C. Devendra and G. B. McLeroy, *Goat and Sheep Production in the Tropics*
Provides comprehensive coverage of how to rear and maintain healthy, productive goats and sheep in the Tropics. Includes sections on breeds, nutrition, reproduction, health and breed improvement.

D. H. Hill, *Cattle and Buffalo Meat Production in the Tropics*
Covers key aspects of tropical cattle and buffalo meat production, from different breeds to management systems and methods of slaughter.

D. S. Hill and J. M. Waller, *Pests and Diseases of Tropical Crops. Volume 1: Principles and methods of control*
A comprehensive coverage of chemical control including methods of application together with information on biological and integrated control methods.
Volume 2: Field Handbook
Outlines the damage to plants resulting from attack by pests and diseases. Major crops of tropical regions are listed and their pests and diseases detailed with reference to symptoms, distribution and treatment.

E. Heath and S. Olusanya, *Anatomy and Physiology of Tropical Livestock*
Based on body systems, this covers a wide range of agricultural animals including less familiar livestock.

D. Gibbon and A. Pain, *Crops of the Drier Regions of the Tropics*
Part 1 deals with basic ecological principles while Part 2 is a survey of different crops. Problems and potential for future development are considered in the final section.

Titles in preparation:

R. L. Humphreys, *Tropical Pastures and Fodder Crops*, Second Edition

A. Chamberlain, *Milk Production in the Tropics*

Preface

This text on Agricultural Economics and Marketing is aimed at the needs of students in agricultural colleges who are taking a subsidiary course in the economics of agriculture. For students who are specialising in agricultural economics we hope that this proves to be a valuable first book. We have also aimed the book at agricultural administration and extension staff, people concerned with the work of private and cooperative marketing enterprises, input distribution agencies and marketing boards, and at progressive farmers.

While the main principles of economics in relation to agriculture still hold good, this second edition of *Agricultural Economics and Marketing in the Tropics* includes substantial new material. The chapter on marketing has been strengthened by the addition of a second part on management and operations. Government price policies receive special treatment. The chapter on Development reflects changes in thought and practice over the past decade. Illustrations and texts recommended for further reading have been brought up to date.

The book will introduce readers to economic principles as applied to agriculture, farm management techniques and marketing methods and it will show how they can be useful in day-to-day operations. It should provide an insight into, and deepen understanding of, the continuing inter-relationship between agricultural production and marketing.

We have chosen to show the application of the principles and techniques to conditions in the Tropics, because of the rapid increase in the numbers of students in colleges there, and because of interest in assisting the development of such countries. Most books on agricultural marketing and farm management available at present are written in terms of temperate agriculture and of conditions where it is better to economise on labour than capital.

A book adapted to the conditions of the tropical countries and focusing on their problems, institutions and employment conditions was lacking. With the deepening experience of development activities in the tropical countries over the last decade, and greatly increasing interest in research into agricultural production and marketing problems, the authors have had access to a rich source of information. While necessarily some of the data and examples presented in the text will be overtaken by events, it is hoped that they will have served their purpose of illustrating the principles under discussion.

To help the reader make best use of this book and find easily the material most suited to his purposes, the main headings of each chapter are listed in the table of contents. At the end of each chapter there is a summary of the main points and conclusions. Issues calling for further discussion are set out to stimulate thought and study on the part of the reader. Each chapter constitutes part of an integral whole with each section helping the reader to understand the next one better. Though the subjects treated are different, readers may be surprised to see how the same economic principles find expression in different contexts.

To support the written explanations of the subject matter presented, the authors have made considerable use of charts, photographs and tabulated data; they have also called on the skills of professional communicators to help present their message. The tables appearing in this book should not be regarded as a source of up-to-date statistical information for quotation elsewhere: their purpose is to support a point made in the text. For current information, reference should be made to recent United Nations, World Bank and FAO Yearbooks and specialised studies; to the reports of national governments, banks and marketing institutions; and to studies from universities and research institutes.

A selection of material for further reading is presented at the end of each chapter. These books are listed not so much to reinforce points made by the authors, but because they help to provide a broader coverage of the subject. Please remember that these references make up only a small part of a rapidly growing literature on agricultural economics and marketing in the tropical countries.

Glossary

activity Any specific form of agricultural production, e.g. maize, cattle or yam production.

arbitrage The movement of supplies between one place and another until prices come into balance, taking into account transport costs.

average cost The total costs of production or marketing, divided by total output or amount handled.

average revenue The total receipts or amounts paid for goods or services, divided by the total quantity of goods or services sold.

broker An agent who brings buyers and sellers together and receives a fee for this service.

budget A detailed quantitative statement of a plan for a farm or marketing enterprise together with the costs involved and the returns expected.

capital Goods which have not been used up including land, equipment, livestock and money. (See also **fixed**, and **working**.)

capital gains Increase in the value of capital items due to a rise in their market price.

capital investment Money spent on equipment, stock or on improvement which has a life of more than one year and which adds to the productive capacity of the farm.

capital output ratio (or capital coefficient) The relationship between the capital put into a project and the value of its annual output when the project is fully operational.

cash flow The movement of money in and out of the hands of an enterprise or individual farmer. (See also **net**.)

c.i.f. Cost, insurance, freight. The buyer pays for a product which is delivered to an agreed destination, the cost being met by the seller.

commission agent He receives and sells produce for another person and is paid for his service as a percentage of the price obtained.

compounding Adding interest to a sum of money at the going market rate, including interest on the interest accumulated each year.

contingency allowance Allowance to cover unexpected events, e.g. a drought resulting in severe losses of cattle or crops.

costs (see **average**, **marginal**, **operating**, **opportunity**, **overhead**, **variable**.)

cyclical price variations Recurring movements in average prices over a period of years, due to changes in demand or supply conditions and delayed production response.

demand The amount of a product or service that will be bought at a given price.

depreciation The loss in value of capital equipment, etc. as it becomes older.

depreciation allowance The sum of money which is deducted from income each year so that funds are available to replace equipment, etc. when it is worn out.

discounting Estimating the present value of money available at a later date by allowing for the interest that would accumulate on it at going market rates.

elasticity of demand The responsiveness of demand to a change in price or a change in income.

external economies Advantages gained by an enterprise or country through easy access to supplies, markets, skilled labour, financial research and service facilities or other productive resources that are already available. An enterprise benefits from these when it locates in an area where they are already available.

fixed capital Land, buildings, wells, irrigation equipment, etc., which cannot easily be moved.

f.o.b. Free on board. The buyer is responsible for freight charges, insurance charges and risks incurred during transport of the goods to his receiving point.

futures Quantities of a commodity of defined quality for delivery at an agreed future date.

gross domestic product (GDP) Total value of all goods and services produced in a country during one year. It differs from GNP by excluding external earnings from investments and services.

gross margin Activity gross income minus variable costs of activity.

gross national product (GNP) Total value of all goods and services produced by a country during one year, including foreign earnings from investments, payments for services and remittances home by workers in other countries.

hedging Insuring against a loss on holding stocks of a commodity due to a price change during the period of ownership.

income elasticity The responsiveness of demand to changes in income.

inflation An increase in the supply of money in relation to the goods and services available and, in consequence, a decline in its value.

infrastructure Facilities and services. The material infrastructure of a country includes roads, vehicles, ports, stores, factories, capital equipment. The social infrastructure includes health, education, housing, welfare and community services.

internal economies Advantages gained by an enterprise or country through its ability to use existing equipment, management, advertising and other productive resources, over a large volume of output.

internal rate of return The discount rate at which the present value of a future income from a project equals the present value of total expenditure (capital and annual costs) on the project.

marginal cost The extra cost incurred in growing or selling an additional unit of product.

marginal revenue The extra net income obtained from growing or selling one additional unit of product.

marginal utility The extra benefit obtained from acquiring one additional unit of a product or service. Generally this utility tends to decline as additional units are obtained.

marketing margin The difference between the purchase price and resale price of a product retained by either a marketing agency, or the marketing system as a whole.

monopoly There is only one seller of a certain product or service.

monopsony There is only one buyer of a certain product or service.

net cash flow The difference between the money received and the money spent in any one period (week, month, year).

oligopoly There are only a few sellers of a certain product or service so that each will be affected substantially by a change in policy on the part of another.

oligopsony There are only a few buyers so that each will be affected substantially be a change in policy on the part of another.

operating costs Variable costs plus overhead costs.

operating profit Gross income less operating costs.

opportunity costs Income foregone by keeping a given set of resources out of the most profitable alternative use that would be practicable.

overhead (fixed) costs Costs which do not vary greatly as the level of production or mixture of activities changes.

parameter Any factor which has an important effect on operating profit (yield, price, hectarage, direct cost).

price variations (See **cyclical** and **seasonal**.)

retailer An enterprise which sells in relatively small quantities to consumers.

revenue (See **average** and **marginal**.)

seasonal price variations Movements in average prices within one year generated by the bunching of output during a limited production season or seasons.

secular trends Tendencies which show up over very long periods and for practical purposes can be considered permanent.

spot price The price for a product available for immediate delivery.

supply The amount of a product or service that will be offered for sale at a given price.

variable (direct) costs Costs which vary as the level of production varies.

warehousing Provision of a guaranteed storage service in return for a fee.

wholesaler An enterprise which sells in relatively large quantities to retailers or other merchants rather than to consumers.

working capital Capital needed to finance the production or marketing cycle, from the initial outlay on preparing the ground, or making an advance on a purchase, to receiving the proceeds from selling the product.

1 Introduction

Meaning of economics

Economics is the science of analysing the use of limited resources to achieve desired ends. As with most disciplines, considerable skill is required in applying economic principles to solve practical problems. Such application involves:

(**a**) deciding between alternative ways of using resources;
(**b**) satisfying different needs and wants for which there are varying degrees of preference;
(**c**) above all, taking into account human behaviour and decision-making on the best way to use available resources.

Although economics is a science of material considerations, it is not just concerned with money. Practical economics can help people in tropical countries obtain better food and services, more goods and a higher level of living in general.

Application of economics to agriculture

The discipline of agricultural economics adapts the principles of economics to the problems of agriculture and people engaged in agriculture. It is of very great help to people who have to decide what kind of food, and how much of each type of food should be produced in order to supply the needs of a country. It also aids decisions about which crops will be the most profitable for the farmer to grow. Economic theory can explain why the price of many foods goes up and down during the course of a year and why the price paid by the consumer is usually much more than that received by the farmer. Through the insights of economics, which sometimes have to be reinforced by keeping certain records and accounts, a farmer can obtain a higher income from his land. Similarly, a marketing enterprise, a cooperative or a marketing board can raise its earnings and provide a better service.

Governments of tropical countries also depend greatly on the practical guides provided by the discipline of agricultural economics when they formulate their policies. Agriculture is usually the main national resource. Governments are responsible for fostering agricultural development so that the domestic needs of their own country are best supplied. They may also want to produce a type and quality of goods desired by other countries. Exports are needed to earn foreign exchange to pay for the importation of products and services that cannot be provided domestically. To meet this responsibility, governments need sound advice. Such advice depends, to a great extent, on a skilled use of agricultural economic analysis.

Proposed treatment of agricultural economics

The application of economic principles to agriculture, and the marketing of agricultural products, is explained in the chapters which follow. Chapter 2 explains how prices are determined. It describes the factors that influence the level of prices and shows how differences in price may occur between one time and place and another. Chapter 3 explains the role of the marketing system in finding outlets for farmers' crops and livestock products. It examines common problems and weaknesses in marketing organisations and marketing methods in the tropical countries and points to ways of improvement. Guiding principles in the planning and management of an enterprise engaged in marketing agricultural products or inputs are provided.

In Chapter 4, the focus shifts to the economics of agricultural production and the management of farms. It shows how land, labour, capital and risk-taking can be combined in varying proportions. It shows how to decide which combination is most profitable under a given set of conditions. This type of analysis may seem most useful to the larger farm units in the Tropics, which are more commercially oriented. Yet it is equally applicable to small farms. Many peasant farmers are already utilising farm management techniques, though not necessarily in such precise terms. Chapter 4 also explains accounting methods that can help a farmer to maintain close financial control over his business. He can then see quickly which sections are most profitable and which ones are suffering a loss. The principles and accounting procedures introduced in this chapter can be adapted to serve private cooperative or state farms as well as various kinds of agricultural marketing and supply enterprises.

The contribution of agriculture to the overall rate of development of tropical countries is examined in

Chapter 5. Pitfalls to be avoided in government intervention and ways of mobilising domestic and external resources to advantage are examined. This chapter is intended mainly to help those who expect to work in government departments, or in public development agencies. It will be useful, however, to leaders of farmers' organisations and all those who are in a position to influence government policies through the expression of their opinions. For their voice to be effective they must speak the language of the people they want to convince. We suggest that the language used be that of agricultural economics.

Agriculture in the Tropics

The tropical countries are those that lie approximately between the latitudes 23.5° North and South. In America the Tropics range from Mexico and Cuba in the North, to Paraguay and Brazil in the South. In Africa the range is from Mauritania and Sudan in the North, to Botswana and Madagascar in the South. In Asia the Tropics range from Bangladesh and Taiwan in the North, to Indonesia and Queensland, Australia in the South. Most of the Pacific Islands are also included in the Tropics. (See Fig. 1.1.) Tropical countries are characterised by the absence of seasonal changes in day length,

by high average temperatures and, especially in the arid and semi-arid regions, by high radiation.

These conditions usually determine the crops that can be grown efficiently, although the range may be modified by altitude. In East Central Africa, and in many parts of Latin America, there are substantial areas over 2 000 metres above sea level. Thus, while coffee, cocoa, tea, sugar cane, groundnuts, coconuts, pineapple, bananas and rice are typical products of tropical agriculture, cotton, maize and millet are also widely grown. Even temperate crops, such as wheat and 'European' vegetables, can be found in areas which are climatically favourable because of the altitude. Table 1.1 shows the variety and quantity of vegetables offered for sale during one year in a typical tropical city. The wide range of types is an indication of the choice open to consumers, and also of the crops which farmers produce and which the marketing system must be equipped to handle.

Figure 1.2 shows the relative value of different products in the total agricultural output of Mexico before the petroleum boom of the 1970s. This illustrates the balance reached in a fairly well-developed tropical economy. The relative importance of different products in a country's economy is also a guide, other things being equal, to the attention they should receive from agricultural economists.

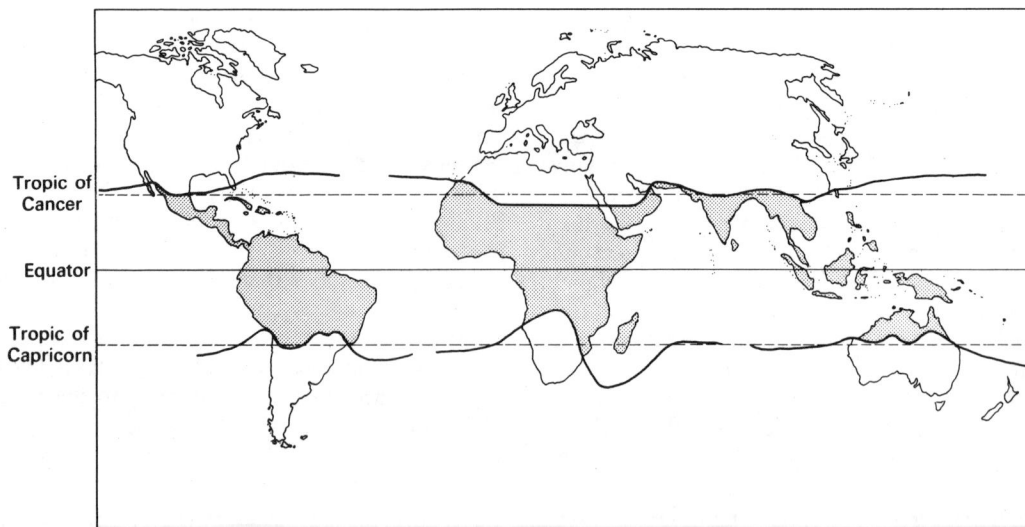

Fig. 1.1 Map of the world showing the areas of the Tropics (shaded)

Table 1.1 Vegetables offered in city markets, Dhaka, Bangladesh. (*Source:* **Khan F. K.** (1963) 'Food markets of Dacca city' in *Oriental Geography*, 7(2))

	Tonnes per year
Pumpkin and gourds	5 800
Potato	5 660
Aubergine (egg plant)	3 900
Tomato	1 700
Radish	1 550
Taro (*Colocasia* spp.)	1 450
Green papaya (pawpaw)	1 230
Beans	1 200
Patal (*Trichosanthis dioca*)	1 200
Okra	770
Jhinga (*Luffa acutangula*)	690
Cauliflower	670
Plantain	480
Sweet potato	470
Peas	430
Cabbage	380
Spinach	290
Turnip	265
Carrot	260
Data (*Amaranthus* spp.)	241
Cucumber	183
Other local vegetables	263

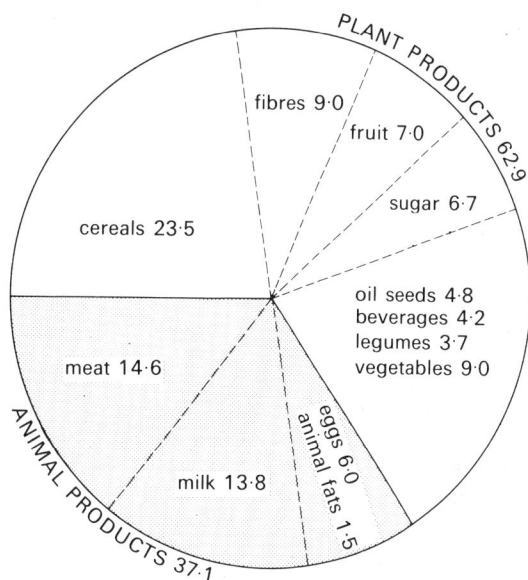

Fig. 1.2 Composition of total agricultural output in percentages by value; Mexico, 1957–61

Income levels

What is the economic status of the tropical countries and what kind of a market is available to farmers wishing to sell their products? The measure of economic development usually employed in international comparisons is gross national product (GNP) per person. This is the total value of the goods and services produced by a country during one year, divided by the number of people living there. These figures include an allowance for food grown and consumed on the farm and are a fairly good measure of cash income. Estimates by the World Bank are shown in Table 1.2. Incomes in most tropical countries are less than one-quarter of those in Western Europe. This does not mean, of course, that the level of living of the people is that much lower. Much of the higher income in the Western countries is taken up in paying for housing and services. These cost more, precisely because of these income levels and correspondingly high wage costs. Furthermore, they are counterbalanced in part by the direct disadvantages of living in highly industrial economies: traffic congestion, long distance to travel to work, polluted atmospheres, noise and reduced personal services.

The tropical countries have made great progress since the 1950s in services for living. There are four times as many children at school. The infant mortality rate has fallen by three-quarters. The multiplication of hospital beds, village water pipes and all-season village roads has been faster than at any period in the history of the countries now developed.

Market for agricultural products

The level of money income in the tropical countries does, however, determine the market offered to agricultural products. The mass of the population may have no money to pay for high-value foods such as milk, eggs and meat; for commercial fruit and vegetables; for elaborate marketing services; or for expensive foods that have been processed.

Wage rates for unskilled workers in India, for example, are only 60 to 80 US cents per day. The average amount that a person can spend on food

Table 1.2 Income per person in the tropical countries, 1984. (*Source:* **World Bank**, *World Development Report 1986*)
US $ per year

Bangladesh	130	Ecuador	1 150	Mauritania	450	Somalia	260
Benin	270	El Salvador	710	Mauritius	1 090	Sri Lanka	360
Bolivia	540	Ethiopia	110	Mexico	2 040	Sudan	360
Botswana	960	Ghana	350	Nepal	160	Tanzania	210
Brazil	1 720	Guatemala	1 160	Nicaragua	860	Thailand	800
Burkina Faso	160	Guinea	330	Niger	190	Togo	250
Burma	180	Haiti	320	Nigeria	730	Trinidad & Tobago	7 150
Burundi	220	Honduras	700	Pakistan	300	Uganda	230
Cameroun	300	India	260	Panama	1 980	Venezuela	3 410
Central African Republic	260	Indonesia	540	Papua New Guinea	710	Zaire	140
China	310	Ivory Coast	610	Paraguay	1 240	Zambia	470
Colombia	1 370	Jamaica	1 150	Peru	1 000		
Congo Republic	1 140	Kenya	310	Philippines	660		
Costa Rica	1 190	Liberia	470	Rwanda	280		
Dominican Republic	970	Madagascar	260	Senegal	380		
		Malawi	180	Sierra Leone	310		
		Malaysia	1 960				
		Mali	140				

is around US $100 per year, i.e. about 22 cents per day. Sixty per cent of this is required to purchase basic cereals. Of course, there is always a proportion of the population with incomes well above the average. Five per cent of Indian households, a total of about 40 million people, have an annual income exceeding $1 000. These people, together with those who benefit directly or indirectly from petroleum prosperity, and cocoa farmers in West Africa, have more money to spend. They could afford say, 6 cents per day each to buy high protein or vitamin foods—if they could be convinced that this was the best way to spend it. But their first preference in the use of such 'surplus' income may well be to buy beer or Coca-Cola.

People buy what is most important to them. The head of a family in Pakistan, for example, may go far beyond his current income and borrow money to pay for wedding celebrations that bring him prestige. His spending power will be much reduced subsequently. Increasing attention is being focused on the need to raise incomes at the lower end of the scale but, especially where large numbers are involved, progress can only be slow.

The most important influence upon agricultural production in the Tropics is the demand for basic cereals and pulses for domestic consumption and for specialised crops for export. Such crops include coffee, cocoa, tea and bananas which are in demand in non-tropical countries where they cannot be grown for ecological reasons.

Agriculture: a mainstay of most tropical economies

In most tropical countries agriculture is the major source of revenue. This means that it has to carry a correspondingly large share of the cost of running the country. Only countries such as Indonesia, Nigeria and Venezuela, with their petroleum exports, have large earnings from a non-agricultural

Table 1.3 Contribution of agriculture to total output, employment, and land availability. (*Source*: **World Bank**, *World Development Report 1986*)

	Share of agriculture in domestic output (%)	Proportion of labour force engaged in agriculture (%)	Arable and permanently cropped land per person in agriculture (ha)
Africa			
Ghana	52	56	0.90
Malawi	37	83	0.77
Uganda	52	86	1.00
Asia			
Bangladesh	48	75	0.1
India	36	70	0.40
Philippines	25	52	0.62
Sri Lanka	28	53	0.40
Thailand	20	70	0.58
Latin America			
Brazil	13	31	3.15
Ecuador	14	39	1.35
Honduras	27	50	1.36
Venezuela	7	16	2.26

sector. Such revenue is sufficient to support major public investment or to subsidise agricultural programmes. But in most tropical countries, agriculture must find funds for development from within its own resources. In many countries it must go further and be the source of development capital for other sections of the economy. The industrial development of Japan, and more recently of Taiwan, was financed from agriculture through taxes, savings and payments for land.

Table 1.3 shows for some representative tropical countries, the share of agriculture in domestic income, the proportion of the total working population engaged in agriculture, and the average amount of arable and permanently cropped land per person in agriculture. In many countries, agriculture provides work for 50–60% of the labour force, and in Malawi and Uganda for over 80% of the work force. The last column of Table 1.3 shows the amount of arable land available per person.

Land can vary greatly in productivity. For example, irrigated land may be cropped three times a year, whereas other land may bear only one or two crops and must then be left to lie fallow. This is therefore only a very rough guide to the agricultural resources available and people's dependence upon them.

In Europe, expanding industrial and commercial employment has reduced the number of people working in agriculture so that now each person cultivates more than two hectares. In Latin America land is still relatively plentiful. In Southeast Asia, one-third to one-half a hectare of arable land per person employed is usual.

Efficiency of tropical agriculture

The leaching effect of heavy rains in the humid parts of the Tropics and the high rate of evaporation in the dry zones, are continuing handicaps to productive agriculture. Short growing seasons and variable rains raise costs and increase risks in some places. Nevertheless, tropical agriculture need not necessarily lag behind the temperate zones in productive efficiency. This is evident from the agricultures of Hawaii and Queensland, and from plantation-type enterprises growing tea in Assam or bananas in Central America. Efficient tropical agriculture on a small scale may be seen in Taiwan. With only 0.15 hectares of arable land per worker, agricultural incomes in Taiwan are among the highest in the world. This has been achieved through intensive use of fertiliser, growing two or more crops a year and concentrating on high-value products, and there is ample scope for innovation.

Where tropical agriculture is backward, the reason lies largely in a lack of education and technical knowledge; weakness in administration and related services; and inadequate management of financing, marketing and related enterprises. It is only a matter of time before shortages of qualified personnel are overcome. In Egypt every village can be provided with a man with four years of university study in agriculture. Most tropical countries are setting up badly-needed schools and colleges.

A more intractable problem is that of developing adequate management. Although training can help, managerial ability is mainly learned from on-the-job experience, and is only really tested by proven performance.

Corruption

Low standards of integrity in officers of central and local government services, and in officially sponsored organisations, are another, much quoted handicap. In some countries corruption has reached a level that prejudices effective administrative performance.

Custom is important. There are societies where persons in high position are expected to be lavish in their public appearance, and generous to friends and political supporters. They can only maintain this style by exploiting the opportunities that their authority provides. Attitudes contributing to this problem are further examined in the section on socio-economics in Chapter 5. Certainly, those who exploit positions of authority cannot be excused on the grounds that their salaries are low, when salaries are low all around them. At the same time

it may be questioned whether corruption in the tropical countries is responsible for more serious misuse of economic resources than its more sophisticated forms evident in some developed countries. Indeed, when it opens a way through bureaucratic delays and obstacles, and aids the establishment of enterprises that are themselves efficient, its effect may be directly positive.

It is sometimes said that people living in a warm climate are likely to put high value on leisure, i.e. they prefer a short working day to higher earnings. While it is possible to live in a mud house and wear the same few garments all through the year, it is wrong to assume that the residents of the Tropics would not appreciate the comforts of an air-conditioned house and take pleasure in having a range of alternative clothes. Similarly, little value may be attached to leisure by people who have little opportunity to engage in a salaried job. Leisure is appreciated most by those who have a full work programme which has already made them quite rich.

Politics and economics

The economist lives in a political world. The price of basic foods; the level of taxes; who can have access to land, and on what terms; can farmers choose between alternative market outlets for their crops; these are all issues that affect many people. When many people complain, a politically-sensitive government is bound to take action. Such issues can also be used by ambitious politicians who make promises in order to obtain support. The agricultural economist may not be in a position to make the decision on policy. He can usually influence it, however, by assessing the consequences of a particular government action. He can then point out the long term implications and whether these seem likely to be harmful or helpful to the economy of the country. He is both a scientific observer and a source of information on pressing issues.

National aspirations

Many tropical countries have attained their independence relatively recently. National aspirations of people to manage their own affairs have shown up in many ways which concern the agricultural economist. Much has depended on the orientation of the personalities who led a country to independence and the environment in which it was attained. Some reaction against the former colonial rulers was to be expected. Often this was expressed in measures to take over agricultural production, marketing and input supply enterprises which were not operated by nationals of the country.

Pent-up resentment of alien immigrant domination of agricultural marketing and processing also found vent. In various countries the aliens were obliged to leave or to hand over their enterprises to bodies representative of the indigenous population. Some leaders of newly independent countries have been committed to Marxist political philosophies. They used political authority to implement collective and state enterprise 'solutions' to intricate agricultural production and marketing problems.

The establishment of state, official cooperative and development authority production, marketing and support service systems has been the main action line of many governments of tropical countries. In addition to backing their political preferences, national leaders sought to achieve something quickly. They had also to please strategic pressure groups. Often they lacked reliable information on the realities of production and marketing performance at the local level.

Under the tension of ambitious projects with slow achievement, advice that is critical is rarely welcome. A planning adviser in one country with limited resources who observed that funds earmarked for a new presidential palace would be better spent on agricultural development was given 48 hours in which to leave. However, since 1981, dissatisfaction with the incentive to food and agricultural production provided under parastatal marketing and supply systems and difficulties in meeting their cost, have stimulated awareness of the need for more competitive systems.

It is now increasingly being recognised that confining important input supply and marketing functions to cooperative and parastatal systems may not be in the best interest of the farmers concerned. These bodies may operate on a non-profit basis, but their costs can be high and their procedures slow and cumbersome. Family firms and other independent enterprises may perform better through seeking a profit, provided that there is competition. Foreign firms can contribute significantly both in production and marketing where they bring capital, market outlets, technology and management that are not otherwise available. Del Monte in Kenya has enabled the country to earn valuable foreign exchange selling canned pineapple on competitive world markets. Such firms have raised substantially the skills and incomes of local farmers growing produce for them under contract. The Charoen Pokphang broiler enterprise has been a notable growth point in the agricultural economy of Thailand. It has competed successfully with US exporters in the expanding Japanese market for boneless chicken parts.

Many tropical governments are reluctant to see a foreign enterprise earning profits which may eventually go out of the country. But there are advantages in working with such enterprises on appropriate terms. For example, they train nationals of the country, re-invest there a proportion of their profit, etc.

High development in restricted areas is precarious, however, unless benefits are also felt in the surrounding countryside. The Dolefil pineapple production, processing and marketing operation in the Philippines earned needed foreign exchange for the country. It also raised incomes locally in a narrow enclave of employees and suppliers. This provoked discontent in the area around. A fast pace of development often means that some people become richer than others in the early stages. Stability comes from the greater spread of a cash economy and increasing involvement of peasant farmers. Major goals for most governments are to promote employment and avoid large differences in income that cause social resentment.

Economic principles hold good whatever the political system

There are people who say that the principles and techniques taught by the economists of Western countries are based on a specific political view. They suggest that for other kinds of political structures, radically different economic approaches are needed. Since modern economists tend to come from the more developed countries, it is sometimes argued that they are part of an 'imperialist' plot to keep down those who are not so well off. Experience shows that there is no basis for this belief. For example, loans to buy equipment and supplies from the lending country are proposed just as much by the communist countries as by the capitalist ones. A farm may be operated by a private enterprise, a cooperative, or a state enterprise, but the main economic problems remain the same. Decisions will have to be made on how much land to allocate to alternative crops; how much fertiliser to apply; and what balance of machinery and labour is most advantageous. Whatever the political system, national interests will be served best when the available resources are used in the most economic way.

To ensure that the managers of enterprises achieve the most economic use of resources, they must in most cases be offered some incentive. A spirit of cooperative idealism or political crusading may inspire some managers for a time. In the longer term, however, and for most managers, the most effective incentive is likely to be an economic one. It is basic human motivation to expect a reward commensurate with the input of labour, planning, organisation and degree of risk assumed. If no such reward is forthcoming, then people will be less willing to provide such inputs and carry such responsibility, and the overall level of efficiency will decline. The enduring quality of the economic incentive is shown by the fact that most communist governments allow collective farmers to share the income achieved above some established amount. It is recognised still more clearly in communist countries such as Hungary and Yugoslavia. There the manager of a collective farm has a great measure of freedom in planning the production and marketing the output of the farm. To guide him, the government uses credit policies exercised through the banks rather than direct controls.

Under the production responsibility system adopted in China, the land remains in public ownership. Its use is subcontracted out to family groups: each has a direct incentive to manage it as efficiently as possible. This programme has brought rapid increases in agricultural output.

An economist working in an environment of political slogans may take heart from the fact that when a 'revolutionary' party has assumed office and made some token changes, it will be increasingly ready to follow sound economic principles.

Frequent government changes are often far more disturbing in practice. Such changes often affect the management of public enterprises and the financing of development projects. A rapid turnover of senior staff who have been appointed by political patronage; diversion of development funds to serve political party ends; the raising of price subsidies to unrealistic levels because of an impending election; and arbitrary changes in policy to serve the private interests of influential ministers; these are perhaps the worst political impediments to sound development planning and efficient implementation.

Summary

This chapter opened with an explanation of the meaning of economics and its relevance for development and modern living in the tropical countries. It then indicated some major features of agriculture in the tropical countries and the markets open to its products. It was then shown that in most tropical countries agriculture must be self-financing, and even provide resources for the development of other sectors of the economy. Factors slowing down the pace of development were identified and some counter-measures discussed.

In a section on politics and economics it was shown that economic principles are equally applicable whatever political system prevails. The spirit of independence can sometimes lead countries to sacrifice immediate economic advantage for the goal of national identification. However, such aspirations can still be pursued while taking advantage of outside know-how, experience and capital on specified terms.

It is incorrect that alternative political systems call for differing sets of economic principles. Sound economic analysis is universally applicable and this is becoming increasingly recognised.

Issues for discussion

1 What are the main economic issues in relation to agriculture for (a) individual farmers, to agriculture for (a) individual farmers, (b) agricultural marketing enterprises,

2 Are there aspects of tropical agriculture which call for a different economic focus than that applicable to agriculture elsewhere?

3 What are the main obstacles to the development of agriculture in the Tropics? How can they be overcome?

4 To what extent do payments made to persons in official positions, in order to influence their decisions, expedite or hamper development in your country?

5 Do people living in tropical countries have the same interest in material progress as those living in colder climates?

6 What are the main areas where politics have a bearing on the work of agricultural economists? How far can such economists expect to influence government decisions?

7 How far should national ambitions to control all sectors of an economy prevail against the economic advantages of allowing skilled enterprises to operate and earn profits? What combination of 'idealistic' and 'profit' motivations is likely to promote the fastest rate of development in a tropical agricultural economy?

Further reading

Bates, R. H. (1981) *Markets and states in tropical Africa: the political basis of agricultural policies*, University of California Press, Berkeley.

Eicher, C. H. and **Staatz, J. M.** (1984) *Agricultural development in the third world*, Johns Hopkins University Press, Baltimore.

Kamarck, A. K. (1976) *The tropics and agricultural development*, John Hopkins University Press, Baltimore.

Killick, T. (1978) *Development economics in action*, St Martin's Press, New York.

Levi, J. and **Havinden, M.** (1982) *Economics of African agriculture*, Longman, London.

Livingstone, I. and **Ord, H. W.** (1981) *Agricultural economics for tropical Africa*, Heinemann, New York.

Webster, G. C. and **Wilson, P. N.** (1986) *Agriculture in the tropics*, 2nd ed., Longman, London.

Wrigley, G. (1981) *Tropical agriculture*, 4th ed., Longman, London.

Youdeowei, A., Ezedinma, F. O. C. and **Onazi, O. C.** (1984) *Introduction to tropical agriculture*, Longman, London.

2 Pricing

Price fixing

Who fixes the price of agricultural products and production supplies such as fertiliser? This question is always in the farmer's and consumer's minds. In this chapter we will try to show how the pricing system works in a free economy. The basic economic forces which operate in free economies also operate in directed economies. Therefore the main principles of pricing apply to both free economies and directed economies. But the way prices are fixed is not significant if there are no supplies or if there is no demand at that price. We must balance the cost of production and the price that the consumer can pay or we will end up with excess goods or with a shortage. Price is the factor which brings a market to equilibrium. In the long term, price encourages people to use resources to produce what consumers want.

This chapter explains who fixes prices. It also explains how monopolies can obtain higher prices or pay less than they would in full competition. Such a monopoly may be a single enterprise, a group of producers or traders, or a government-owned organisation, which has a monopoly of farm supplies or market outlets. The principles which are discussed here will help farmers and managers of agricultural marketing and supply enterprises to make decisions.

Demand

Demand is the amount of a product that a buyer will buy at a particular price. Demand tells us the amount of money a buyer is prepared to pay for a product, even though he needs and likes other things.

For the seller, demand means that buyers are able and willing to purchase at a particular price. We call this effective demand. Consumers may need or want much more than effective demand. Effective demand is different from the nutritional requirements of the consumer. In most countries there are people who are under-nourished, not because food cannot be produced, but because it is too expensive.

The following figures show the demand of an individual for palm oil at different price levels. We call this sort of comparison a demand schedule.

Price (cents per tin)	Individual demand (number of tins)
12	1
10	$1\frac{1}{2}$
8	$2\frac{1}{2}$
7	3
6	4
5	5
4	6
3	8

The graph in Fig. 2.1 gives a continuous picture of this demand schedule. The price of the tins is shown on the vertical axis and the number of tins bought (the dependent variable) is shown on the horizontal axis.

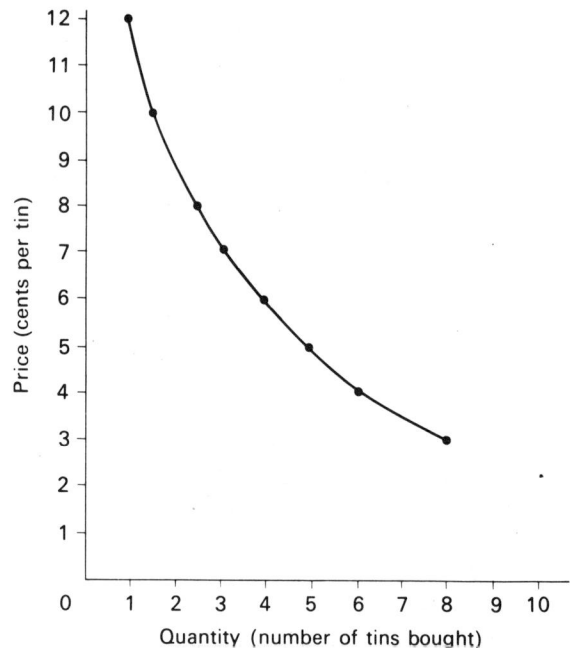

Fig. 2.1 Model demand curve for palm oil

The curve shows the demand of a single individual. We can calculate the total demand of a group of consumers by adding the demands of all individuals in the group. The total market demand curve would be the same as Fig. 2.1 if the individual demand was the same as the average of all consumers. For example, if the total number of consumers was 100 000, we would have to change all the quantity figures to hundreds of thousands.

Factors influencing demand

A number of factors help to determine how much a consumer will buy. The following are some of the most important factors.

Income This is the major factor. Income limits what a person can buy.

Price This is always important; usually the higher the price, the lower the quantity purchased. This is because there are substitutes for most commodities. Therefore, if the price of palm oil rises, some consumers will use other cooking oils whose price has not changed.

Religious teaching Moslems and Jews do not eat pig meat. Many Hindus do not eat beef, and some of them are completely vegetarian. In Ethiopia, the demand for meat is greatly reduced during the long periods when Christians fast.

Traditional taboos Some groups in Africa will not eat eggs and poultry.

Habits People enjoy the food they are used to. Our liking for certain foods depends on the food our parents gave us when we were children; the types of food which are available locally; the family's social status; the cultural background; etc. Influences like these may be more important than income. Many people continue to eat the food they are used to after their income has increased.

Tastes and preferences Rice is a good example of the importance of individual preference. Basmati rice grown in Pakistan is very popular in Pakistan and nearby Arabian markets. It is often 50% more expensive than other rices. Many people prefer well-milled or polished rice to unpolished rice which is of higher nutritional value. Some of the early high-yielding varieties of rice developed in the Philippines were very unpopular because the people there did not like the taste and cooking quality. Of course, apparent preferences may be related to price. Many Egyptians eat round grain rice because it is cheaper, but they would prefer long grain rice if they could afford it. Consumers everywhere prefer rice which has only small amounts of broken and spoiled kernels. However, the percentage of broken and spoiled kernels accepted in rice may be very high if the price is low. For example, in Sierra Leone consumers accept 40% of broken and spoiled kernels in imported rice.

Changes in demand

We have so far discussed demand at one point in time. Demand should not, however, be considered as a constant. When a person's income increases he can buy more (if price is unchanged) and he can buy things which he could not afford before. When this happens the overall demand curve moves to the right (see Fig. 2.2). In this illustration there has been no change in price. But in the new demand curve D_2D_2 the quantity of palm oil demanded at 6 cents per tin rises from 4 to 8 tins.

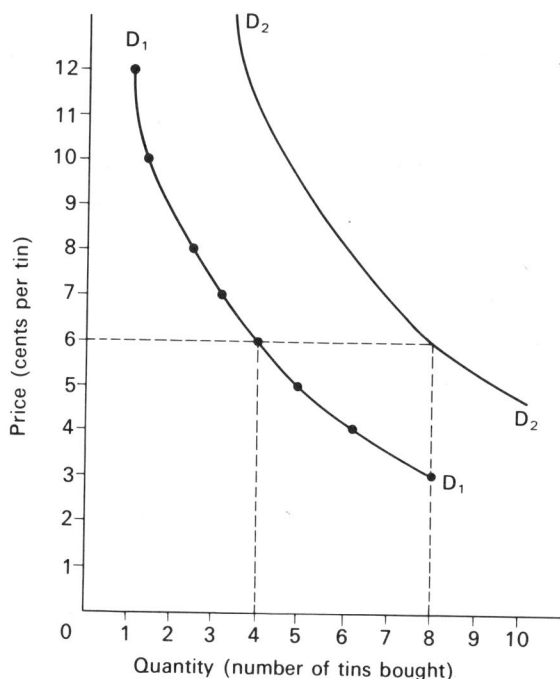

Fig. 2.2 Demand curves showing a shift in demand

Demand changes with a change in income. For a market as a whole, demand will change with a change in the distribution of income. In most countries there is great inequality of income. FAO has estimated that total demand for food would rise by 10% in some Latin American countries if there was a moderate redistribution of income. There would be a rise in overall demand for some foods if there were improvements in job opportunities and in social services for the poor.

Effective sales promotion can also change the pattern of demand. Advertising can change market demand by creating a fashion for certain products and by persuading people that the products have valuable and attractive properties. Not so long ago, avocados were unknown in England. By 1972 they had become very popular luxury foods. Sales promotion is more difficult when most consumers are on low incomes. However, the amount of Coca-Cola drunk in tropical countries shows that sales promotion can be very successful.

Price and elasticity of demand

Anyone who has to price a product must know how much more he will sell if he lowers the price and how much less he will sell if he raises it.

Elasticity of demand means the effect that small changes in price have on the amount of demand. Elasticity of demand is the way that the amount of a product sold depends on rises or falls in its price, other things being equal. Thus elasticity of demand measures the way that people reduce their consumption of a product if its price rises and buy more of the product if its price falls.

Various degrees of elasticity are illustrated graphically in Fig. 2.3. Fig. 2.3(a) shows that the percentage change in quantity demanded is larger than the percentage change in price. In Fig. 2.3(b) you can see that demand is inelastic when price changes have little effect on sales. Fig. 2.3(c) shows what is called unit elasticity. Unit elasticity is where the percentage change in demand exactly corresponds to the percentage change in price. Unit elasticity occurs when a consumer has only a fixed sum of money to spend on a certain product. If the price per unit of product rises he buys less of it.

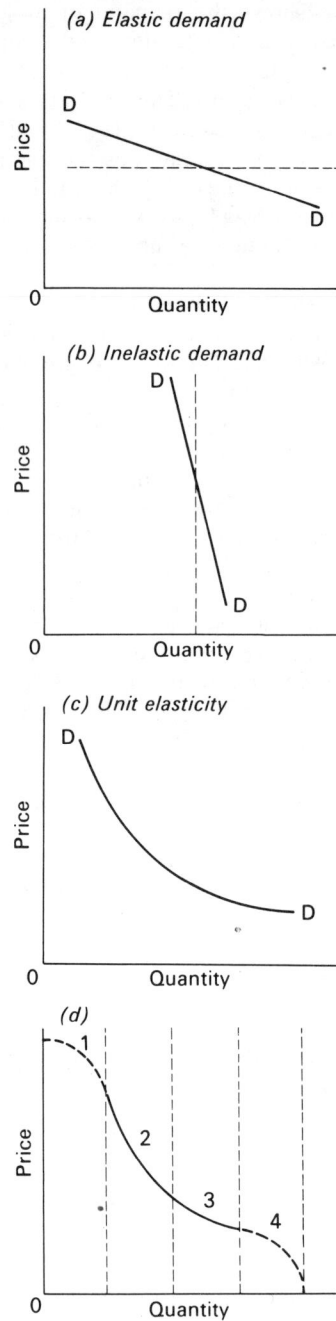

Fig. 2.3 Degrees of elasticity of demand with respect to price

Elasticity of demand can be estimated by observing actual reactions to price changes.

Elasticity of demand =
$$\frac{\text{percentage change in quantity demanded}}{\text{percentage change in price}}$$

Thus if the price falls from 5 cents to 4 cents per unit and the quantity which is bought increases from 10 to 13 units the percentage change in quantity demanded is:

$$\frac{3}{10} \times \frac{100}{1} = 30\%$$

The percentage change in price demanded is:

$$\frac{1}{5} \times \frac{100}{1} = 20\%$$

Elasticity of demand = $\frac{30}{20}$ or E = 1.5

Where E is greater than 1.0, demand is elastic. Where E is less than 1.0, demand is inelastic. Where E is equal to 1.0 there is unit elasticity.

The elastic demand shown in Fig. 2.3(c) refers to a fixed range of prices. Beyond this price range there might be different demand reactions for many products. Where substitutes are available a very high price indeed could reduce demand to zero. On the other hand, demand would not keep increasing indefinitely in response to very low prices. Eventually a saturation point would be reached. These extreme situations are shown as phases 1 and 4 in Fig. 2.3(d).

A very low price can create new demand for some products, for example when farmers can use rice for animal feed because its price is very low. In this case demand would be very price elastic.

The degree of elasticity of demand is determined by: (a) the availability of substitutes; (b) the importance of the product; (c) the consumer's income; (d) the strength of the consumer's habits. If substitutes are in the same price range as the product then the closer the substitute, the more elastic is the demand. Demand is likely to be inelastic where there are no substitutes and where people think that the product is essential. Demand for rice is relatively inelastic in many Asian countries where it is the basic food and is consumed daily. Demand for rice becomes more elastic, however, at lower levels of income. For example in parts of Indonesia lower income groups eat tubers instead of rice. Rich people have a less elastic demand for most foods than lower income people. They do not pay much attention to available substitutes. But the poor man always has to consider the best way to spend his income and he is immediately affected by changes in price.

Income and elasticity of demand
This is very important when planning agricultural production and marketing. Income elasticity of demand is the way that demand responds to changes in income.

Income elasticity of demand =
$$\frac{\text{Average percentage change in quantity demanded}}{\text{Average percentage change in income}}$$

In Sri Lanka the income demand elasticity of rice has been estimated at 0.5. This means, for example, that a 10% rise in income leads to a 5% rise in demand:

$$\frac{5}{10} = 0.5$$

Such formulae refer to a particular level of income. At a higher level of income, demand for rice as a basic food will probably be less elastic. In Japan, annual rice consumption reached a peak at 140 kg per person around 1920. Since then incomes have risen and demand for rice has declined because consumers could afford more interesting food.

Table 2.1 shows how a few years ago income affected the consumption of various foods in Mexico. Demand for starchy foods tended to go down as income rose. People at the lowest income level consumed 117 kg of maize annually and people at the highest level consumed 67 kg. Thus we can say that demand was very income inelastic.

Table 2.1 Relation between family income and consumption of various foods; in towns in Mexico. (*Source:* Government of Mexico)

Monthly family income ($)	Up to 24	120 to 240	360 to 480
Foods	**Annual consumption per person** (kg)		
Maize	117	74	67
Wheat	41	53	50
Beans	36	23	20
Vegetables	22	34	41
Fruit	16	50	76
Sugar	21	24	25
Beef	8	22	26
Other meat	2	15	22
Milk	33	110	147
Eggs	5	12	16
Butter	5	6	3
Vegetable oil	2	6	10
Coffee	4	4	4

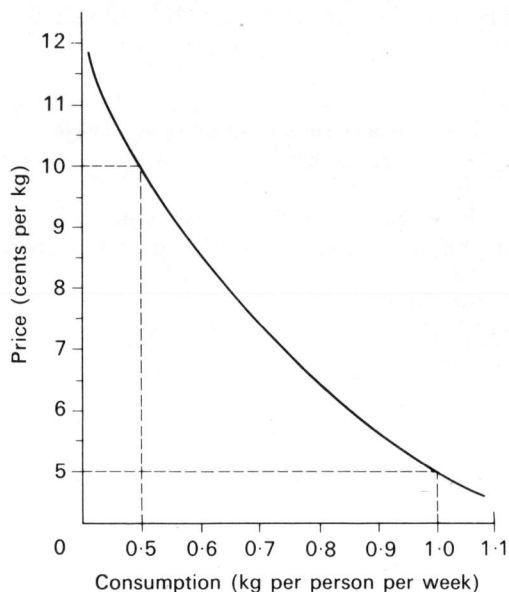

Fig. 2.4 Relation between consumption of plantains and their price; Bogota, 1967

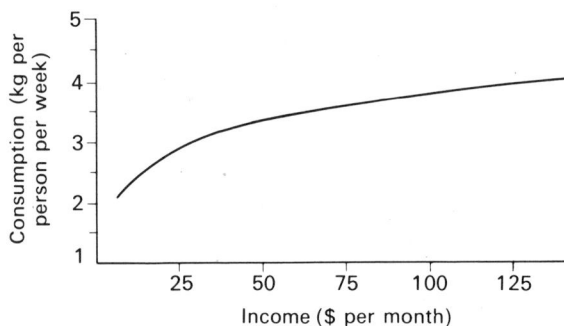

Fig. 2.5 Relation between consumption of plantains and income; Bogota, 1967

In contrast milk is very income elastic. Milk was consumed at the rates of 33 kg per person by the lowest income groups and around 150 kg at the highest income level. Demand for meat and fruit is also very elastic in Mexico.

Figs. 2.4 and 2.5 show the effect of price and income on the consumption of plantains in Bogota, Colombia. The curves show how consumption varied with changes in price under 1967 conditions. At 5 cents per kg, consumption averaged 1 kg per person per week. At 10 cents per kg consumption fell to 0.5 kg. Thus price elasticity was quite high. Fig. 2.5 shows how consumption rises as incomes rise. This type of information can be very valuable to people who are responsible for making marketing decisions and those who are planning long range investments in production.

Fig. 2.6 shows factors which affect the demand for bananas in export markets. The diagram is interesting to banana growers because of the influ-

ence of export demand on the prices which producers receive. Thus consumption per person in countries which import bananas increased rapidly as annual incomes rose to a level of $2 000 per person. But the average consumption level of 8 kg per capita did not increase further. Although the

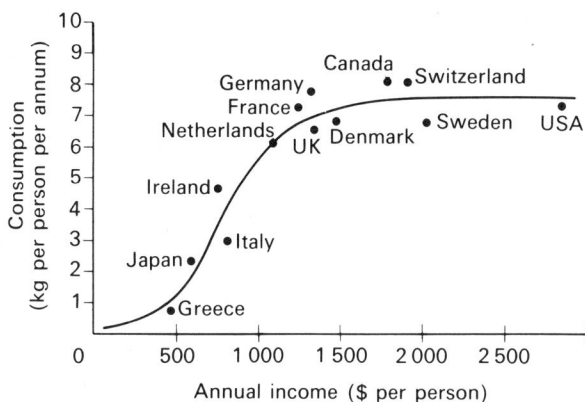

Fig. 2.6 Relation between consumption of bananas and income; selected countries, 1964–65

average income in the USA was nearly $3 000 per annum the consumption of bananas was no higher. In the mid 1960s banana producers and exporters were very encouraged by the situation in Japan. Japan's 100 million population was shifting to a higher average income level and economists expected the shift to result in increased demand for bananas. They were right, Japan's annual imports of bananas rose from 358 000 tonnes in 1965 to over one million tonnes in 1972. At this point consumption averaged 10 kg per person; subsequently it fell back to around 6 kg.

Supply

The amount of a product that will be offered for sale at various price levels is called the supply. Usually the higher the price, the more will be offered for sale and the lower the price, the less will be offered for sale. Supply is not the same as total output or production. This is because a large part of a crop is consumed on the farms where it is produced. For example, half the world's rice output is eaten on the farms where it is grown. Therefore supply is the quantity of output which particular prices attract to the market.

We might expect that the higher the price the larger the supply which will be attracted to the market. This is largely true, especially over a long

period of time. However, some farmers only sell their produce when they have to pay rent or taxes or to buy something which they cannot produce themselves. These farmers want to achieve a certain target income. Once this target has been reached they see no need to sell any more, and consume more of their produce themselves. The number of producers like this may be quite large in some countries. But the proportion of produce which comes from such farmers is usually only a small part of the total market supply.

Some producers and traders hold back supplies when they see prices rising because they believe they will rise still further. This is normal economic behaviour, though it may be criticised as hoarding.

An example of what is generally considered a normal market supply schedule follows:

Price (cents per kg)	Quantity of product offered (kg)
12	100
11	90
10	80
8	60
7	50
6	40

Fig. 2.7 shows the supply curve for this schedule. The curve from right to left indicates that a higher price draws a larger quantity into the market.

In contrast Fig. 2.8 shows an inverse or backward sloping supply curve. This depicts the reaction of semi-subsistence farmers. These mainly market their crops to pay for fixed expenses and can therefore afford to sell less when the price is higher. With the inverse curve, supply first increases as the price rises. Then, gradually, the rate of increase slows down. Eventually supply declines sharply as the price rises.

Supply must always be considered in terms of time — the very short term, the short term and the long term. In the very short term, supply is the amount of goods which are actually in the market. The production costs of these goods do not count because they are already in the market. Their

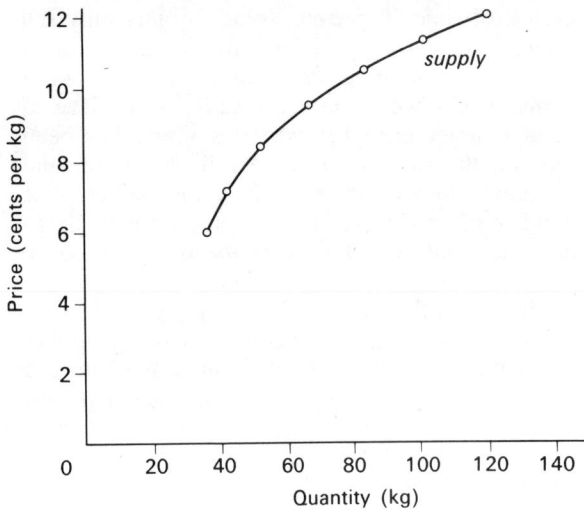

Fig. 2.7 Relation between supply and price

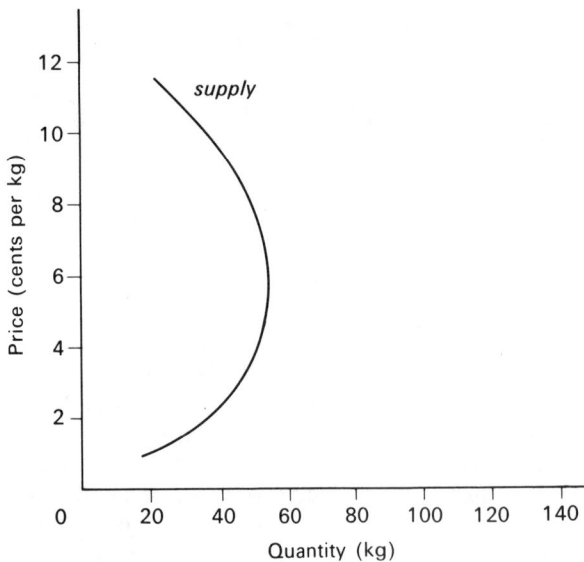

Fig. 2.8 Inverse supply curve

We must take production costs into consideration when we look for future supplies. The short term is regarded as the period during which goods can be supplied using land and equipment which is already available. During this period overhead costs are not an immediate factor when the seller decides how much to sell. This is because overhead costs are incurred at all levels of production. The seller may continue to supply provided that his variable or direct costs (the cost of inputs, services and labour) are covered.

In the long term a producer takes into account all his costs, including overheads and the amount he regards as normal profit. If returns from a product do not cover all these costs the producer is likely to abandon that product and look for another.

There is a considerable time lag before adjustments in supply have any significant effect on the market. This is because the period of production is very long for many farm products (4–6 years for some beef cattle, 8–10 years for some fruit trees). Likewise, supplies of some products may only be expanded slowly when agricultural prices are high. These special features in the supply of agricultural products cause agricultural products to vary irregularly in price, more than industrial products.

Several agricultural products may come from a single origin. A change in the supply of one causes a change in the supply of the other. For example, meat and hides and skins are linked in this way. Increasing the supply of vegetable oil from groundnuts or soya beans necessarily increases the supply of oil seed cake and meal.

The supply of some products may also be in direct competition with the supply of others. There are, for example, regions of India where rice and sugar are alternative crops. In the 1950s a guaranteed market was established for sugar. At that time the market for rice was uncertain and this led to a reduction in the production of rice. In Bangladesh rice is grown in rotation with jute. But if there is an economic incentive farmers will concentrate on one at the expense of the other.

Responsiveness of supply

This may also be thought of as elastic, like demand. Egg and poultry supply is very elastic in countries

owner might even give them away if he would be involved in further charges for storage and transport if he kept them. Sellers in organised markets try to prevent others from giving their produce away, because they think it will depress demand still further. Nevertheless sellers may sometimes have to give away perishable fruit and vegetables.

where there are commercial hatcheries and farmers can obtain equipment, chicks and feed on credit. Beef supplies are much less elastic. If a rise in demand attracts a large part of the available supply to market, there will be considerable delay before breeding herds can be expanded to keep up a steady supply on a higher level. In tropical agriculture, supplies from the large commercial farm sector are generally considered to be the most elastic. A farmer in Zambia, for example, once said that he could expand the supply of onions from his farm to meet the whole country's needs within a year.

For some crops however, the less commercial sector may be more elastic. This is true for cassava which can be left in the ground as a reserve and harvested for market when needed. In Indonesia some small-holders only tap their rubber trees when the price is attractive. These growers are more responsive than commercial plantations with overheads that must be paid for every year.

The marginality principle

Economic analysis should help farmers and marketers to make better production and sales decisions than those who depend only on local tradition and past experience. Marginality is one of the most important economic concepts and aids. It means that choices of how much to buy, how much to produce and how much to sell are usually made between a given and an additional (or marginal) quantity.

Marginal utility

The consumer does not make his choice between, for example, 1 kg of meat and a whole carcass. He is interested in the quantity of meat he can consume with pleasure. Additional quantities of meat after the first kilogram will be of declining value unless he is able to store or resell it. This is the law of diminishing marginal utility. Diminishing marginal utility means that with each additional unit of a goods or service which you buy, the next unit becomes less useful until you reach a point where you do not want any more. In this case the last unit bought is called marginal. This principle is very important when we are assessing the elasticity of demand for a product.

Marginal revenue and marginal cost

These are both equally important when we are deciding how much of a product to produce or sell. Determining marginal revenue and marginal cost involves comparing the extra revenue and the extra cost of producing and selling each additional unit of produce. The most profitable level of output and sale is when the extra revenue from producing one unit and the extra cost are equal. To produce less would lose more in revenue than it saved in cost. To produce more would cost more than the addition to revenue. The example in Table 2.2 shows how this principle works in practice.

Price × units sold = total revenue
Total revenue − total cost = profit.

Table 2.2

Price ($)	Units sold	Total revenue ($)	Total cost ($)	Profit ($)	Marginal revenue ($)	Marginal cost ($)
6	100	600	200	400		
5	300	1 500	400	1 100	900	200
4	600	2 400	700	1 700	900	300
3	900	2 700	900	1 800	300	200
2	1 400	2 800	1 300	1 500	100	600
1	1 800	1 800	1 600	200	−1 000	300

By reducing the price from \$6 to \$5 per unit the seller stimulates an increase in demand from 100 to 300 units. This adds \$900 to his revenue as against an additional \$200 to his costs and he makes \$700 more profit. At a price of \$3 per unit the point of maximum profit is reached. Reducing the price to \$2 per unit sells another 500, but this incurs \$400 of extra costs and brings only \$100 of extra revenue. The marginal revenue and marginal cost columns have been calculated from the total revenue and cost columns respectively. Marginal revenue and marginal cost are nearest to being equal at the price of \$3, which is where profits are highest.

It is normally difficult to use this kind of analysis because there is usually a lack of accurate information on how demand will respond to a change in price. The seller can only estimate how demand will respond to a change in price from his experience of price changes in the past. He can, however, usually assess his costs, and the relative balance of overhead and variable costs will be an important factor.

How many farmers are aware of marginal costs and are guided by them when they make production decisions? In fact, most farmers are greatly influenced by them, although they may not know how to describe them. An African farmer may cultivate only one hectare of maize because this is all that his family can manage. If he cultivates half a hectare more he will need to employ labour and he knows that if he does, his marginal costs will increase beyond one hectare of output.

The production of rice in some parts of Africa is limited by the high cost of using anything but traditional methods. Cultivation by ox plough or tractor is the alternative to cultivating, planting and harvesting by hand. But the change of technique would set a new level of costs because of the initial outlay on the ox and plough or on the tractor. A tractor must be used to capacity to justify its high overhead cost, therefore average costs are lowest when output is high and the area which is cultivated is large. Marginal costs will decline as larger and larger areas are cultivated. Under these circumstances it will pay the farmer to keep his tractor working every hour of daylight during the seasons of cultivation. If the farmer is using an ox and plough and he tries to do too much, he may strain his ox and have to get outside help. His marginal costs may then rise sharply and he may find it difficult to get cultivation finished on time. The farmer may thus decide to cultivate only that area of land that can be handled by family labour.

The principles of marginality also apply to providing marketing services. Any marketing enterprise will use these principles in assessing how much time and money to spend on preparing and packaging, storage, personal contacts and promotion, etc.

Some review questions

The principles which have just been explained are very important. Make sure that you fully understand these principles by answering the following questions.

1 What are the main factors in the demand for food? How does demand for food differ from nutritional requirements? Why does demand for a product usually fall as its price rises? What are the main traditional influences on demand in the area where you live? What are the main consumer preferences in your area?

2 What is meant by price elasticity of demand? Name five food products for which demand is elastic in your country. Name five foods for which demand is relatively inelastic. What group of consumers are you thinking about when you list foodstuffs which have elastic and inelastic demand?

3 How is agricultural supply determined? How is agricultural supply influenced by production costs in (a) the short term, (b) the long term? What lines of production in your area are most responsive to changes in demand? Why are they so responsive? Do you know any group of producers in your country whose reaction to demand follows a backward sloping curve?

4 For what agricultural products in your country is supply interlinked and for which is it competitive?

5 What is meant by the law of diminishing marginal utility? What is the significance of this law for demand?

6 What do we mean when we say that profit will be maximised when marginal revenue equals marginal cost?

The determination of market price

In the market, demand and supply meet. There is an equilibrium price at which buyers take all that sellers can offer and the market is cleared. When goods are moved from places where prices are low to places where prices are high, we eventually reach a stage when prices everywhere are so close that further movement is unprofitable. When this stage has been reached we say that an equilibrium price has been reached. The process of moving goods to reach an equilibrium price is called arbitrage. The balancing of supply and demand at a certain price level may be illustrated with the following example for meat.

Price per kg ($)	Meat demanded (kg)	Meat supplied (kg)
2.50	85	200
2.00	95	185
1.50	120	120
1.00	140	60
0.50	165	45
0.25	195	0

A price of $2.50 per kg will attract plenty of meat (200 kg) but the consumers can only afford to buy 85 kg. At a price of about $1.50 per kg consumers will take up 120 kg of meat and this is just what is attracted from suppliers. So $1.50 is the equilibrium price and 120 kg the equilibrium quantity. In Fig. 2.9 these figures are plotted on a graph to form supply and demand curves. The point where the two curves intersect is the equilibrium price.

The process of market price determination can be simplified in order to show its basic principles. In free markets equilibrium price is very much dependent on the operation of wholesalers. Take the example of fresh fruit and vegetables. Wholesalers usually try to buy produce which they can sell within its normal keeping period with a profit to retailers. If the supply seems insufficient wholesalers will bid against each other to get supplies from growers. Wholesalers will then pass this extra cost on by raising their prices to retailers. If

supplies are plentiful wholesalers may be able to buy from growers at lower prices and keep the difference. But if other wholesalers are charging less they may have to reduce their prices to retailers in order to sell.

Price fluctuations at the wholesale level have a decisive influence on the price which consumers have to pay. This is because retailers usually try to sell in accordance with the price they have paid to the wholesaler. Retailers will buy the amount they think their customers will need within the keeping period of the product. Unforeseen factors may upset these calculations, such as weather conditions or a larger number of tourists than was expected. If this happens the retailer may raise or lower his price in response to shortage or excess of supplies.

When a market is over-supplied, the prices paid to producers often tend to fall more than those paid at intermediate marketing stages. Consumer prices follow the downward trend more slowly and to a lesser degree. This is partly due to the fact that many marketing costs such as transport charges or market fees do not vary with the price of the product.

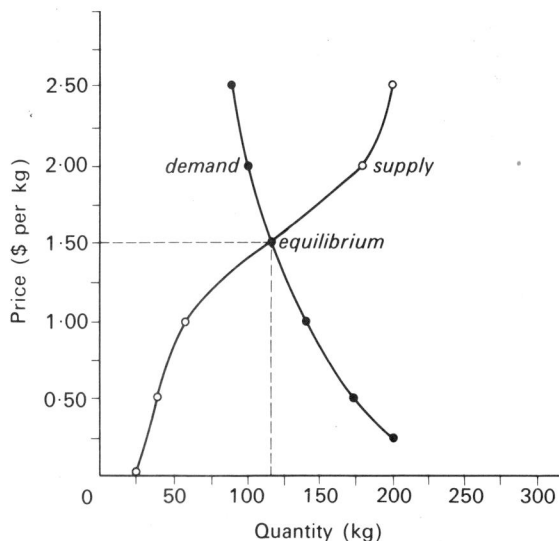

Fig. 2.9 Balancing supply and demand at an equilibrium price

Seasonal and cyclical variations

Most farm products are available only in small quantities at the start of the maturing season. After that their supply builds up to a peak, following which supplies gradually diminish until the crop is finished. Every kind of fruit and vegetable has a production calendar. A production calender shows the dates when the crop matures in a given locality. These seasonal increases and declines in deliveries are matched by inverse movements in prices. The first supplies at the market usually fetch a good price because of their novelty, although quality may improve later. At this stage only the rich can afford to buy. As the season continues, deliveries increase, prices fall and lower income consumers are able to buy. But if prices fall so far that market supplies are discouraged, and if consumers are still interested in buying, prices should improve. Eventually, deliveries will fall off steadily until the crop is finished. The seasonal movement of potato prices in Colombia is shown in Fig. 2.10. There are two peaks before the new crops come in, May/June, and December. In areas where seasonal changes of climate are less marked, variations in price are less noticeable.

seasons of the year, but are based on the reactions of supply to changing market conditions. In principle, these changes originate from the short term inelasticity of supply of certain crops. Low prices for several seasons lead many producers to reduce the amount they plant. This action causes prices to go up again. Eventually the area planted and market supplies will expand once more and so the cycle continues. Cyclical changes in the price of rice in Colombia over a number of years, is shown in Fig. 2.11. The detailed analysis of the tendency for prices and supplies to fluctuate continuously around an equilibrium level has been formalised into what is known as the cobweb theorem.

Secular trends are caused by a number of factors: advances in production and marketing techniques; the development of new ideas about what we should eat; other products which can be used as substitutes; changes in the preferences of consumers. An example of this is the disappearance from West European markets of the greenish brown eating apple because consumers prefer apples with red or golden skins.

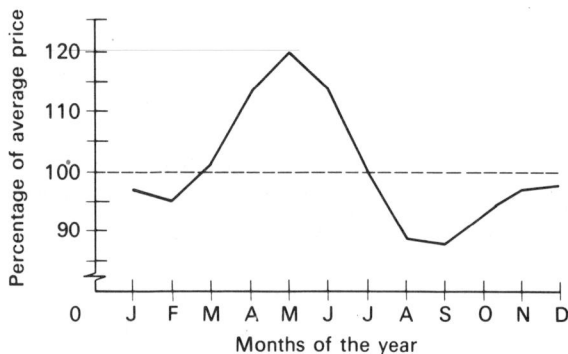

Fig. 2.10 Seasonal price variation for potatoes; Bogota

In addition to variations in price and supply during a single season, there are constant changes between one set of years and another. These changes are usually called cyclical changes. There are also long term changes known as secular trends. Cyclical price changes are not linked with the

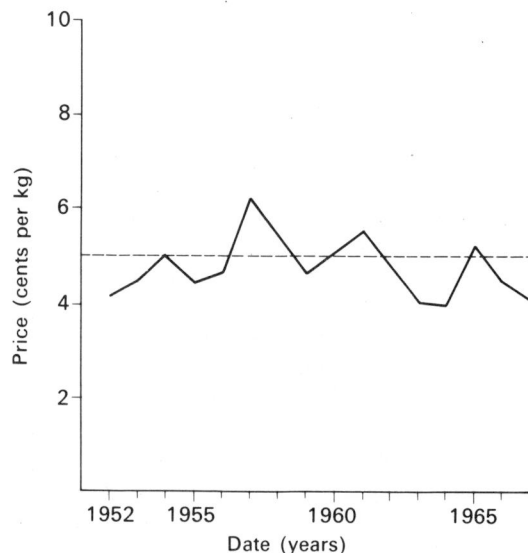

Fig. 2.11 Cyclical price fluctuation for rice; Bogota

Competition

In a fully competitive situation a firm can sell all its goods at the market price, but it cannot, by its actions, affect that price. If it asks a higher price it will sell nothing. If it offers its goods at a lower price it will receive more orders than it can handle. It will attract orders from all other sellers and force them to reduce their own prices. The result of this will be that equilibrium is re-established.

The demand curve faced by an individual producer or seller is infinitely elastic under such competition (see Fig. 2.12). This is because of the small share he contributes to the total market. However the total demand faced by suppliers as a whole will also be related to price and this is shown in Fig. 2.13. The shape of the supply curve is likely to be nearly the same for all suppliers as it is for individual suppliers. Cost of production does not have much influence on price in the short term. This highly inelastic supply condition is responsible for rapid falls in price that sometimes occur in free agricultural markets.

In principle, competition encourages efficiency. Under competition, all a firm can do is try to cut its costs to a minimum. New enterprises can open up at any time. Therefore an enterprise must always keep up to date with technical developments that may enable them to cut costs. Moreover, if an enterprise is able to reduce the cost of its product, it must reduce its price to the consumer. If it does not it will lose business to firms who reduce their price when they make use of the new development. This is the situation in which many small farmers and marketing enterprises find themselves.

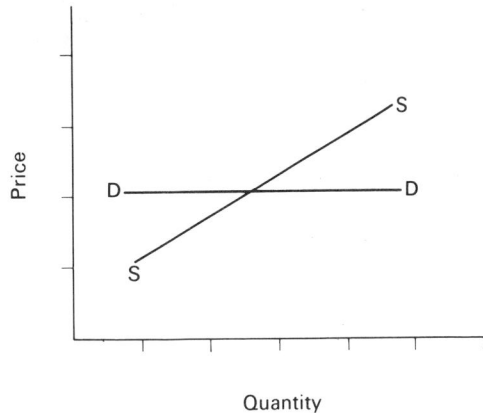

Fig. 2.12 Individual supply and demand curves

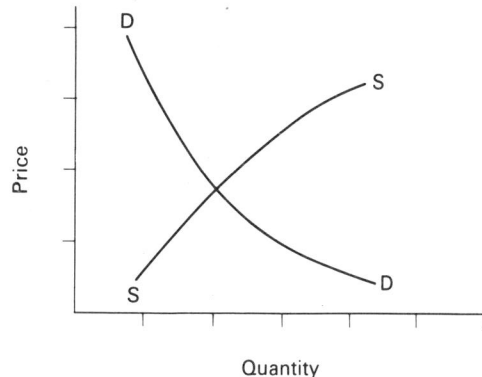

Fig. 2.13 Total supply and demand curves

Monopoly

This is the opposite of competition and means that there is only one seller. This seller controls all the sales of a product and can influence the price through this control. Monopolies face the total demand curve as shown in Fig. 2.13, not the demand curve facing the individual in competition as shown in Fig. 2.12. As a result the monopolist will take into account the effect of his volume of sales upon price. The monopolist can choose the level of sales and price that offer the greatest returns relative to his operating costs. The price

and output upon which he decides are governed by the elasticity of demand for the product.

The monopolist obtains maximum profits when the growth of output, or sales, adds just as much to revenue as it does to costs. Fig. 2.14 illustrates this by showing how maximum profits are obtained when marginal revenue equals marginal cost. Marginal cost equals marginal revenue at the level of output Q_1. The price is obtained from the average revenue for this quantity, i.e. P_1. Firms in competition would have had to sell at the price

21

where average cost and average revenue meet, i.e. P_2. This would mean that the quantity sold, Q_2 would be greater and the price obtained much lower.

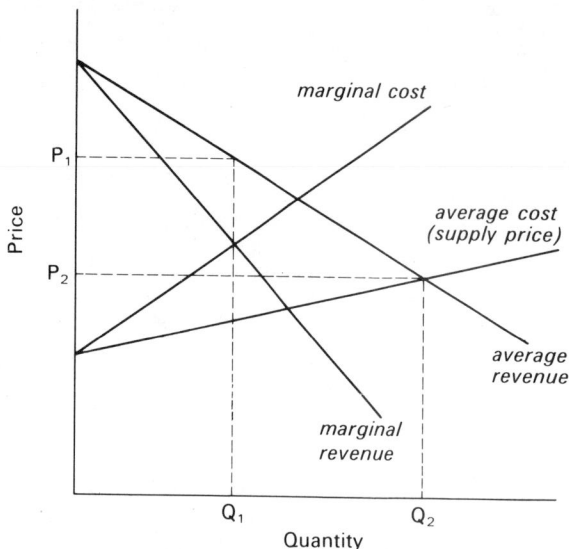

Fig. 2.14 Monopolistic pricing

Monopsony

The opposite face of monopoly, where there is only one buyer, is called monopsony. Farmers who grow produce for processing often find that there is only one processing plant in their area. This plant can, within limits, set its own buying price because it has no competitors. Under normal circumstances the more it buys the higher the supply price. Therefore the plant will buy that quantity at which its marginal cost equals the demand price. This is shown in Fig. 2.15. The quantity purchased is Q_1 at the price P_1. Thus it buys less and pays less than if it faced competition. Several firms competing against each other would buy the larger quantity Q_2 at the higher price P_2.

The limit to which a monopsonistic enterprise can keep down the prices it pays depends on two factors. The first factor is the need to safeguard invested capital and profit opportunities by keeping its suppliers in business. The second factor is the ease with which a new enterprise can set up in opposition.

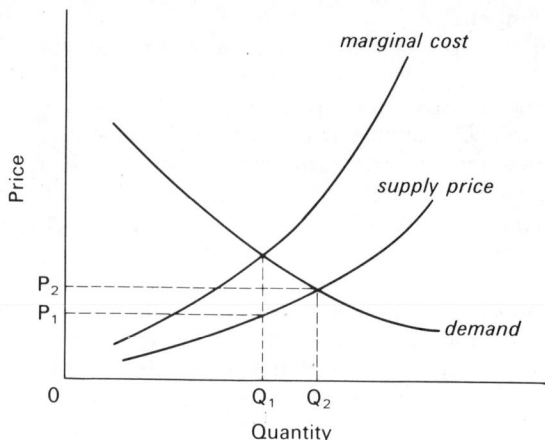

Fig. 2.15 Pricing under monopsony

Many governments have made abattoirs, marketing boards, state companies and cooperatives, monopolies. Other private and public enterprises are almost monopolies because they are protected from competition by high duties, exchange control and other limitations on imports. But monopolies and monopsonies are not necessarily bad. They may be able to operate at lower costs and promote sales more effectively than smaller firms because of economies of scale. That is to say they can apply better management, equipment and sales promotion because overhead costs are spread over a larger volume of business. In practice these lower costs are only achieved if the monopolies are firmly controlled by their management and whatever bodies are in a position to influence its decisions. Official monopolies in tropical countries are often criticised for the low quality of their service and the fact that illicit payments to their staff have to be made to get service at all.

Oligopoly

There is an intermediate stage between monopoly and competition in areas of marketing and farm supply which is not subject to official monopolies. This stage is called monopolistic competition or oligopoly (Greek, meaning *sale by a few*). In many countries a few firms dominate the supply of products such as fertilisers. These firms are all aware of each others' positions and possible reactions. They tend to avoid direct competition because it would result in the competition being returned. But they compete in other ways, for example by offering credit, by entertaining their customers, by advertising and making their products and services look more attractive. Fig. 2.16 is included to help make clear the relationship between monopoly, oligopoly and competition.

Separation of markets

Organisations that are able to control the total output for sale of a product can increase their returns in a number of ways that competing enterprises cannot. They can limit the total quantity of a product put onto the market. They can control the release of supplies by planned storage. They can control the amounts sold in separate markets. And, if they can prevent movement between these markets, they can change exactly what each independent market will bear.

Discriminatory pricing, as this system is called, takes advantage of differences in demand in different markets. The monopoly seller charges a high price in a high-income or inelastic demand market and a lower price in a low-income market where demand is more elastic. He could not do this if the markets were not separate because he would have to charge the same price to all customers. This means that high-demand buyers might buy at a lower price than they would have been willing to pay; while at the lower demand end, sales would decrease because the price would be too high for some customers.

Separation of markets may be complete where movement of a product is restricted by public authority. Separation may also be complete within certain price ranges if there are tariff barriers. It may be effective to varying degrees where it is based on differences in appearances, grading, packaging and advertising of the same basic product. Separation of markets by this last method is possible provided that sellers can convince their customers that different brands of the same product merit the payments of different prices. Individual farmers or small traders rarely sell enough to benefit from such methods. It is for this reason that they can often benefit from joint sales control arrangements.

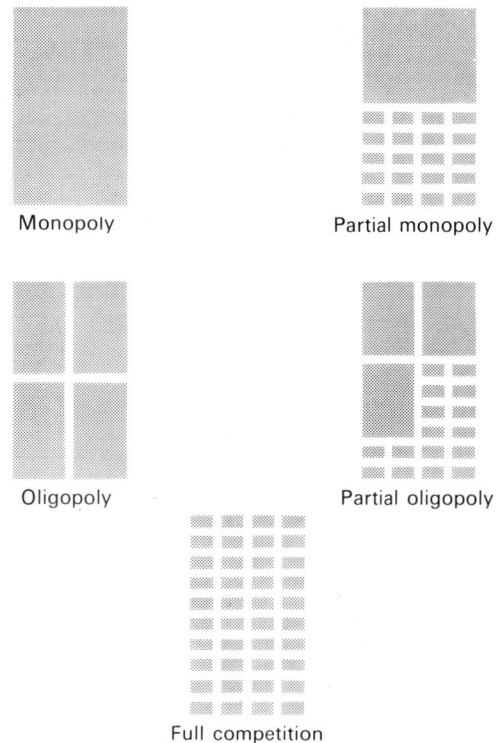

Monopoly   Partial monopoly

Oligopoly   Partial oligopoly

Full competition

Fig. 2.16 Levels of competition between buyers and/or sellers

Agricultural markets can also be separated by means of import quotas and controls to prevent the transmission of pests and diseases. The marketing of Californian oranges is an example of this. The movement of fresh oranges into California is prohibited on the grounds that they might bring pests or diseases to Californian orange groves. So the Californian growers have a protected market in their own State. They can sell their low-grade product for prices which are only governed by the local elasticity of demand. Meanwhile, higher quality oranges are exported to more distant markets where California fruit must compete with fruit from other sources.

Optimum allocation of resources

The function of a pricing system is to direct resources where they are needed. If the price of a product is high this attracts land, capital, labour and entrepreneurship into increased production. In this way demands reflected by higher prices are satisfied. The continuous adjustment of resources in response to demand is a sign of a healthy and flexible economy. It means that demands are met as they occur. It also means that resources are not used in the production of foods that are not wanted, which is very wasteful for an economy.

The following is needed for prices to guide agriculture towards producing what is needed:

(a) Prices should be known early so that production programmes can be adjusted to them.
(b) Prices should cover a sufficient period of time to allow production plans to be completed with reasonable certainty.
(c) Information on prices should be clear enough to allow farmers to interpret them for their own individual situations.

The price level should encourage the right amount of production that can be handled by the market at an acceptable price. If production is maintained at a higher level than is needed, by means of support prices for example, resources will not be used efficiently. Production capacity is retained which would be better shifted to some other product or activity.

How well this system works depends on the efficiency with which prices are reflected back to producers. Retail prices are often so high that they restrict consumption yet do not cause producers to grow more of what is needed. This may be because the impact of higher prices is not felt due to defects in credit and marketing. For example, farmers may be obliged to sell most of their output at harvest time to repay loans. If this happens they will receive a much lower price than the average throughout the year in wholesale markets. This may establish an effective brake on expansion of output.

At the same time the prices paid at each marketing stage must encourage the most effective allocation of resources to marketing. For example, prices should normally rise during the period after the harvest to cover storage and interest costs. Also, payment for transport must be attractive if there is to be enough, well-maintained transport available. On the other hand a monopoly of transport, along a key route from producing area to market could have a bad effect on production resources. If the monopoly resulted in exaggerated transport costs, production would be discouraged and the economy would suffer. The function of the marketing system is to shift produce from place to place, store it and change it to a form that consumers want. Market prices indicate what people want and thereby encourage efficient use of resources. Resources are not likely to be allocated in the best way where the natural movement of prices is hindered by movement controls, tariffs, monopolies and arbitrary fixing of prices and margins.

Governments and prices

In most countries governments intervene to modify prices for agricultural products that, without such intervention, would be set by the market. To pay for public services they may levy taxes on agricultural exports; it is relatively easy to collect taxes on products that must pass through a limited number of frontier control points. To placate influential urban consumers they may keep down the price of some strategic food products. This is done by setting maximum retail prices enforced by the police, by restricting exports with the expectation of increasing the supply on the domestic market, by importing supplies available free under aid programmes or at concessional prices. They can also reduce the price of fertiliser and credit by subsidies so as to favour particular groups of farmers.

Governments can also pursue macro-economic policies in support of overall development that impact negatively on prices to farmers. A common failing is to maintain an exchange rate for the national currency that is too high. This keeps down the price in local currency of materials that must be imported, e.g. petroleum and supplies for domestic industry. However, an overvalued exchange rate reduces the prices that farmers receive for export crops and, at the same time, makes it cheaper to import agricultural products. The exchange rate thus exerts pervasive downward pressure on the prices received by farmers.

It is the responsibility of governments to ensure that the prices of agricultural products and supplies are not distorted in a way that inhibits the growth of output and incomes. This does not mean that agriculture should not be taxed. In low-income countries, especially, agriculture constitutes the main tax base. Farmers must therefore contribute to help finance many government activities — not least the investments in infrastructure and irrigation from which they themselves benefit. For commodities such as tea, coffee and cocoa — which are produced mainly for export, and for which demand is more sensitive to quality than to price — it makes sound economic sense for governments to impose export taxes. Such taxes should be applied intelligently so that they do not act as a disincentive to production. The export taxes on Argentine beef during the Peron period, for example, were economically 'bad'.

Thus the issue is not whether to tax agriculture, but how and how much. Export taxes on tropical beverage crops have clearly been set too high in a number of African countries. Production has stagnated or declined, and market shares have been lost to other exporters.

Prices to farmers for domestic food products should not be kept artificially low. There would have been no food 'crisis' in 1973, it is claimed by World Bank analysts, if farmers in developing countries had been allowed to obtain the prices prevailing on international markets.

The rate at which a national currency is exchanged with the currencies of world trade is the most important price of all. If there is a black market rate then, with allowance for the degree of risk involved in illicit currency exchanges, this is an indicator of the equilibrium rate at which goods and services inside and outside the country have equal value. Bringing exchange rates into line with actual conditions in markets is critical for appropriate agricultural pricing.

As to the prices of agricultural inputs, the bulk of experience cautions against subsidies. Subsidised fertiliser prices may well encourage farmers to adopt fertiliser-using cultivation methods more rapidly than they would otherwise, but that is not a sufficient reason for subsidies. New practices that offer high economic returns are rapidly adopted by farmers, even without subsidies. And once instituted, subsidies are politically difficult to lower or remove. Credit also is often subsidised, in some cases at negative real interest rates. Thus farmers may be charged 6% interest for money that, because of inflation, has devalued by 10% by the time they are asked to repay it. Such a policy may stimulate investment in agriculture, but it is all too often of the wrong kind: subsidised interest rates, lower the effective cost of capital goods and lead to labour-displacing investments that are not warranted where labour is plentiful and capital is scarce. In any case, subsidised credit seldom reaches small farmers, since it is generally pre-empted by the larger and more influential ones.

Summary

There is a story of a man who claimed to have taught his parrot to be an economist. The parrot could repeat two words: 'supply' and 'demand'. This indeed is the heart of economics. However, the balancing of supply and demand is a process of great detail and subtlety and forever continuous. This chapter has set out some of the basic principles and shown how they apply to production and marketing.

The mechanism that brings supply and demand together at an equilibrium market price has been introduced. And we have discussed the allocation of resources through the pressures of profit incentives and competition. The limitations of competition in determining major issues affecting human welfare are clear enough. There are many areas where the application of competition is restricted. In others it might be considered undesirable. Even so it is an enduring force, never to be neglected in any realistic economic analysis.

Agricultural marketing and supply is full of monopolies and quasi-monopolies, so it is useful to know how a monopolist makes his pricing decisions and what techniques he can use to obtain higher returns. It is also important to be aware that the staff of state and cooperative organisations can exploit a monopoly as well as local traders.

Prices are the basic mechanism for directing resources into producing what society wants. This process can be modified by government intervention — by taxes and subsidies, import and export controls, and by keeping particular rates of exchange. There is a danger that such interventions become accepted government practice. Because of internal pressures governments find them difficult to relax. The result can be to delay shifts in the use of resources in accord with changes in comparative advantage and so obstruct development. As Marshall said half a century ago, 'Those who defy the market's rules eventually will be the fools.'

Issues for discussion

1 How are prices determined? What is meant by an equilibrium or market clearance price? Why do the prices of agricultural products which are sold in free markets often fluctuate rather widely? What are the main seasonal movements in your country for rice, maize, meat, eggs, milk, and other major farm products? Which enterprises in your area have the main role in price information for each of the main crops and livestock products? How have their wholesale prices varied over the last five years and what are the main factors influencing variations?

2 What is the degree of competition in the marketing of grains, other major crops, livestock and fertilisers in your area? Have there been significant changes in the share of the total market taken by different enterprises? What were the reasons for these changes?

3 Do you know of any enterprises that have a monopoly at the village level, the market level or the town level? On what is this monopoly founded and what are its limits?

4 What public agricultural, marketing or supply monopolies are there in your country? What advantages do they obtain from their monopoly position? Are there disadvantages for farmers? How can farmers in your country fight against any poor service and exploitation by employees of official monopolies that may occur?

5 For what major agricultural products would it be advantageous and possible to use market separation techniques in your country?

6 Is there a 'free' or black market exchange rate for your country? If so, what is your currency worth in US$? Work out the advantages and disadvantages to farmers were the government to shift to this rate.

7 In what ways does the government of your country influence the prices of food and agricultural products? How far do the prevailing prices differ from those that could be expected with an open ('free') market?

8 What are the advantages and disadvantages of free competition and government price fixing in achieving the best use of resources? What mixture of the two would you recommend for agricultural production and agricultural marketing in your country? Give the reasons for your recommendation.

Further reading

Jain, S. C. (1971) *Principles and practice of agricultural marketing and prices*, Vora, Bombay.

McArthur, A. G. and **Loveridge, J. W.** (1986) *Economics, theory and organization*, 2nd ed., McDonald, London.

Ritson, C. (1977) *Agricultural economics: principles and policy*, Granada, London.

Samuelson, P. A. (1974) *Economics: An introductory analysis*, 19th ed., McGraw-Hill, New York.

Simoons, F. J. (1961) *Eat not this flesh: Food avoidances in the Old World*, University of Wisconsin Press, Madison.

Stigler, C. J. (1966) *The theory of price*, Macmillan, New York.

Street, P. *What price food? agricultural price policies in the developing countries*, St. Martin's Press, New York

Timmer, C. P. (1986) *Getting prices right: the scope and limits of agricultural price policy*, Cornell University Press, Ithaca.

Timmer, C. P., Falcon, W. P. and **Pearson, S. R.** (1983) *Food policy analysis*, John Hopkins University Press, Baltimore.

Tolley, G., Thomas, V. and **Wong, C. M.** (1982) *Agricultural price policies and the developing countries*, John Hopkins University Press, Baltimore.

3   Marketing

How does food which may be produced on thousands of small separate farms, reach the consumer? How is it graded, prepared and packaged for the consumer to cook and eat? Who buys the excess that the farmer grows beyond his own family needs? Who provides storage space for produce that is not immediately required by consumers? The purchase, transport and storage of produce costs money. Where does the money come from to finance these activities? What kind of enterprises transport food from the producer to domestic consumers? How does produce reach markets in other countries? How do processing plants obtain their raw materials? What can farmers do to improve the prices they receive for their products and the services from the marketing system? What can consumers do to obtain a better service? What should the government do to improve the working of the marketing system as a whole? What is a marketing system? Why is it necessary and how is it organised? What information is required by the man who wants to run an agricultural marketing or supply enterprise? What are the problems he will face and how can he solve them?

Most people see only one part of the marketing process. Many farmers have contact only with those buyers who attend assembly markets near their village. Consumers generally shop at their favourite retailers, unless they come from the country and then they may obtain produce from the point of origin. Unfortunately, many governments seem to know very little about the marketing systems for which they are responsible. In many countries there are social and professional barriers between the staff of government departments and those who engage in commerce.

The purpose of this chapter is to show how to break down some of these barriers and to answer some of the questions. This should enable both farmers and consumers to make better use of the marketing facilities available to them. This chapter is also a guide for those who are thinking of going into marketing as a career, either on their own or with a cooperative or state organisation.

Many of the issues involved in improving marketing systems have implications for government policy. This chapter will, therefore, be of particular importance to those who work with governments on programmes aimed at marketing improvement and all those who will some day be in a position to influence government decisions.

Meaning of marketing

Marketing means different things to different people: to the housewife it means shopping for food; to the farmer it means the sale of his produce; to the fertiliser distributor it means selling to the farmer. Some people think of marketing as high pressure salesmanship. Teachers of marketing practice include all those business activities associated with the flow of goods and services, from production to consumption. All of these views reflect different aspects of the marketing process and constitute parts of the whole.

Agricultural marketing
The marketing of agricultural products begins at the farm when the farmer plans his production to meet specific demands and market prospects.

The product, when it is harvested, cannot usually go direct to the consumer. Firstly, it is likely to be located some distance from the place of consumption. Thus transport is required to bring the product to the right place. Secondly, agricultural production is generally seasonal while consumption is regular and continuous throughout the year. Thus storage is required to adjust supply to demand. Thirdly, a product when it has just grown, is rarely in a form acceptable to consumers. It must be sorted, cleaned, and processed in various ways, and must be presented to the consumer in convenient quantities. Finally, the farmer expects payment when his produce leaves his possession. Some financial arrangement must be made to cover all the various stages until the retailer sells the product to the consumer. It is marketing which provides these services between production and consumption.

As the economic development of a country

proceeds, the gap between farm and consumer widens and the tasks of marketing become more complex. Modern methods of storage and processing, including refrigeration, and forms of retail distribution are required. These may even become separate specialisations, although they still remain elements of marketing. Storage and processing facilities must be part of the marketing process if the system is to be used to full advantage. Retail enterprises have a direct link with the consumer and tend to reflect the needs of the consumer. The structure and sale methods of retailers can have an important influence on the marketing procedure linking the retailer to the farmer.

Agricultural marketing also includes the selling to farmers of supplies needed for production. These include fertiliser, pesticides, other agricultural chemicals, livestock feed, farm machinery, tools and equipment.

Special features of agricultural products

There are certain inherent characteristics of farm products which make special demands on marketing systems and organisations.

Farm products tend to be bulky. Their weight and volume is great in relation to their monetary value, especially when compared with many manufactured goods. As a result transport and storage charges for such products tend to be high in relation to their value.

Some crops, such as rice (in the form of paddy) retain their quality for a long time but most farm products are perishable. Fruits and vegetables rapidly become over-ripe and begin to decay if they are not consumed or kept in special storage. Milk is especially perishable. In hot climates and without special treatment, it may keep for only a few hours.

The seasonal nature of farm products imposes strains on a marketing system. At harvest time

(a)

(b)

Fig. 3.1 Where there is no effective marketing system there may be (a) high prices for the consumer, while (b) the farmer cannot find a buyer

there is a heavy demand for marketing facilities such as storage and buyers' credit. At other times of the year these facilities may be hardly used at all. This situation is made worse by the small size of the average production unit. Over the greater part of Asia, for instance, the average size of a holding is not more than two hectares. So many farm products start their journey to market as the small surpluses of many thousand separate farms.

Part A: Analysis

Marketing functions and services

There are various ways of looking at the functions and services involved in marketing. One way would stress the successive phases of concentration and distribution; another the stages of assembly, wholesale and retail (see Fig. 3.2). The nature of the tasks and responsibilities involved in marketing appear most clearly in the following:

(a) finding a buyer and transferring ownership;
(b) assembly and storage;
(c) sorting, packing and processing;
(d) providing the finance for marketing and taking the risks;
(e) assortment and presentation to consumers.

Finding a buyer and transferring ownership
The heart of marketing is finding a buyer for the product on sale, and the negotiation of acceptable terms. The simplest form of marketing is the bartering of surplus products for products that are needed. It may be difficult to find someone to provide exactly what is needed who will accept a specific product in return. It is convenient therefore for the farmer to sell to someone who is prepared to pay cash and who will himself look for a customer needing the product. This is the origin of the trader, and the entrepreneur specialising in marketing.

In many countries the town market square is the scene of direct transactions between producers and consumers. Here each producer accepts full responsibility for advertising his produce, finding customers and obtaining information to guide him in bargaining over the price. His task is made easier

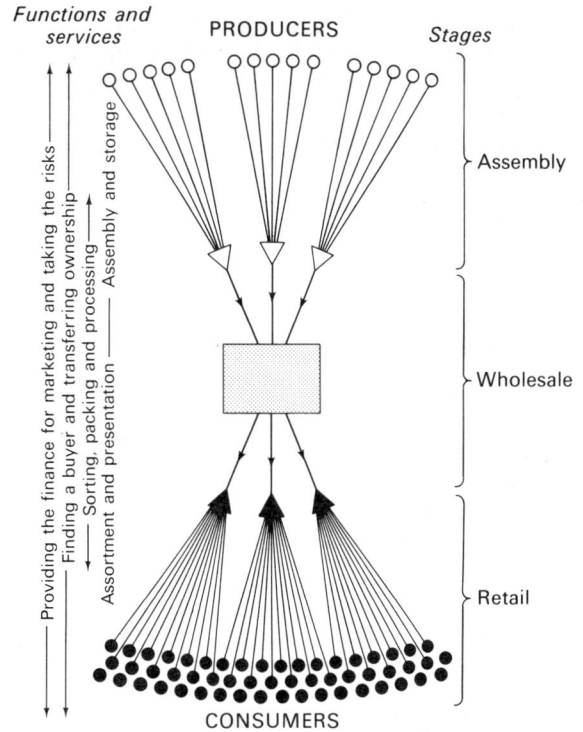

Fig. 3.2 What does 'marketing' mean?

by the presence of specialised traders who buy more than the consumers need and who will later offer the goods in a market where there is an unsatisfied demand.

In larger markets the producer and consumer may be separated by distance, time, and form requirements. Purchasing and selling services may then be furnished in conjunction with other services such as transport, storage and processing. Such services may be provided by specialised commission agents, brokers or auctioneers. These people do not usually handle or take possession of the goods sold, but simply negotiate sales in return for a fee.

People engaged in buying and selling products need certain information about the products that they deal with. Buyers need to know the character of the product and its suitability for various purposes. They also need to know its price in various markets since they do not want to pay too high a price to the seller. The sellers seek corresponding information. Where are the people who want to buy this produce? In what form do they want the product? What is the best time to sell, and what is the best price to ask? Advertising and market news systems have developed to help answer these questions.

Assembly and storage

The concentration of produce at convenient points attracts buyers who could not spare the time to make small purchases at scattered farms. It also enables the buyers to use larger, more economical transport and processing equipment. Special trucks, trains or boats can be provided to transport certain types of produce at a stated time, if the quantity moved is large enough to make up a full load.

The storage time required for some agricultural products will be only a few days, while the product is awaiting sale. Other products however may need to be stored for more than a year as when the surplus of a good crop is carried over to the following year. The type of storage varies widely with the nature of the product and the climatic environment. Grain requires protection from damp, mould and insect or animal pests. Eggs and meat generally need refrigeration.

Storage facilities are needed at various stages in marketing. Farmers can benefit if they can keep part of their crop to await seasonally higher prices. Most traders who take possession of produce need some storage space so that they can choose the best time to resell. Processing plants must have stocks of their raw material conveniently at hand. It is very expensive for machinery and staff to stand idle because of a delay in the arrival of supplies. Wholesale distributors and retailers need to maintain adequate stocks of all their items to cover variable day-to-day demands from customers.

Sorting, packing and processing

Harvested supplies coming from farms usually need sorting in some way so that consumers can choose the kind of produce they want. The characteristics used for sorting include size, shape, flavour, degree of ripeness, length of staple or some other quality which influences the commercial value of the product. Buyers are prepared to pay a higher price for produce when they are sure of its quality.

Many farm products must be enclosed in some

Fig. 3.3 Lightweight veneer boxes with corner supports protect fruit, reduce transport costs and make good presentation

kind of container if they are to be marketed widely and efficiently. These containers help to prevent physical deterioration. They make theft, adulteration or substitution more difficult. They ensure cleanliness. They facilitate measurement, labelling and the attachment of sales instructions and descriptions. Finally they may promote sales because of their attractive appearance to the consumer and suitability as an advertising medium (see Fig. 3.3).

The type of container used varies widely with the character of the product, the physical and climatic environment and the phase of marketing served. Generally the container is changed as the produce moves from the producer to the consumer. A product may leave the farm in sacks or baskets. During long-distance transport and storage it may be handled in bulk. For distribution to individual customers it may be presented in small packages of attractive appearance, in cans or bottles.

Some products undergo changes in form to adapt them to the householders' needs and tastes. Such changes are services provided by marketing. Some commodities such as grains, livestock and sugar cane cannot be used at all without processing. Paddy must be pounded or milled into rice. Meat animals are slaughtered, dressed and divided into convenient cuts and joints. Much milk is pasteurised and bottled or converted into butter and cheese. Perishable fruits and vegetables can be marketed over a much longer period if they are processed. Processing may include canning and drying and the extraction and bottling of juices.

Financing and carrying risks

Goods cannot pass through the marketing system without financial support. The owner of goods at any stage must either sacrifice the opportunity to use his own capital elsewhere or he must borrow the necessary capital from some other source. Thus, wholesalers must spend money buying the produce they handle. They must also finance the marketing facilities, such as processing and storage plants, and the transport equipment and office premises needed for their business. Retailers must pay for their sales premises, for storage of part of their stock which wholesalers will not carry, and in some cases their customers' purchases. All these financing needs involve interest costs on the money used.

There are important marketing risks to be carried. Farmers generally want to be paid a fixed price in cash before they hand over their produce. The buyer must carry the risk of finding a customer who is prepared to pay enough to cover both the purchase price and the other costs he is likely to incur. The risk of an unfavourable change in the price level is considerable. There is also the risk of deterioration of the product. The burden of these risks also contributes to the cost of marketing and must be covered by the profit margin obtained.

Assortment and presentation to consumers

Distribution systems also aim to meet the demands of the consumer. The supplies delivered to assembly points — warehouses, mills, etc. — vary in quantity and quality. Consumer demand also varies according to season, climate, income, religious teaching, local customs and many other factors.

Experience and access to market information let distributors release supplies from storage and move them from one area to another, so that the flow of goods to consumers will match their demands. Exchanging information with market contacts, the wholesale trade adjusts and equalises supply and demand. Some wholesalers simply provide the appropriate quality and quantity of supplies for use in mills or factories. Other wholesalers may be involved in splitting up loads into smaller quantities that are suitable for sale by the retailer to individual consumers at local shops.

A very small retailer may concentrate on selling a single product. But most retailers offer a selection of products that are conveniently brought together. The ultimate form of this is the supermarket which offers under one roof, all the food items in general consumption. In this case it is especially important to match the assortment of items to what the majority of consumers want.

Marketing agencies and channels

Marketing agencies carry out marketing functions or offer marketing services. To understand the part they play in marketing it is important to distinguish each type by the functions and services it undertakes, rather than by the nature of its ownership. For instance, a farmer may also be a wholesaler. Many merchant-moneylenders in India and West Africa were originally, and sometimes still are, farmers. Marketing agencies may be individuals acting independently, or they may be partnerships, large firms, cooperatives or government corporations. Any one of these various types of economic unit may also act in several capacities at the same time.

Local assemblers

These buyers undertake the initial task of assembling produce from farms or local country markets. They may be farmers who collect the produce of other cultivators. They may be landlords, village shopkeepers, itinerant traders, wholesale merchants and processors, cooperatives or government procurement agencies.

The local assembler may either act on commission or purchase on his own account. He may furnish credit to the farmer. He will probably arrange for the transport of his purchase to a central processing or wholesaling point. In any event he relieves the producer of further direct marketing responsibilities.

Wholesalers

The wholesaler has a central role in a marketing system. Wholesalers take produce from farmers or local assemblers. They sell to retailers, to other wholesalers in domestic and foreign markets and to manufacturers. Wholesalers may finance the movement of goods themselves, or with the aid of banks; in general they bear most of the marketing risks.

Wholesalers who are willing to take greater risks than others are often called speculators. They also perform a useful service, known as arbitrage. They buy when demand is low and resell when demand is high. They may also buy and sell in different areas where the demand differs. If there is competition, this kind of buying and reselling is useful because it can prevent prices from fluctuating between even wider extremes.

A wholesale marketing enterprise may be owned and operated privately, cooperatively, or publicly. Examples of each type are to be found in most countries.

Commission agents and brokers

Producers and wholesalers frequently want to offer their produce on markets which they cannot conveniently attend in person. Commission agents specialise in buying and selling for such people and take charge of goods on their behalf. They are encouraged to do well for their client by being paid a percentage of the price obtained. Commission agents run no risk, but must do better for their clients than the clients could do themselves, if they are to attract business. Commission agents are used mainly where direct offers tend to be low, as for perishable fruit and vegetables for sale on distant markets. By continuing to carry the risk, the seller retains the possibility of obtaining a much higher price.

Brokers bring potential buyers and sellers together. Their service is to provide an intimate knowledge of supplies, requirements and prices in various markets. The term 'broker' is best restricted to agents who do not own or physically handle goods. The actual transfer of ownership takes place between the original buyer and seller, with the broker acting as counsellor and intermediary in return for a fee. Brokers are in touch with a wide selection of specialised dealers and are well supplied with up-to-date information on markets. Brokers can thus offer a wider market to a buyer or seller than would otherwise be accessible to him.

Retailers

The function of the retailer is to obtain supplies and display them for sale in forms and at times and places convenient to consumers. Usually the retailer buys from one or more wholesale distributors, often on credit, and serves consumers buying small quantities on a day-to-day basis.

Frequently retailers sort, process and repack food to suit consumers' individual requirements. This may take place while the customer watches, as in the cutting of meat, or behind the scenes where prepackaging is acceptable. One management may control a number of retail outlets, and it may set up its own buying organisation which acts as a wholesale supplier. Such chain store buying agencies may deal directly with processors, large producers or producer groups. In this way the retailer obtains price advantages through large-scale buying. He can also maintain closer control over the flow and uniformity of his supplies.

Specialisation and integration

A continuing issue in marketing is how far to specialise. For example, an enterprise may undertake one function for one commodity in one place, or on the other hand combine a number of different activities or products in what is called an integrated enterprise. The retail chain with several branches in different parts of a town is horizontally integrated. If it sets up wholesale purchasing, packing, and processing units and buys directly from farmers, it is considered to be vertically integrated.

There are advantages and disadvantages for both specialised and integrated enterprises. Management requirements and abilities are often deciding factors. A specialised enterprise can:

(a) attract customers by offering a wide range of qualities;

(b) become very familiar with the product handled, its sources of supply and the nature of demand;
(c) give direct personal attention to management and pricing.

The enterprise will be efficient in conditions where these considerations are important. Where, for example, rice is a major consumption item and consumers attach great importance to fine shades of quality, there are likely to be specialised retailers. But where rice is only purchased occasionally and in a few standard grades, it is best handled along with other foods.

The integration of a range of marketing activities in one enterprise can offer advantages in:

(a) assuring supplies and outlets, thus reducing business risks and the cost of purchasing and sales;
(b) enhancing bargaining power either through handling a larger volume of business or having more alternative market and service opportunities;
(c) making fuller use of management, buildings, or equipment, e.g. transport vehicles, that are already available;
(d) obtaining greater returns from the money spent on advertising and sales promotion.

Thus a retail chain in Recife, Brazil, acquired a rice mill in a producing area and was then able to offer rice at lower prices than other retailers.

It is important that the separate elements of an integrated enterprise do in fact complement each other. It is often suggested, for example, that farmers marketing cooperatives should integrate with consumers' cooperatives. They rarely do so in practice because the nature and timing of sales by the farmers' cooperatives do not match the supply needs of the consumers' cooperatives.

In tropical countries, integration is often arranged through members of a family. A brother located in the producing area sends produce to a brother who retails it in town. A particularly successful Chinese rice trader in Malaysia had several mills located in different villages, each managed by one of his wives whom he visited in turn.

Marketing channels

Contacts with farmers in a number of villages or a visit to a typical African market might give the

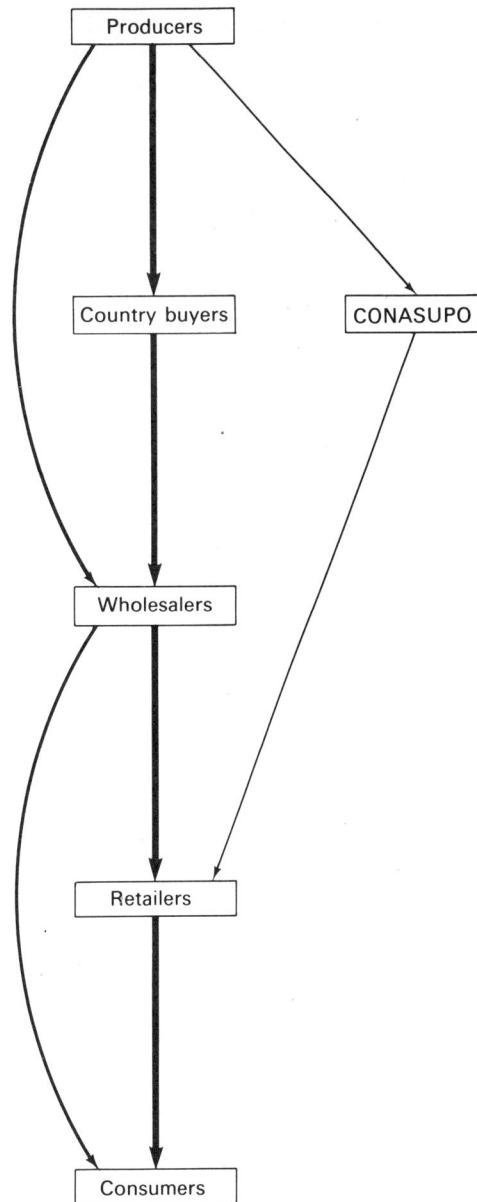

Fig. 3.4 Marketing channels for beans; Mexico

impression that myriads of people are engaged as marketing 'middlemen' and that products go through many hands from farm to consumer. Marketing does indeed offer employment to many people and often there are many small one-man or family enterprises. This does not mean, however, that a single batch of produce passes through so many hands. Usually it follows a fairly well established channel from farmer to consumer. A major marketing channel such as that shown for beans in Mexico (Fig. 3.4) is often made up of many smaller channels in parallel. From Fig. 3.4 it may be seen that some beans bypass some intermediaries; they are bought by wholesalers who also retail to consumers. There is also a channel provided by one enterprise, CONASUPO, set up by the Government to provide an outlet at specified prices.

Sometimes a marketing channel made up of many small enterprises may not be very significant in terms of the volume handled. As a basis for planning new investments or other programmes to improve marketing, information of the kind presented in Fig. 3.5 should be available. This shows the main marketing channels for fruit and vegetables and the share that each channel handles of the total.

Marketing institutions

These generally develop to meet a specific need or to provide a service for which there is a demand. They can be very helpful to the farmer in selling his crops. He should find out what services they can provide and where to look for the help he needs. Marketing institutions are also intended to help consumers and all those engaged in marketing operations. It is up to these three categories of users to see that the marketing institutions in their areas are adapted to their requirements.

Markets

People conduct most of their trading activities at recognised places and times because this makes it easier to find exchange partners. Thus farmers take their produce to town on the day when most buyers will be there. In this way market days have developed as an institution. The next step is the establishment of some market authority to keep order and supervise conditions of sale. Later, stalls for protection against the weather, and other facilities may be provided by public bodies or through private initiative in return for fees paid by users.

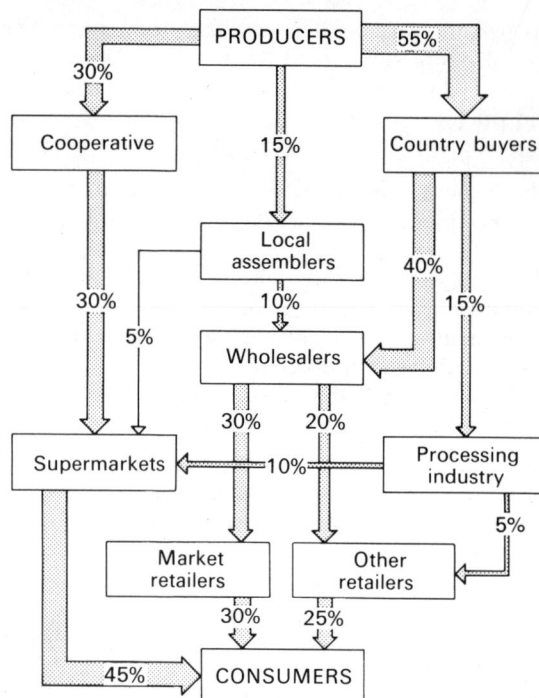

Fig. 3.5 Marketing channels for fruit and vegetables

A market can be defined as an area in which exchange can take place. It also means the people living there who have the means and desire to buy a product. Thus there can be a 'local' market, a 'domestic' market and a 'world' market. The limits of this kind of market are set not by a physical boundary fence, but by ease of communications, and transport. There may also be political and monetary barriers to the free movement of goods and money. A country which has high tariff barriers or allows no foreign exchange for imports, effectively seals off its internal market from all others. For cotton exported from India, Sudan and Uganda, the importing countries constitute a single world market in which each supplier competes.

Local assembly markets

Much local assembly is undertaken by buyers who go to the farmer in his village to bid for fruit on the tree or for grain after harvest. This saves the farmer trouble but he is at a disadvantage in bargaining unless he knows what other possible buyers would offer. At an organised market where various buyers and other farmers are present, he has a better chance of obtaining full value for his produce. Usually a local authority provides an enclosed space for the use of buyers and sellers, display pens for animals, and perhaps also a covered sale area and some impartial information on prices. Sales may take place by public auction or by private negotiation; there are rules which protect the buyer against fraud, and which ensure payment to the seller before his property leaves the market.

Central wholesale markets

These develop to meet the supply needs of large cities. They provide a convenient buying point for retailers. Some wholesalers may also buy there for other towns. In this way such markets may become the centre for setting prices for a large area.

Usually the site has good transport access and is equipped with display premises which are rented to wholesalers or commission agents. Sales proceed quickly. The smooth operation of such markets depends on the experience of the users, their need to maintain a reputation for fair dealing and on public regulation. Most such markets are managed either by a city authority or a special body set up by market users. This body provides some protection against fraud and arbitrates in cases of dispute.

Commodity exchanges

These are wholesale markets at which the goods traded never appear. They are bought and sold by description. As long as communications are good, they can serve a vast market area as well as being sensitive to local changes in supply and demand. Offers and orders to buy may be received by telegram or telephone. There must be recognised quality standards and specifications, and confidence that the market authority will require the responsible parties to make good any discrepancies.

A cargo of groundnuts on a ship bound from West Africa to Liverpool may be sold during the journey and the destination can be switched to, say, Antwerp. Such a sale could be specified 'free on board' (f.o.b.). This means the final buyer must pay for freight charges to his receiving point. Alternatively, a shipment may be sold 'cost insurance freight' (c.i.f.) at a rail terminal or port where the buyer would receive it free of all transport charges.

Commodity exchanges may also operate 'futures markets'. Warehouse operators, flour millers, feed manufacturers, processors and exporters, plan their operations with a view to making a normal profit in return for the marketing service they offer. They may not necessarily wish to carry the risk of a sharp change in the value of their stocks. Buying 'futures' provides a means of insurance against such risks.

The procedure may be illustrated as follows. Assume that, in late November, a merchant buys 500 tonnes of maize. He pays a price which allows for transport charges, etc., and his own normal operating profit. This would equal the spot price — at that time say $25 per tonne. To protect himself against the risks of price decline, he immediately sells 500 tonnes of the December future at a price which might be $25.30 per tonne. Whether grain prices move up or down does not matter to him now because a loss in one market will be largely offset by a gain in the other. If the price has fallen by $5 per tonne when the grain is resold, this loss will be offset by a profit of $5 per tonne in the futures market. Through hedging, as this is called, to avoid price risks wholesale operations on free markets can proceed on a smaller profit margin than would otherwise be possible.

There are important futures dealings in grains, cotton, oilseeds and other products. However, not all commodity markets lend themselves to futures trading. The essential requirements seem to be a standard form of product, unrestricted movement to market, suitability for storage, and uncertain supply and demand. The production of the commodity must be sufficiently widespread for an adequate volume to be available at all times. There must be many and varied outlets for the commodity, so that there is always a substantial group ready to buy. Restriction of either production or buying may lead to market manipulation and sharp fluctuations in prices. If the price of a commodity is stabilised by effective government programmes, there is little need for a national futures market.

Retail markets

These are established on sites that are easily accessible to the consumer. They enable a variety of retailers to display their produce for sale. The advantage to consumers is that they find in one place a range of suppliers from which to choose. Without much effort and expense, the sellers can expect a number of consumers to contact them. As retail markets become institutionalised, municipal authorities build permanent stalls with protection against sun and rain; these stalls are rented to retailers for a fee. Producers are usually allowed to take up places in retail markets if they wish, and sell directly to consumers. They can also set up roadside markets and sell direct to town people travelling in rural areas.

Marketing support services

Market regulation
Marketing goes well where there is legal enforcement of contracts and protection against fraudulent practices. Of general benefit are standard weights and measures and quality specifications which minimise disagreement among traders and reduce the need for individual inspection of every lot. Such measures reduce risks and costs, and may extend the market by making it possible to do business by letter and by telephone. There are minimum health and sanitation standards required for workers, premises and handling procedures. This protects consumers and also helps the better trader in competition with less scrupulous rivals. Transport and other market operations may be regulated to ensure honesty in vital services. Where products are sold in distant markets, an official certificate of quality may bring higher returns. Seeds offered for public sale may be limited to lots which are certified as reaching an approved standard. This will ensure the production of standardised varieties well suited to large scale processing and marketing. It is essential that the contents of fertilisers and pesticides are shown correctly on the package and there should be penalties for misrepresentation.

Rules should be laid down for the use of public storage and warehousing. The operator should obtain insurance coverage and safeguard the produce against loss by fire and theft. This aids the development of services by reducing risks to users.

The enforcement of such regulations requires an effective inspectorate. Generally it is only worth while to attempt enforcement if the majority of traders and market users are likely to support it.

Market information and intelligence
This is essential for producers, traders, and consumers, if market mechanisms are to work efficiently. Information helps them to balance supply and demand in particular markets and thus avoid gluts and surpluses with their corresponding fluctuations in prices. Farmers need information about probable supplies and prices in order to make decisions when planning their production and sales. The knowledge that a farmer can compare one price offered by a trader with another price elsewhere, also influences buyers in offering fair prices.

Access to better information enables wholesalers to develop those consumer demands and producer supplies which might otherwise have been neglected. This reduces their business risks and enables them to operate profitably on lower margins. This brings benefits to both producers and consumers. Consumer purchases can also be influenced by market news. They can be encouraged to leave products that are in short supply and buy alternatives that are plentiful. Programmes of price and supply stabilisation are more effective when based on reliable estimates of production, storage carry-overs, internal movements and prices. To collect and broadcast such information is a complex operation. It must be processed rapidly to avoid becoming out-of-date. It must be presented in a simple style which can be understood readily by all interested parties. This calls for a government sponsored service with a permanent staff and budget.

Research
Research both to improve marketing and to develop markets is needed. Market research may be undertaken by marketing enterprises to guide their investment and sales policies and reduce their costs (see Part B). By raising their own efficiency, such enterprises help to improve the overall system. Marketing research which does not benefit a particular enterprise is usually carried out by a government or university research unit on funds provided publicly, or by a trade association or marketing board.

A practical marketing research programme might include the following:

(a) preparation of plans for marketing facilities in production areas, at wholesale concentration points, and in distribution centres;

(b) determination of the best handling methods, equipment and use of equipment under local conditions, for the various stages of marketing — transport, storage, packing, etc. — in order to minimise loss and damage and reduce operating costs;

(c) development of improved methods of wholesaling and retailing;

(d) ways of improving the marketing of products of regional or national importance.

Extension and training

In most of the tropical countries there is a lack of trained personnel and this is a major constraint on marketing development. Marketing courses can be included in college teaching programmes and concentrated courses can be offered at various levels. People must be encouraged to work in marketing when their training is completed. Maximum use should be made of in-service training opportunities offered by efficient enterprises. Preferably there should be at least one institution that combines practical research and training, for these two activities reinforce each other.

Bringing research results, practical advice, and government policy to the larger body of farmers and marketing workers, calls for extension techniques. An obstacle to the organisation of agricultural marketing extension in most countries, has been the need to focus on operations between the farmer and the consumer for which no single ministry is responsible. It is hardly possible to send a marketing adviser to each farmer and small trader. However, a limited number of marketing specialists can collaborate with general extension staff in organising programmes to help farmers and local assemblers and market personnel.

Sales promotion

Promotional campaigns are now an integral part of marketing. They may involve advertising by posters, in the press, on radio and television, or provide special displays and introductory prices through retailers. They can be very powerful in influencing traders and consumers in favour of a particular product. These techniques are now widely used, particularly for produce sold in export markets where there is much competition. The Spanish exporters' syndicate was spending $1 million annually on the promotion of Spanish oranges in European markets already in the 1960s. While most sales promotion is undertaken by enterprises in a position to benefit from it directly (see Part B), it can also be an important way in which governments can support agricultural marketing. Export promotion centres have been set up in many countries funded from customs revenues. Sometimes they are effective, sometimes not. This depends very much on the calibre of their staff.

Governments can assist export promotion campaigns by direct financial contributions. They may also sponsor participation in trade fairs and exhibitions and make available commercial services through embassies, etc. School and other educational programmes can promote domestic consumption of products that improve health. Such products include fresh fruit, vegetables and milk.

A qualified sales promotion agency would normally be employed to design and implement a promotion campaign. Familiarity with the conventions and viewpoints of the people that the campaign is intended to influence is essential. Knowing the agricultural product concerned is important. Ideas, and experience of the promoters of other products can also be valuable.

Sources of credit

Access to financing institutions is essential at all stages of marketing.

(a) Growers need credit before and during production to meet the costs of seed, fertilisers, and pesticides. Further credit may be needed after harvest so that the farmer can hold part of his crop until prices rise.

(b) Wholesalers need short term credit to pay the farmer before reselling the goods. Longer term credit is required to finance business premises, storage depots, transport and equipment. In the case of wholesale processors, further specialised equipment would be needed and the turnover of working capital would take a much longer time. The processor of a perishable crop may have to buy the produce during a short harvest season. During this time he may sell almost nothing because it coincides with the peak season for the fresh produce.

(c) The retailer needs short term credit to acquire stocks before he is paid by his customers. He may even give credit to them.

The normal source of credit for these purposes is the commercial bank. The wholesaler often acts as an intermediary and guarantor for the farmer from whom he buys, and for the retailer to whom he sells. Because of the risks involved, such credit may be very restricted in quantity, and involve heavy commitments on the terms of resale. This may become a bottleneck for development.

Governments can assist by making funds available for developing agricultural and food marketing. They can also require that the existing banking system lends to 'marketing' a specific proportion of deposits on terms on a par with those available to other favoured borrowers.

Marketing enterprises

Marketing enterprises fall into three broad categories. First and most common in most countries is the independent private enterprise. It may range in size and complexity from a one-man firm to a multinational corporation. The distinguishing feature is that its capital is provided by individuals at their discretion. Participation in its decision making and eventual profits is on the basis of capital contributions.

The second category is the cooperative, founded on the principle of equal participation by its members in its capitalisation and its directing committee. Initially it may be run by an elected chairman and secretary. For continuing operations a salaried manager is usually needed.

The third is the parastatal, established and funded by government. Its directing body normally provides for agricultural, commercial and government representation. A manager is appointed to carry on its business. While subject to government policy directives it is autonomous in day-to-day operations.

Private enterprise

Over a wide range of conditions indigenous private entrepreneurs have shown that they are well suited to the following:

(a) Starting up and going a long way with little capital. They are great builders of capital assets. Their operators tend to be economical, even parsimonious, in their personal expenditure. Outlays on equipment and other capital expenditures are kept to the minimum and delayed until proven indispensable.

(b) Operating at low cost. Full use is made of family labour. They are stringent in their requirements for paid staff. Only those who make a positive contribution to the enterprise are paid.

(c) Following up new ideas and exploiting unforeseen opportunities. Because decision making is concentrated, these entrepreneurs tend to show ready initiative and quick response to changing situations.

(d) Using family ties and kinship linkages to extend their marketing operations with high confidence and low risk. Where the infrastructure for marketing is at an early stage of development, reliable means of communicating information, sales commitments and financial proceeds are important.

A continuing sanction against inefficiency in a private enterprise is that, unless there are barriers to the entry of new firms, it will lose customers and go out of business.

There are four main areas of marketing where private enterprise tends to perform well.

Perishable products Variability in quality, a tendency to deteriorate quickly if not held in special storage or processed, and sharp changes in price in response to variable supply, call for rapid responses on the part of enterprises marketing such products.

Livestock and meat The variability of the product, the need for judgement in appraising quality and value and for care in handling to avoid losses gives an edge to direct decision making. The predominance of private enterprise in marketing livestock and meat also reflects a reluctance of many people to come close to the realities of this trade.

Combined purchase of produce and sales of farm inputs and consumer goods When the quantities supplied and taken by each customer are small and varying, considerable local knowledge, patience and willingness to work over a wide range of hours and locations is needed. Prices may have to be

Fig. 3.6 (a) A low-cost private buying agency for the Kenya Cereals and Produce Marketing Board

(b) Direct sales by truckers at San José wholesale produce market, Costa Rica

adjusted at each transaction, and complex small scale credit arrangements maintained if such an enterprise is to serve its clientele well. Often, only a family enterprise, with a wife or child minding a shop while the husband goes out on rural purchasing and sales rounds, can provide this service economically.

New and highly specialised activities in marketing Characteristically these are the outcome of an individual initiative, not a planned development by a committee or a government department. Not all such initiatives succeed in the longer run. However, leaving no legal scope for private initiatives can shut the door on exploiting opportunities

that would be directly contributive to development (Fig. 3.6).

Collaboration with foreign private enterprise in transnational joint ventures can also hasten the pace of marketing development. It can bring in the following:

Finance This can come in as equipment, improved seeds, strategic supplies and skilled management and technology for which foreign exchange would be needed in any event.

Applied technology Developing countries face the risk of choosing unsuitable designs and equipment and face problems in putting new plants into operation and maintaining them. Engaging an enterprise with demonstrated experience in applying a desired technology and in a position to keep it up to date is often the safest and, in the longer run, the least expensive way of getting it.

Management When qualified management experienced in specific lines of processing and marketing comes with a transnational project, there is an immediate advantage. Local personnel can learn by working with the project. The cost of keeping expatriate managers will lead the transnational to promote nationals to their place as soon as they are competent enough.

Quality standards and presentation The transnational experienced in maintaining high standards can help a developing country to meet such needs to sell successfully on export markets. It can also reduce quality risks to domestic consumers and help adapt domestic agriculture to produce raw materials with the required attributes.

Market access In export sales, a close link with an enterprise which has established outlets in major import markets is a great advantage. Experience shows that when prices turn down, exporters with continuing distribution arrangements in the importing countries hold on to their market and the independents lose out.

Brands These carry great weight with consumers, and the wholesalers and retailers who serve them. An agreement to sell through the owner of an established brand lets the producer share in the benefits of past outlays on its promotion.

It is in export marketing that a transnational venture can be most helpful. Knowing the import market's requirements and having an established

39

position there are strategically important. The products most favoured by such arrangements are branded processed items such as canned pineapples and soluble coffee, and perishables that can meet the quality requirements of a distant market under integrated management, e.g. bananas. Economies of scale favour transnationals in the development and distribution of higher yielding seeds and poultry strains, and specialised livestock feed ingredients, pesticides, etc.

Private marketing enterprises supply fruit, vegetables and meat to consumers in most tropical countries. They are the basic food suppliers of the big cities of Nigeria. After B.U.D./Senegal failed to organise large scale movements of out-of-season produce to Europe, it was local private entrepreneurs who continued shipments by air.

Transnationals developed many of the main export lines of the tropical countries; they continue to lead with canned pineapples, bananas and tobacco. A more recent development is the Charoen Pokphan broiler operation in Thailand. A local firm combined with Arbor Acres, providing productive strains and feed ingredients and with Japanese importers who assured them of a profitable market. In 1981 it was earning $30 million in foreign exchange; it also became the major supplier to the domestic market.

Limitations of private enterprise in marketing are:

(a) difficulties in access to capital;
(b) variability in management;
(c) a propensity to collude over prices, if there are only a few traders in a particular market.

To get the best performance from a private enterprise structure, therefore, a government should:

(a) make their access to credit and information easier;
(b) promote management training that is practical and convenient;
(c) stimulate competition by removing barriers to the entry of new firms, assisting new entrants and penalising collusion.

Attitudes towards private marketing enterprises are prejudiced in a number of tropical countries by the fact that many of them are in alien hands. The best policies in such circumstances are (a) to learn from the 'aliens' and (b) to absorb them. Where religious and other factors inhibit integration, the aliens can still be obliged to take on local partners and form registered companies in which local interests have a specified minimum share.

In the case of transnational ventures there is the risk that:

(a) the foreign partner will withdraw if trading conditions become unfavourable, so leaving a gap in the market;
(b) if the foreign partner has financial power it might be used to wield political influence.

These risks may be more apparent than real. Transnational operations are highly susceptible to organised labour and political pressures. For each transnational there is an alternative to take its place. The government of a developing country can now assess the benefits that transnational collaboration can bring to its economy and bargain over the terms. In so concluding we do not intend to be apologists for the transnationals. They are a fact of life. They have a lot to offer on the marketing front. One may as well take advantage of their experience (which is often bitter).

Cooperatives

In principle a group of farmers should be able to market their produce more advantageously by selling together. This enables them to:

(a) benefit from economies of scale in the use of transport and other services through increasing the volume of produce handled at one time;
(b) increase their bargaining power by offering a larger quantity concentrated under a single management.

Establishing cooperative marketing arrangements necessarily calls for some time and patience from the farmers concerned. Their motivation is generally a reaction against felt ill treatment, i.e. they believe that the existing channels of marketing are not providing satisfactory prices and service. The Cotia Cooperative in Brazil, which now holds a dominant position in the supply of fruit and vegetables to the city of Sao Paulo, developed from such an origin. It reflects the determination of an ethnic group of settlers to band together against felt market exploitation.

In many tropical countries, governments have set up farmers' cooperative credit and marketing systems. They saw them as a useful mechanism for rural development and assisted them with tax exemptions, concessional credit and a range of support services. They were also a convenient base for political patronage and mobilising external aid. Often they were made monopoly agencies for marketing board purchases and for distributing farm inputs. Experience with such cooperatives in Asia and East Africa has led to the following observations:

(a) Traditional ethics which require loyalty to a family and clan do not carry over to cooperatives promoted by distant governments.
(b) The interests of cooperative employees lie in preserving and expanding their hierarchy. Local committees, chairmen and managers are tempted to exploit their monopoly position. This can be quite contrary to the interests of the farmer.
(c) Creating cooperatives from above according to administrative districts is unlikely to stimulate democratic participation. More likely it will encourage attitudes of dependence or apathy.
(d) A continuing obsession with cooperatives can become a major obstacle to agricultural development. Cooperatives frequently fail to achieve their goals and this results in a catastrophic defeat of integrated programmes built round them.
(e) The cost of marketing through a monopoly cooperative marketing board structure can often be much higher than that of the private enterprises it replaced (see Fig. 3.7).

Government policies towards cooperatives need to be pragmatic and realistic. Conditions favouring farmer cooperative marketing are:

(a) specialised producing areas distant from their major markets;
(b) concentration, specialisation and homogeneity of farm production for market;
(c) groups of farmers dependent on one or a few crops for their total income;
(d) availability of local leadership and management;
(e) an educated membership;
(f) members with strong kinship or religious ties.

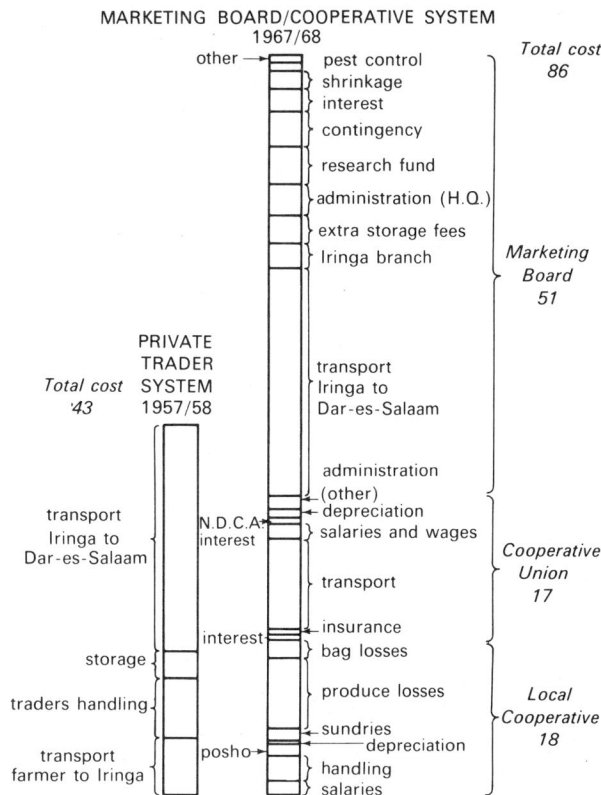

Fig. 3.7 Maize marketing costs; Iringa to Dar-es-Salaam, 1957–58 and 1967–68; ($ per tonne). (*Source:* **Kriesel, H. C.** (1971) Statement to the International Conference on the Marketing Board System, Ibadan, Nigeria)

On these bases some outstanding cooperative marketing operations have developed. The Anand Milk Producers' Cooperative in India markets over 750 tonnes of milk per day for 120 000 producer members. The Hae-ee Vegetable Marketing Group in Korea sells squash grown out of season under plastic and has obtained outstandingly favourable terms from wholesalers and transporters.

Cooperative systems established at the initiative of governments have difficulty in competing with private enterprise performing the same functions. Yet experience shows that after a cooperative disappears the cost of the service offered by private enterprise tends to rise. One solution is to ensure, by some measure of protection short of monopoly, sufficient turnover for the cooperatives to keep them in business. This has been done in India by allocating 40% of the total supply of fertilisers to them for distribution, backing this up with funds from a cooperative bank to provide credits to their members. This constitutes an operating base from which an individual cooperative with strong leadership can take on a range of other marketing activities to help its members.

In most tropical countries special government departments have been established to support the development of cooperatives. The principle of equal shares makes it difficult for them to mobilise capital if most members are small farmers. The incentive they can offer to paid staff is limited. They are committed to a complex accounting system. A need for continuing assistance in financing, management and staff training must be foreseen.

Parastatals

These include boards, state corporations, development authorities and other marketing bodies given authority, capital and a source of income by government. In the developing countries they have consolidated into three broad groups:

1 Those with legal powers over other participants in specified commodity markets.
2 Those with responsibility for stabilising specified commodity prices by operating buffer stocks alongside other enterprises.
3 Those with a legal monopoly of a defined area of marketing.

Parastatal enterprises are a convenient mechanism for government policy because they:

(a) are directly responsible to a designated ministry;
(b) have the autonomy to respond to operational marketing requirements;
(c) can be considered acceptable bodies to assume monopoly powers.

Enterprises in Group 1 are generally empowered to undertake promotion and quality control, and manage market flows and price stabilisation funds; they do not engage in marketing operations. The organisation which controls the flow of winter tomatoes from Mexico to maximise returns from US markets allocates quotas and minimum size specifications. Implementation is via the packing stations which despatch shipments. A limited number of border crossing points facilitates control. This type of parastatal may also stabilise prices to producers of export crops by requiring the exporters to pay into a fund when prices are high. The fund is then drawn on to make up prices to producers when export markets are unexpectedly low. This approach has been used widely in francophone Africa. It is adapted to situations where there are a relatively few independent exporting firms and there is confidence that the stabilisation fund will retain its value. It is in disfavour where currencies are subject to inflation and there is experience of accumulated reserves being diverted to other uses.

To moderate supply and price fluctuations in food grains on domestic markets, a parastatal stabilisation agency (Group 2) can buy into and sell from a buffer stock. Most African, Asian and Latin American countries have established such mechanisms to implement minimum prices to producers of major food grains and to protect consumers against prices likely to cause hardship. Sharp variations in price can be caused by marginal surpluses and deficits; buying into and selling from a buffer stock some 5 to 15% of the total quantity marketed is normally sufficient to eliminate price extremes. Confining the operation to such proportions limits the capital and subsidy required from the government. It leaves the bulk of the trade to private marketing enterprises, which are generally able to operate more economically because they have lower overheads and can select transactions to match their resources and convenience.

Nevertheless, the need to subsidise food grain stabilisation parastatals can become a continuing burden. It can be reduced by maintaining a wider margin between buying and selling prices and applying price differentials to cover transport costs and promote quality maintenance and local storage. Private buying agents can be used instead of direct purchasing stations. Buying costs per bag of maize for the marketing board in Kenya were estimated in the early 1980s at 4.80 shillings for private agents, 6.15 for direct buying and 7.0 for a cooperative agency.

Parastatals with a monopoly of the marketing of a certain product (Group 3) can obtain higher returns for export products if they control enough of the total supply on their markets to be able to influence prices. Within its particular seasonal niche on the UK market, the Cyprus Potato Board has such a position. Supplying 40% each of the long staple export markets, the cotton monopolies of Egypt and Sudan can release supplies at a pace that maintains prices. Where buyer preferences vary, however, a monopoly board may obstruct price signals seeking to adjust production to their needs. It can also become a discriminatory vehicle for taxation.

Monopolies in domestic marketing are assigned to parastatals to concentrate sales of produce through a particular processing plant to justify the investment, to facilitate collection from small farmers of credit repayments and other dues, and to implement market separation programmes whereby higher overall prices can be obtained.

If a parastatal is given a monopoly it is in a favourable position to avoid losses that must be met by government, but checks on its efficiency are difficult to devise. While it is fairly easy to add staff, many parastatals find it very hard to terminate them. Management must also cope with competing staff loyalties and the depredations of politicians.

In the absence of legal alternatives, producers and consumers are obliged to use the services of a monopoly parastatal. It is on them that the burden of its costs will fall. Significantly higher shares of the price which consumers paid for the major food grains were taken by marketing organisations in Tanzania, Kenya and Malawi during the 1970s, as against Nigeria and Sudan and some Asian countries. The marketing monopolies maintained in these three countries were responsible for much of the extra cost. (See Fig. 3.7.) This can result from higher costs forced onto parallel marketing enterprises by the restrictions they imposed, from the higher staff and transport costs of their own operations and from the costs of additional services such as maintaining strategic reserves and pan-territorial pricing. Over the years 1971–79, the costs incurred by the monopoly board of Jamaica in marketing bananas in the UK averaged $100 per tonne higher than those of bananas marketed in Germany from Ecuador. Along this latter channel a national private enterprise was in competition with two transnationals.

If a parastatal monopoly is maintained there should be a clear technical and economic justification: that it permits a certain marketing function to be carried out more efficiently than would be feasible otherwise.

In determining the most appropriate marketing enterprise for a particular situation, local conditions can be decisive to an extent that is often glossed over. Where family allegiances are dominant and the commercial infrastructure is uncertain, the more elaborate organisations are handicapped.

Marketing efficiency

It is in everybody's interest that marketing should be efficient. The producer looks for efficiency in the auction market or commission agency through which he sells his produce. The consumer wants an efficient service from the retailers he uses. Those who run marketing enterprises certainly want to be able to earn enough to pay good salaries and receive good profits. Only a few people, however, are in a position to do much about raising the efficiency of a system as a whole. These are research workers whose investigations and analyses create informed opinion, and the marketing specialists in government organisations who are responsible for formulating policy. This section on the efficiency of the marketing system as a whole is intended mainly for such readers. First it examines the meaning and some of the features of efficiency in marketing. Then it goes on to outline approaches that have been found useful in appraising efficiency in actual market situations.

To farmers the sale of their products at the highest possible price would be efficient marketing. Consumers would see efficiency as the provision of high quality supplies at the lowest possible price. Yet too high a price for the farmer would limit sales to consumers, and too low a price would discourage the production of future supplies. The satisfaction of consumer requirements at the lowest possible cost is linked with the maintenance of a high volume of farm output.

Neither party stands to benefit from unnecessary marketing charges, wasteful methods and inconvenient structures. The interests of both groups are reconciled if marketing efficiency is defined as the movement of goods from producers to consumers at the lowest cost consistent with the provision of the services that consumers desire and are able to pay for. Thus a reduction in the cost of maintaining the same standard of service represents a clear increase in efficiency. At the same time additional marketing services that raise the cost of marketing, may also represent increased efficiency. That is if consumers value the extra service more than a corresponding saving in cost.

Technical and economic efficiency

It is important to avoid confusing these two aspects of efficiency. New methods of packing and processing, for example, may reduce waste and prevent deterioration in quality. Labour economies may be achieved by the adoption of new machinery. However, the use of machines or storage designs which are more efficient in terms of volume handled per hour, may not necessarily be economically efficient under all sets of conditions.

Technologists from economically advanced countries often fall into the trap of attributing to other societies the same demands for services and the same capital-to-labour ratios as apply in their own countries. Many persons may be engaged in distribution because of limited earning opportunities elsewhere and in consequence, saving on labour may be neither profitable nor socially desirable. The use of sophisticated equipment may cause difficulties such as obtaining spare parts and performing adequate maintenance. New techniques must fit into existing systems. Storage and processing units that are efficient, from an engineering point of view, have stood empty and unused for much of the time in various tropical countries, because the marketing system was not geared to their use.

Economic efficiency means that marketing is proceeding on the lowest cost basis feasible with the techniques, skills and knowledge available. This will be reflected in prices and quality of service. All the enterprises involved should continually look for new ways of carrying out their tasks and improving services. They should adopt new methods as soon as they seem likely to reduce costs or encourage a better service. The most effective incentives for securing this are the financial rewards due to attracting more business, and the penalties of being left behind in competition. The pressure of such incentives can apply whether enterprises are privately, cooperatively, or publicly owned. However, there must be scope for competition. If there is no competition, an enterprise is likely to continue in the same way that it has followed in the past. Pressure for efficiency has then to come from the prospect of a government inquiry and the consequences that may follow. Pressure can also come from young men inside the enterprise proposing new ideas to further their personal reputation, but this generally needs outside support if their views are to be heard.

The obstacles to economic efficiency in marketing are: lack of information; the resistance of established institutions; and monopoly. In-built forces for efficiency will have their way, provided they are not held back by these impediments. For this it follows that the priority questions to ask regarding the efficiency of a marketing system are:

(a) Have all persons concerned with marketing access to all the information that could help them? Have they had a chance to see the methods used in other countries and to study all potentially useful techniques?
(b) Are the decision makers restricted by old, established legislation and customs? Are they hindered by vested economic, social and political interests, or by political or religious dogma, in choosing new marketing systems or procedures?
(c) Are there private, cooperative or state monopolies which shield the managers of marketing enterprises from pressures to change and improve?

Measures of efficiency

How can one evaluate the efficiency of a marketing situation? One approach would be to analyse existing channels according to the following criteria.

Prices The prevailing prices should reflect costs plus a profit margin. The profit must be just sufficient to reward investment at the going rate of interest, to repay risk-bearing and to provide an incentive for new ideas designed to save costs or improve services.

Service provided The quality of service should be neither too high nor too low in relation to cost and consumer desires. There should also be a range and variety of services to match the variety of consumer incomes and preferences, in so far as this is consistent with economies of large scale operation.

The factors that count for efficiency can also be evaluated by examining marketing enterprises for structure, conduct and performance.

Structure This includes all the firms engaged in a particular marketing channel. There are two strategic features. The first is the number and relative size of the firms involved. Are one or two so large as to dominate the others? The second is the business relationships between them. Are they independent or interlinked in ownership and management? Are they connected by formal contracts or informal understandings? How easy is it for new firms to come into the system? In some West African countries, for example, there might appear to be half a dozen firms engaged in exporting agricultural produce. In fact, the majority may be found to be subsidiaries of Unilever and competition is only slight.

Conduct This refers to the market behaviour of these firms. In what ways do they compete? Are they looking for new techniques and do they apply them as early as practicable? Are they looking for new investment opportunities, or are they disinvesting and transferring funds elsewhere?

Performance This is an assessment of how well the process of marketing is carried out and how successfully its aims are accomplished. Is produce assembled and delivered on time and without wastage? Is it well packed and presented attractively? Is its quality reliable and are contracts kept? Is the consumption of the products increasing and are sales in competitive markets expanding? There are many such practical indications of how well a certain marketing system is operating.

Because there can be no absolute indicators of efficiency, evaluation depends very much on comparison between enterprises, between marketing sectors and between countries. The marketing system for rice in Taiwan was much quoted in the early 1970s as an example of an efficient marketing system. Average prices, costs and margins for this are shown in Table 3.1. The bran was retained by the polisher and its value, 75 cents from 100 kg of polished rice, constituted his margin. The producer obtained about 80% of the price paid by the consumer for polished rice. These figures are now being matched in several South-east Asian countries. In contrast, surveys have shown prices paid to rice growers averaging 54% of that paid by consumers in Nigeria, and in the USA 43%. In the USA milling took 8%; packaging 14%; transport 6%; and wholesaling and retailing 28%.

Table 3.1 Prices and margins in marketing rice; Taiwan 1971. (*Source:* Joint Commission on Rural Reconstruction, Taipei)

	Price ($)	Margin ($)	Percentage of retail price
Farm price of paddy (140 kg at 11.5 cents per kg)	16.00		80
Margin for milling, transport, etc.		1.60	8
Wholesale price of husked rice (111 kg at 15.8 cents per kg)	17.60		88
Margin for wholesaling, etc.		1.10	5.5
Wholesale price of polished rice (100 kg at 18.7 cents per kg)	18.70		93.5
Retailer's margin		1.30	6.5
Retail price of polished rice (100 kg at 20 cents per kg)	20.00		100

There are several factors behind the low margins in Taiwan.

(a) The cropping pattern in Taiwan averages 2.5 crops per year and the harvest season varies from south to north within the country. This reduces the need for storage.

(b) There is a close integration of marketing and processing, e.g. wholesale purchasing is combined with husking, and polishing with retailing in towns. There is total integration in the rural areas.

(c) A relatively dense population and a high rate of consumption make rice marketing a very stable business with quick turnover and little risk.

(d) Rice retailing is a competitive, part-time family business with low opportunity costs.

(e) The retail sale unit is quite large, usually 15 kg or more. Packaging is provided by the customer.

(f) A government-sponsored marketing channel is maintained in parallel with that constituted by private enterprise. Well-established farmers' associations assemble as agents for the Provincial Food Bureau which stabilises prices through buffer stock operations (see Fig. 3.8).

Marketing costs and margins

The costs incurred by marketing enterprises are made up of: wages and other running costs; overhead costs; and fees paid for services. A marketing margin is the difference between the purchase price and the price received on re-sale. The overall marketing margin is the difference between the price paid by the consumer and that received by the producer. Usually this difference is made up of margins taken by wholesalers and retailers, plus transport and other charges. The relationship between margins and costs stands out clearly in Fig. 3.9.

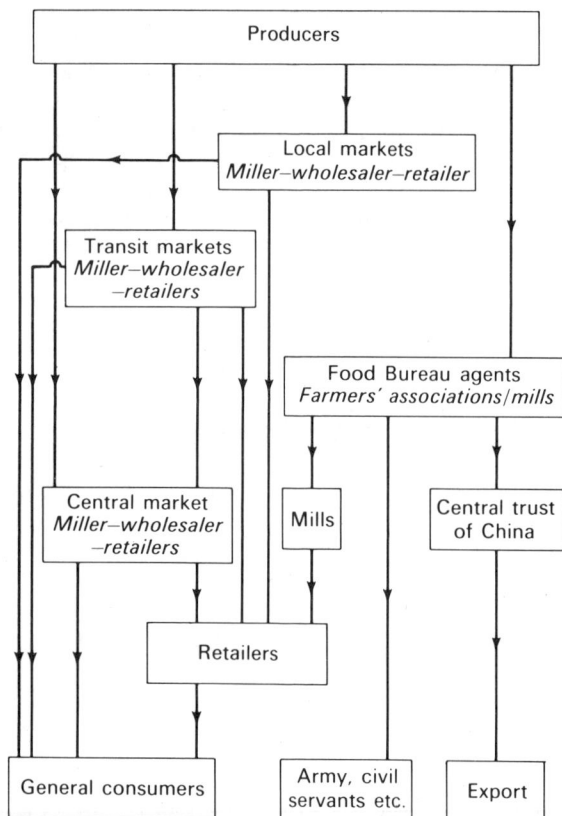

Fig. 3.8 Rice marketing channels; Taiwan

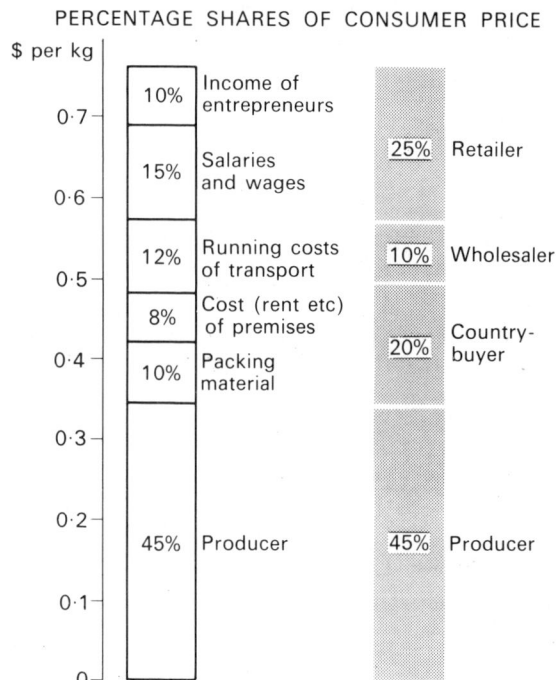

Fig. 3.9 Marketing costs and margins (fruit and vegetables)

Three broad approaches are used to estimate marketing margins:

(a) Representative samples of a certain product are followed through the whole marketing system; prices and charges are noted at each stage and averages are then computed.

(b) The gross receipts and outlays of each handler along a marketing channel are divided by the number of volume-units handled.

(c) Prices at each stage from producer to consumer are averaged for a standard quality over a period of time.

Only (a) and (c) are much used in most developing countries. It is difficult to obtain the collaboration from trading enterprises needed for method (b). Method (c) was used to obtain the data shown in Table 3.1. It is based on 100 kg of rice sold to consumers and the corresponding quantity of husked rice at the wholesale level, and paddy as sold by the farmer.

Great care is needed in drawing conclusions from comparisons of marketing margins. Data presented above show that rice growers in Nigeria and Taiwan receive a larger share of the retail price paid by consumers than the growers in the USA. Superficially it might appear that the American farmer is worse off because of the share of the total margin taken by the cost of packaging. However, under United States conditions the retailing of rice without prepackaging would both discourage consumption and increase the total margin because of the high cost of retail labour.

International comparisons of margins are always dangerous. The margin may be higher in one country than in another because more services are provided. A higher percentage marketing margin may simply indicate that production costs are especially low. Comparisons of absolute (or cash) margins raise the problem of selecting an appropriate exchange rate. It is most meaningful to compare analyses of costs and margins in the marketing of similar products over comparable distances and under similar conditions. There should also be equivalent processing and service inputs for a clear comparison. Sharp discrepancies between one channel and another, point to a situation which merits investigation in terms of services, costs, conditions and alternatives.

Only too often, policy decisions are influenced by an over-simplified impression of the margins taken by marketing enterprises and the costs incurred. A simple comparison of the producer and consumer price, without an examination of what has happened to the product after it leaves the farm, can only lead to many erroneous conclusions.

While the tropical countries will naturally want to make the best use of new technological developments, economic efficiency often calls for a compromise. New techniques must fit the prevailing conditions. Perfect competition, with full knowledge and freedom of movement, is the economist's model for economic efficiency. However, to attain economies of scale, to enforce government control and to meet political pressures, many governments have set up monopoly marketing and supply structures. It is all the more important, therefore, to have criteria of efficiency that are applicable to such enterprises. The application of these criteria calls for judgement and skill which come with experience. It also needs the support of an independent authority. Very often the enterprises and channels most needing investigation will act vigorously in protecting themselves against it.

Problems of agricultural marketing

The various crops, livestock, dairy and poultry products, seeds and fertilisers, all have their marketing problems. We can here discuss only a few problem areas to indicate their general nature and how they are being handled. Necessarily, this treatment will be along very broad lines. It will have to be adapted to the details of any particular situation.

Production conditions

One of the most persistent obstacles to the improvement of marketing in many parts of the Tropics is the source of supply. In many areas, the bulk of agricultural output comes from large numbers of very small farms, each operated independently. The task of organising an efficient assembly, processing and distribution is immensely more complicated than when farms are few, large and specialised. The supply of improved seeds, fertilisers and pesticides is correspondingly more difficult also. Equally challenging is the task of organising an effective marketing system for meat and dairy products originating from nomadic herds moving irregularly over large distances, according to the availability of pasture and water.

It is probably easiest to organise an efficient marketing system when a new line of production is taken up to serve a specialised outlet. A convenient pattern can then be established from the beginning. This has been possible with meat poultry, in a number of areas otherwise little developed in marketing, because an integrated production and marketing system could be set up as a single unit. Selected poultry raisers were provided with young stock and credit for feed and were instructed on the husbandry and market preparation methods they should pursue. The processor could then count on an assured supply of fairly uniform produce, and could lay out his plant and build up retail connections accordingly. New sugar cane and oil palm production is generally located within easy access of the processing unit.

Efficient marketing demands a fairly high degree of uniformity in most farm products. This uniformity cannot always be achieved later if the crop leaving the farm is variable. Thus, if the farmers in one area cultivate a range of varieties of rice, as in many parts of India, the marketing of the rice is greatly complicated. If the varieties are to be kept separate, this complicates storage. Sales to distant customers are always easier if quotations and promotion can be given in terms of large, standardised lots of a well-known type. A project to establish a new mill for producing export quality rice in Pakistan, specifically included provision of standard seed to the producers who would grow for the mill on contract.

The marketing of tropical fruits is often hampered by a lack of uniformity of the varieties and the small scale of production. The leading international brands of canned fruit have a reputation for high quality and there is a wide demand for their products. This has not been built up on the seasonal processing of small lots which are simply surplus to the needs of local markets for fresh fruit. The major fruit and vegetable processing enterprises are based on the cultivation of large areas of produce in accordance with certain uniform quality and ripening schedules.

Similar policies are also being followed by farmers seeking to maximise returns from fresh market outlets. The Ha-ee Vegetable Marketing Group in Korea plan the production of each crop taking into account expected supplies from other sources, the varieties and quality, and the time of delivery preferred by their wholesale agents. Any member who departs from the agreed sales plan is immediately penalised.

Transport and communications

Inadequate transport facilities are largely responsible for the slow increase in marketing efficiency and for continuing subsistence farming in many areas. Deficient communications limit the range of marketing, and confine sales to nearby consumers. This prevents the growth of specialised marketing agencies as well as the development of more efficient procedures under the stimulus of competition. Many agricultural producers are still confined to village markets, and will remain so until appropriate transport facilities make other outlets accessible. How to move livestock or meat from scattered savanna grazing areas to the cities, where there is a strong consumer demand for meat, is one of the most intractable marketing problems of Africa.

The obvious solution to the transport problem, it may be said, is to build roads and railways or establish air services. But these often involve investment and running costs far beyond those justified for agricultural marketing alone. The proposed solution for the Jebel Marra area of the Sudan, a potential fruit growing area, was to market dried tomatoes and tobacco. These have a relatively high value in relation to their weight and do not deteriorate over a long slow journey.

A specific local transport problem may be overcome through coordinated effort. Lack of a strategic bridge blocked access to fresh produce markets in Bombay for farmers in one village in India. The bridge was built by volunteer labour when the government agreed to provide those materials which were not available locally.

Local beneficiaries can be encouraged to undertake maintenance where, if left to public bodies, there could be long delays. Thus in Zaire, the cooperation of produce buyers and other regular road users has been obtained to maintain agreed sections of public highways. They were entrusted with the management of 'food for work' supplied by the World Food Programme and associated cash wage components.

To help livestock reach a market in better condition, governments have established stock routes, equipped them with watering points and set up fattening stations near their destination. Slaughterhouses have been constructed in the producing areas and the carcasses are flown out. At one time 5 000 tonnes of meat were exported annually from N'Djamena in Chad in this way.

To many of these transport problems the technical answer may seem clear — use refrigeration. However, an attempt to apply such an answer too hastily can bring heavy losses. A mechanical breakdown can mean the complete loss of a consignment. Secondly, a complete cold chain is usually required to obtain the full benefit, and not merely refrigerated vehicles. It should begin with pre-cooling facilities in the producing areas, and end with cold stores at destination. Produce transported under refrigeration is likely to deteriorate rapidly if exposed to high temperature immediately afterwards. There is a need to make prior arrangement for such a consignment to be immediately distributed, or else to go into further cool storage; otherwise the seller is left in a very weak bargaining position (Fig. 3.10).

To justify the capital and maintenance costs of such facilities they should be used to capacity. This is often difficult with seasonal crop and livestock marketing. In addition there is often no economic load for the return journey of such vehicles and this is true also of air transport. Costs and benefits should be carefully weighed in the light of these considerations before major investments are made in sophisticated transport equipment.

Handling, packing, processing
The handling of perishable goods calls for special care. Green vegetables and ripe fruit, for example, cannot be carried in heavy sacks and piled on to lorries in a tropical climate, without loss in quality. This adds to the cost of that portion of the shipment which does reach the consumer.

Sometimes only simple precautions are needed to protect food commodities from contamination and deterioration. Milk waiting for collection can be protected from the direct rays of the sun by the use of shade covers, even where no cool room is available. Customers can be discouraged from handling foods. Produce which is susceptible to contamination and spoilage should be protected by packaging wherever feasible. Flies can be kept off meat by the use of insecticide sprays in the surrounding area or by equipping the sales place with gauze doors and windows.

Improvements in day-to-day handling methods must begin at the farm. Extension services can train producers to avoid rough treatment in picking and handling. Damage to tomatoes caused, for example, by the sharp edges of palm stem crates,

Fig. 3.10 The planner's short cut to export meat

Fig. 3.11(a) Banana bunches vary in size. At one time wooden boxes were made to fit each bunch individually (Somalia)

can be reduced by smoothing the inner edges. Much deterioration can be avoided if picking and marketing are well coordinated. Much produce is picked too long before it is ripe, and thus never achieves its full natural flavour. In other cases the fruit is too ripe, and a large percentage is spoiled because the fruit cannot stand the treatment it undergoes on the way to the market.

Observing mixed lots of variable quality in marketing channels, improvement advisers are inclined to recommend establishing central packing stations. It must be remembered that:

(a) The demand for better graded produce cannot be assumed. In most tropical countries it is valid for retailers serving high income consumers and for export markets. For many domestic markets elaborate standards of quality, size and maturity can even be counter-productive; a mixed lot from which customers can pick may be preferred.

(b) Using a few standard types of container can be encouraged, but they should be adapted to market needs, and preferably be made of materials available locally.

(c) Technical innovations are best demonstrated within existing marketing structures. In various countries, new packing facilities remain unused because they were not operated by the enterprises that buy and sell the produce.

Rather than install sophisticated equipment that will be economic only with a large throughput, existing traders can be helped to try new methods on a scale that they can support. Competition obliged the banana growers of Somalia to shift to vacuum-packing standard finger lots in cartons with cryovac liners. The new packing plants incorporated a minimum of imported equipment and permanent construction, thus making full use of cheap local labour (Fig. 3.11).

Fig. 3.11(b) Now, bananas are cut off the stems, sealed in plastic wrappers and packed in standard cartons

It is common to urge the establishment of processing plants in order to avoid waste and to provide an outlet for seasonal surpluses. In planning new processing enterprises it is essential to make objective feasibility studies. Otherwise more problems can be created than solved. The high cost of sugar and tin cans is often a barrier to the development of preserving and packing industries in many of the less developed countries. Where a large part of the cost of sugar is tax, a rebate on the sugar used in export packs may be obtained. Assurances of protection against competition can give a misleading sense of security. Charging higher prices after the introduction of tariff protection or import restrictions is likely to reduce the total market. Some consumers may no longer be able to afford the higher prices. Others will be reluctant to pay the higher prices for home goods because of a preference for certain imported brands and because of unfavourable quality comparisons. Processing plants should not, just for the sake of engineering economies, be constructed on a large scale when local supplies cannot provide an economic turnover. The developing world is spotted with meat, milk and other processing plants standing idle because investment decisions were based on faulty assumptions and because access to aid capital and manufacturers' credit was too easy.

As opposed to accepting external assistance in the establishment of ambitious centralised meat, milk and other product handling plants, governments of developing countries would often do better to foster local initiatives on a smaller scale and help in providing the necessary infrastructure, credit and support services.

Storage and warehousing

The hot, humid climates of many parts of the Tropics are notoriously favourable to insect infestation and mould growth in grain and the rapid decomposition of more perishable products. Inevitably this makes holding produce over time more difficult. Marketing systems have adapted to these conditions as their resources permitted. Grains are dried by daily exposure to the sun to reduce the likelihood of mould growth and heating in storage. Rice is held as paddy; the husk is resistant to insects. Structures of local materials have been designed to keep grain dry and reduce the entry of rodents. Some losses were tolerated because it was hard and often impractical to achieve total control.

Storage problems have intensified in recent years where:

(a) irrigation permits a second crop to be grown which has to be harvested in the rainy season;
(b) increasing yields and quantities marketed mean that existing storage cannot cope with the supply;
(c) governments undertake to buy all grain offered at a pre-announced guaranteed price.

Harvesting crops during wet seasons has led to an interest in mechanical dryers. Time is needed before suitable models can be acquired and located where convenient. Increasing yields call for the construction of additional storage. Private investment in storage has been held back in various countries by government intervention policies that left the role of the private marketing enterprise uncertain or eliminated the incentive normally given by a seasonal rise in prices. Expanding purchases by government stabilisation agencies have added significantly to storage problems. Here storage is

Fig. 3.12(a) Silo with bulk handling equipment; Hapur, India

very impersonal and losses can accelerate rapidly. The reasons include multiplication of 'pockets' of insect infestation originating from particular lots, the entry of rodents, the natural tendency of producers to sell inferior stocks to a government agency which does not offer a reward for quality, and problems in storage management. Under political pressure the Food Corporation of India once had to accept grain with 18% moisture. There are bumper harvest years when stabilising parastatals acquire stocks far beyond their capacity to store; these go into the rainy season with little protection. In India and Kenya, for example, losses of 25% of the quantity purchased have occurred in this way. Losses of this order have also been reported in stocks held for long periods as reserves in Ghana, Tanzania and elsewhere.

There are short and longer term approaches to the solution of these problems (Fig. 3.12). Sharpening price incentives to dry grain before sale would reduce the burden on stabilising agencies, as would adopting pricing schedules that encourage farmers and local assemblers to make full use of the storage available to them, including their own homes. Losses of grain can be brought down to very low levels by drying before storage, use of insecticides, etc. Even so, if it is to be worth storing grain for eight or nine months, a seasonal price increase of 17 to 20% on the initial value is generally needed (depending on local conditions and ruling interest rates).

Extension programmes on loss prevention for produce in storage can be intensified and backed up with market incentives. Experience in Africa has been that the return on buying, for example, a sachet of insecticide for 30 cents to treat a 90 kg sack of maize worth $10.00 is not enough. If the loss in weight due to insects over a 6-month storage period is 5% and this is avoided, the saving is 50 cents. In many African markets, cereals and grain legumes are sold by volume, not by weight. The principal insect pests leave them cavitated but with the same overall volume. Thus, grain which has lost 5% of its weight may not lose commercial value correspondingly, even though it has deteriorated in quality.

Construction of additional storage is needed as the volume marketed increases. Here the ability of government-backed parastatals to obtain concessional finance has led to a bias in favour of centrally located large scale storage. When the programmes of such parastatals have been modified with changing government priorities, such storage is often found to be misplaced. Over the long run, storage convenient for mills meeting local consumption requirements is likely to prove more economic.

An apparent need for more storage can be eased by changes in production. For instance, the production and marketing of eggs can be made more uniform through the year by adjusting breeding schedules and providing additional feed and light. This is often more economic than undertaking expensive storage. The same principle holds good for fruit and vegetables. Plant breeding techniques may produce varieties that are less suscep-

52

Fig. 3.12(b) Sack type storage used by the Food Marketing Corporation of Ghana

tible to insect infestation. Prospects for this are good in the case of cow peas, for example.

The need for credit on produce in storage is often forgotten. The stores set up by the Central and State Warehousing Corporation in India foresee this. On deposit of his produce the owner receives a certificate with which he can obtain a loan at the bank. There is still the problem that he should repay the loan before he can sell his produce. This may mean going to another money lender. Centralised storage of produce belonging to different people is easiest where their lots are relatively large, or are uniform in quality and can be combined for storage. Developing negotiable credit certificates for produce in storage is important if private marketing enterprises are to take up increasing and variable quantities of seasonal crops.

This service was still lacking in Ecuador, for example, in 1985.

Sharp differences in prices

A criticism often made of agricultural marketing systems is that prices vary too sharply between one place and another, between one time of the year and another, and between years. They reflect an imbalance of supply and demand. They signal to producers, marketing enterprises and consumers a need to take compensating measures. These can be to transport more of a product from where the price is low to where it is high, and to hold stocks from the season when prices are low to when they are higher. Faced with high prices some consumers may be able to shift to substitute products; this will help to bring down the high prices.

Thus differences in price generate their own correction; but the process take time. Producers can be discouraged by very low prices at harvest time in good years. Consumers incur hardship when prices are more than they can pay. Both groups look to governments for help. It is important that the measures taken by governments focus on the cause of the problem: too often they attack its symptoms. Strict controls may be applied to consumer prices. A common result is for the product controlled to disappear from open markets.

Sharp differences in prices for a product between one part of a country and another reflect transport and communication difficulties. Merchants may be reluctant to make shipments to unaccustomed markets because they are unfamiliar with sales conditions there, and they do not know the traders and the prices they will pay. The high locational price differences sometimes experienced in Ghana and Nigeria, for example, are a result of this. In contrast, prices for grain in Indian markets have been close to what could be expected from differences in transport costs. Price differences between areas are likely to diminish as transport becomes easier and less expensive and better communications are established. Increased confidence with greater political stability and continuity of trading enterprises also favours this.

In most countries there are substantial differences in prices through the year for seasonal crops, or for livestock depending on seasonal food supplies. This is a normal feature of agricultural marketing. It reflects the need to spread supplies coming onto the market at one time over a much longer period of consumption. Necessarily this involves costs. The degree of seasonal difference in prices is determined by how far farmers' sales are seasonally concentrated; the perishability of the product; and the storage, credit and risk charges involved in holding it over the time required. For example, the wholesale prices of paddy in the Madras area of India showed an average seasonal increase of some 30% over a recent five-year period. In contrast, the average peak seasonal wholesale price at Patna of potatoes, which are much more difficult to store in India, was 340% of the harvest price. Objective research studies have found little evidence to support the popular view that such seasonal price variations are caused by speculative hoarding by traders.

The total output of many crops varies considerably from year to year. Supplies of rice, for example, reflect the area planted (and this is influenced by producers' price expectations); the amount of water available; and other climatic, pest and disease factors. The figures shown in Table 3.2 make it clear that production of a major food crop

Table 3.2 Year-to-year variations in production of major food crops. (*Source*: FAO Production Yearbooks)

	India paddy	Brazil paddy	Sierra Leone paddy	Kenya maize	Senegal millet
(Millions of tonnes)					
1985	91.6	9.0	0.50	2.6	0.95
1984	88.0	9.0	0.46	1.4	0.47
1983	98.0	7.7	0.61	2.2	0.35
1982	65.9	9.7	0.58	2.3	0.58
1981	82.0	8.2	0.40	2.0	0.74
1980	79.9	9.7	0.51	1.7	0.55

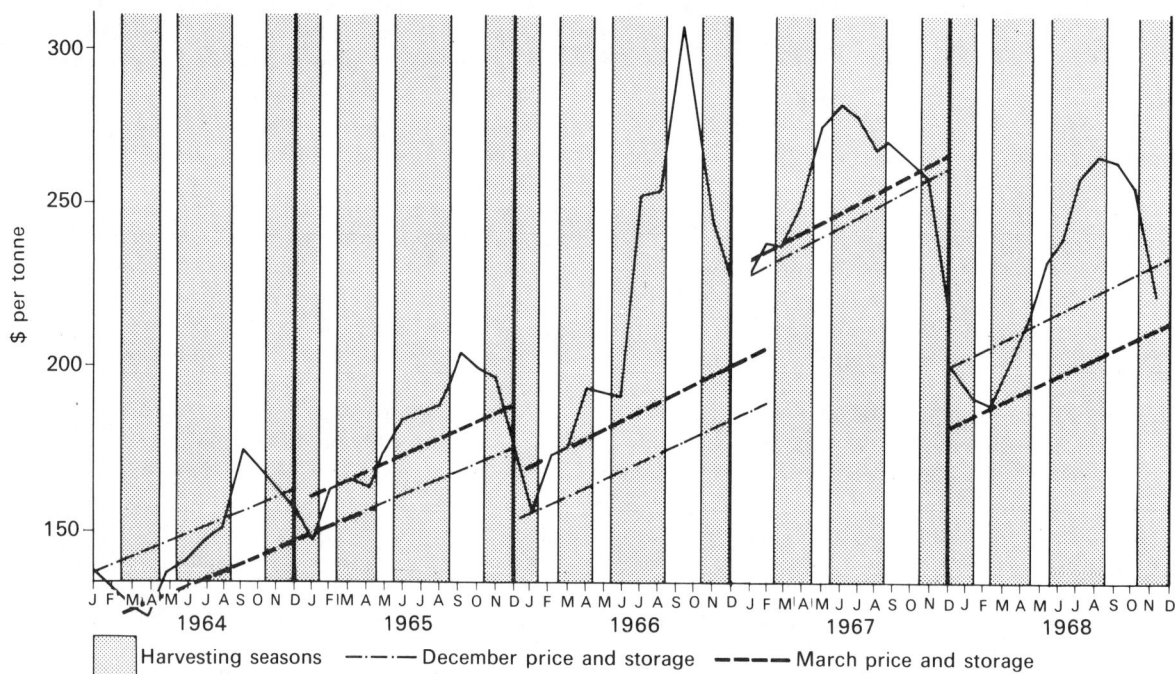

Fig. 3.13 Seasonal price movements of rice in relation to storage costs; Dacca. (*Source*: **Farruk, M. O.** (1970) *The structure and performance of the rice marketing system in East Pakistan*, Cornell University Press, Ithaca)

may well vary in successive years by as much as 25%. An efficient marketing system should incorporate mechanisms capable of cushioning the effects of the variations in output that can be expected in a particular country.

This can be done by exporting in good years and importing when the crop is short. Where the cost of transport to and from world markets is very high — as in landlocked countries such as Burkina Faso and Malawi, and areas distant from ports in China and India — it may be more economic to hold buffer stocks locally. Considerable experience has been gained in the management of stock systems for this purpose. The stock is accumulated by a government-backed stabilisation agency which buys on the domestic market when the harvest is plentiful. This has the effect of supporting prices at a time when otherwise they might fall very low. The stock is sold off when prices to consumers are approaching high levels, thus preventing them rising further.

Commonly they are operated by stabilisation agencies of the type described as Group 2 above (see p. 42). The goal of such an agency would be to moderate price movements to bring them approximately into agreement with the broken lines shown in Fig. 3.13. This represents the producer price plus storage costs. The price patterns for the year 1966 shows what can happen when there is no stabilisation initiative.

This approach is now widely followed in the tropical countries. The traps into which, under political pressures, many governments have fallen are to:

(a) apply the same prices respectively to producers and consumers over a whole country, ignoring the *transport* costs involved;
(b) apply the same prices respectively to producers and consumers through the year, ignoring the *storage* costs involved;
(c) accept a margin between minimum price to producers and maximum price to consumers that does not cover the costs of the storage involved, thus squeezing out commercial enterprise and requiring increasing subsidies.

Reducing price variations on domestic markets of perishable fruit and vegetables is much more difficult. Seasonal surpluses may be diverted into processing uses. There may be restriction of the quantity offered on the market, or direct production controls. These solutions have been used widely in Europe and North America, but the cost and complex administration needed limit their feasibility in many situations elsewhere.

Stabilisation of producer prices for produce sold in export markets is generally easier. Marketing boards types (1) and (3) above (page 42) do this for cocoa, groundnuts and other export crops in West Africa. The central feature is a stabilisation fund built up by deductions from sales returns when prices are high, and drawn upon to supplement producers' incomes when prices are low. Organisational forms and management techniques for such boards are well known. It may prove difficult, however, in the face of political expediency, to maintain the reserve funds. Fluctuations in export prices are treated in further detail in Chapter 5 under International trade.

Urban food supply systems
High rates of population increase and of migration from the country to the cities result in a rapid growth of urban residents in Africa, Asia and Latin America. In 1960 there were 50 cities in these regions with more than one million inhabitants. In 1980 there were 200 such cities. By the year 2000 there will be 20 with populations of over 10 million. All these urban dwellers depend on marketing channels for the whole of their food supply. There are many constraints on the growth and modification of marketing systems to feed all of these people.

Major problems are:

(a) wholesale markets that are inconveniently situated, congested and expensive to use;
(b) rising consumer incomes call for the provision of a wider range of foods including perishables that need rapid handling and special treatment;
(c) increasing numbers of retail outlets that operate at high cost because of traditional individual purchasing arrangements;
(d) urban consumers who lack the means to pay free market prices and no longer have access to family semi-subsistence supplies.

In many cities of tropical countries, wholesaling is combined with the retail operations in congested

Fig. 3.14 Wholesale markets
(a) Congested conditions in Bombay

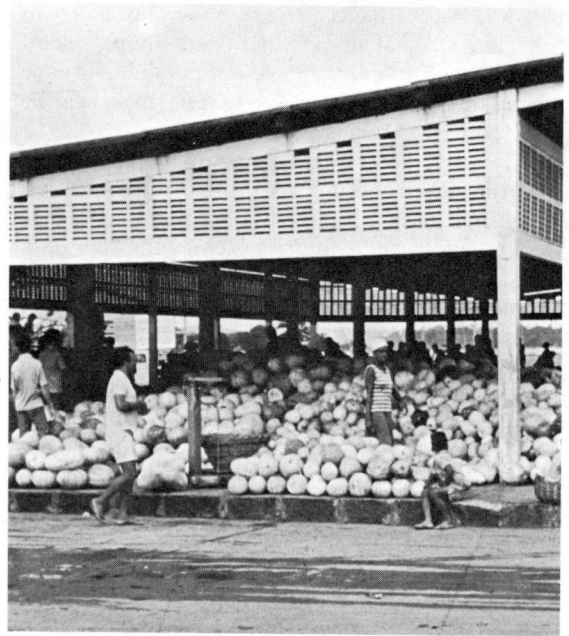

(b) New Market in Recife; here access is good but a more ample roof would give greater protection against sun and rain. (Courtesy of H. J. Mittendorf)

parts of the city. There is thus no space for the introduction of efficient handling, transport and sales methods. Frequently, old-established enterprises and systems are protected and the entry of new firms and the forces of competition are blocked (see Fig. 3.14).

Establishing new wholesale markets calls for a coordinated effort by market users, municipal authorities and marketing development units of central governments. Ease of access from producing areas and supply channels and for urban retailers are prime considerations.

Ample space for the movement of vehicles and the handling of produce into and out of sales places and for future expansion is essential. Flexible, low-cost buildings are recommended. Too often municipal architects crystallise existing marketing structures in standard concrete units.

Increased supplies of higher value products such as meat and milk require separate sets of facilities meeting specific standards of hygiene. Municipal initiatives often lead the way in establishing such plants with regular inspection. They should not, however, remain a monopoly. Too often protection of such plants and the vested interests associated with them, has impeded the provision to growing cities of additional supplies through other more efficient channels.

Lower-cost purchasing for retail distribution has been the great advantage of horizontally integrated food chains. A central buying department procures supplies for all the retail units; it arranges delivery to them directly. In this way the costs of movement into and out of a central wholesale market can be avoided; concentrated bargaining power can bring lower prices; transaction costs are also reduced.

Supermarket chains in the tropical countries with their focus on prepackaged goods benefit mainly higher income consumers. The family-scale retailer serving the less well off lacks such a buying service. The organisation of such retailers into voluntary chains using a single buying agency can be strategically helpful. It can reduce their supply costs, help with presentation, provide promotional materials and offer practical advice on management. Substantial success in this has been achieved in Brazil by the government market development organisation COBAL.

To ensure that low-income urban consumers can obtain essential food supplies at prices within their reach, many governments have kept down the prices paid to farmers. This has been found counterproductive because farmers were deterred from expanding production. To help these low-income consumers and at the same time keep supplies coming from agriculture, special programmes are needed. There is now considerable experience with two price systems designed for this purpose. Specific quantities of wheat or rice are made available in India, for example, at 'fair price' shops on presentation of ration cards. The bulk of the supply continues to flow through free market channels. Supplies are provided by the Food Corporation of India as an adjunct to its price stabilising operation. To confine the benefits to the truly poor and avoid excessive subsidy burdens on the government it is preferable that the food supplied is self-targeting. This means that it should be of a type or quality that, while adequate nutritionally, does not appeal to the average income consumer. Roller maize meal is offered under such a programme in Zambia; higher-income consumers are ready to pay more for maize flour that is more finely ground.

Seed, fertiliser and other input distribution
Most farmers are aware of the importance of good seed; their problem is how to get it. Often they continue to use seed from their own crops because they lack confidence in what is offered to them commercially. In many countries official seed improvement programmes have been launched; they are at various stages of effectiveness. Breeder and foundation seed is grown on government seed farms. The improved seed is then allocated to selected farmers who produce certified seed for controlled distribution to other farmers.

In the early stages, distribution may require direct contact with the farmer by extension staff. They can offer farmers the certified seed in exchange, kilo for kilo, for their own inferior seed. Some subsidy is needed here, though the farmers' seed can be used for milling. The goal, however, is to develop a reliable service through simple commercial channels. Usually certified seed is sold through agricultural service centres, cooperative and private farm supply shops subject to inspection. Where full benefit from improved seed is obtained only in association with applying mineral fertiliser, as for hybrid maize in East Africa, the seed and fertiliser are best sold together as a package.

In recent years transnational enterprise has taken up the development of high yielding agricultural seeds. Advantage can be taken of their products and associated advisory and distribution services in competition with those initiated under government programmes.

In most tropical countries use of mineral fertilisers, pesticides and other agricultural chemicals has now gone beyond specialised producers to the smaller farmers. The issue is how to ensure that they can obtain suitable supplies at the time they are required and on favourable terms.

The tasks involved in marketing fertiliser include: forecasting demand by season, location and type of fertiliser; arranging and financing supplies; storage; transport and distribution including sales on credit; sales promotion; and advisory and demonstration servicing at the farm level. These activities are undertaken willingly by commercial enterprises for large farms and in areas of intensive production of cash crops. Distribution where users are small and scattered involves special problems; the small dispersed market; the high cost of serving it; poor prospects of a return on promotional efforts; and the complications of small scale operations on credit. These are likely to deter many private enterprises. Various approaches have been tried: distribution by government agricultural services because of the important role of extension; establishing special fertiliser corporations as demand increases; distribution by marketing boards; and integrated development authorities and cooperative structures which also purchase the farmers' produce.

There are important points to be taken into account. The distributing agency must be motivated and organised to get the right type of fertilisers to farmers *at the right time*. Discounted prices along the marketing chain for acceptance of stocks in advance ease the burden on transport services at peak times of demand and reduce the risk of late arrival. For retailers, however, fertiliser is cumbersome to handle and store; their preference is to have their customers take deliveries directly from the truck when it arrives in the village. Establishing specialised agro-service centres is desirable because of the technical advice they can provide. In areas of low demand, in particular, the general store is always a valid alternative. The costs are low because it can combine the sale of agro-chemicals with that of other consumer goods demanded in rural areas, and the purchase of farmers' output.

The risks of providing credit for small scale purchases of fertilisers and other inputs are much less where this is part of a contractual arrangement with the purchaser of the crop as practised by the cotton companies in francophone Africa. If the net payment for the cash crop is sufficient it can also be the base for credit sales of fertiliser for use on food crops as well. This is envisaged by the Kenya Tea Development Authority for its 138 000 growers.

In general, a monopoly enterprise which is set up to develop fertiliser distribution to small farmers, eventually proves an obstacle to continuing expansion. In Bangladesh, India and Pakistan it has been found expedient to allow independent firms to compete, if farmers are to get a prompt and responsive service.

Coordination of support services

The role of central and local government in organising markets, regulating the conditions of trading, establishing quality standards and enforcing them through inspection has been indicated (Fig. 3.15). There are also services such as providing crop intelligence and market news, carrying out marketing research, extending advice to market participants and organising marketing training, where a public initiative can help the smaller enterprises. Sales of

Fig. 3.15 Wool baled for export with Indian government quality inspection label

products of national or regional interest can be promoted with government support. We have also noted the need for finance services from banks and other credit institutions. Critically important is government awareness of what is going on in marketing and the implications for market participants of possible interventions in pricing, control of produce movements and assignments of responsibilities to particular enterprises.

Need for a central marketing department In many countries support services for marketing are still at a rudimentary stage. There are others where controls over marketing operations are onerous; traders are harassed by local officials and police road blocks. Decisions by one arm of government may be in conflict with the policies of another. Commodity aid can become a disturbing factor. Commercial importers of fertiliser into Kenya have had to pay for storage over long periods because unforeseen shipments arrived under aid programmes. Rice growers in Nigeria in the 1980s declared their biggest risk to be the arrival of rice imported at concessional prices.

Behind these deficiencies in institutional support for the marketing of agricultural products is a lack of awareness and responsibility in the government. Decisions are based on the experience and opinions of influential individuals as opposed to systematic analysis by informed specialists.

In many governments there is no department

which is specifically responsible for advising on agricultural marketing policy, or for conducting practical research as a basis for such policy. In most Latin American, African and Asian countries, the elements of marketing services and controls are taken care of by different organisations without much coordination. Departments of agriculture, trade, industry, cooperatives, agricultural banks and municipalities are all involved. Lack of an adequate government support service for marketing can also explain why many investments in physical plants for marketing have been misplaced or are inappropriate in scale and design.

The main marketing support responsibilities of governments are summarised under four headings in Fig. 3.16. The kind of staff needed to handle them are also shown. This can be regarded as a model for a government agricultural marketing support department. Where these responsibilities seem irrevocably dispersed among a number of departments and official bodies, a marketing council should be established. This would bring together at regular intervals, or as required, representatives of the units concerned. A secretary should be appointed to provide continuity.

Marketing investment projects Failure to propose projects that were adequately prepared has contributed to the lack of systematic investment in support of agricultural marketing in many countries.

While the costs of marketing investments are generally measured as simply as those of other projects, the range of benefits is not always appreciated. They are tangible, however, and can be assessed. This is illustrated by a World Bank project to finance the construction of rural assembly markets in India.

The total outlay on 125 agricultural markets was to be 750 million rupees. Major lines of expenditure were on land preparation, access roads, auction platforms, fencing and cattle holding facilities, buildings, wholesalers' shops and stores, internal roads and parking lots, electricity, telephones, loudspeakers, radio, drinking water and sewerage, and market equipment including weighing scales, quality testers, grain cleaners and dryers.

The benefits indentified and evaluated were as follows:

(a) Quicker marketing during the glut season would mean that less grain would remain in the

Fig. 3.16 Plan for a government marketing department

Intelligence and policy formation	Marketing development	Quality control, packaging, storage	Market information and extension
Assembles current supply, demand, price and outlook data	Undertakes research and assembles information on marketing enterprises, channels and facilities	Recommends specifications for product quality standards, packaging, transport, storage for voluntary and compulsory use	Organises daily and periodical market news services; prepares advisory material for use by extension services; promotes and supplements marketing training arrangements
Provides prompt advice to the government on current issues and operations of government-sponsored marketing enterprises	Advises the government, enterprises and individuals on marketing conditions, methods, equipment, costs, and on investment projects	Needs marketing and technical staff, inspection personnel, access to laboratories	Needs staff able to present information in a convenient, easily understandable form
Needs marketing economists with practical experience, good judgement and realistic perception	Needs economic, marketing and technical staff with a practical research and advisory orientation		

Table 3.3 Assessment of economic benefits of assembly market improvement

Year	Reduced losses from quicker marketing and drying	Savings from better handling	Savings from reduced congestion	Savings on storage losses	Reduced costs to municipalities	Increased arrivals	Increased prices to farmers	Total
			(Millions of rupees)					
1	—	—	—	—	—	—	—	—
2	—	—	—	—	—	—	—	—
3	1	2	18	1	2	1	6	31
4	2	3	43	2	4	1	9	64
5	3	6	62	3	6	3	13	96
6	4	7	74	4	7	4	18	118
7	4	8	83	4	8	4	20	131
8	4	9	87	4	9	4	21	138
9	5	9	91	4	9	5	22	145
10	5	10	95	5	9	5	23	152
11	5	10	100	5	10	5	24	159
12	5	11	106	5	10	5	26	168
13	6	11	111	5	11	5	27	176
14	6	12	116	6	11	6	28	185
15	6	12	122	6	12	6	30	194
16								204
17								216
18								226
19								236
20								248

field and be damaged by rain — estimated saving 2% of the total crop, valued at Rs 2m annually.
(b) Facilities for drying wet grain at the market would raise the price of some 120 000 tonnes by Rs 16–18 per tonne: total value Rs 2m annually.
(c) Savings from better handling of sales items than in the old, overcrowded, congested markets — estimated at $\frac{1}{8}$ of the total quantity marketed, valued at Rs 8.5m.
(d) Savings in losses due to the provision of 240 000 tonnes of improved storage capacity. This was expected to reduce the average physical and quality loss between farmers and consumers from 10% to 7%, valued at Rs 3.9m annually.
(e) Quicker transport due to easier access for vehicles at new market sites. Formerly trucks and bullock carts were delayed for 1 to 3 hours during peak seasons. At a hire cost of Rs 61.5 per truck/hour, for example, the saving was estimated at Rs 76.2m. Bullock cart savings were estimated at 650 250 bullock cart/days at Rs 10 per day, amounting to Rs 6.5m annually.

Table 3.4 Development costs and benefits, Haryana market project

Year	Expenditure				Incremental benefits	
	Capital outlays	Increment in operating cost	Land rent	Total	Gross incremental	Net incremental
	(Millions of rupees)					
1	197	1.8	1.3	200.5	—	(200)
2	197	3.2	1.6	202.3	—	(200)
3	197	3.2	1.9	202.6	31	(171)
4	99	3.2	1.9	103.8	64	(40)
5	99	3.2	1.9	103.8	96	(8)
6	—	2.6	1.9	4.5	118	113
7	—	2.0	1.9	3.9	131	127
8	—	0.6	1.9	2.5	138	135
9	—	0.6	2.0	2.6	145	142
10	—	0.6	2.1	2.7	152	149
11	—	0.7	2.2	2.9	159	156
12	—	0.7	2.3	3.0	168	165
13	—	0.7	2.4	3.1	176	173
14	—	0.8	2.6	3.4	185	182
15	—	0.8	2.7	3.5	194	191
16	—	0.9	2.8	3.7	204	200
17	—	0.9	3.0	3.9	214	210
18	—	0.9	3.1	4.0	226	222
19	—	1.0	3.3	4.3	234	232
20	—	1.0	3.4	4.4	248	243

(f) Savings in costs to the municipalities due to simpler and more economic electricity, water, sewerage, police and fire control servicing: estimated at Rs 8m annually.

(g) Increased prices to farmers due to reductions in malpractices estimated at a minimum of 1%, plus the consequent incentive to grow and sell more. Assuming a supply elasticity of 0.4 and half the extra production as a net increment to farmer income, the total value after 10–20 years is estimated at Rs 20m annually.

(h) Increased arrivals at the market because of better information available to farmers: estimated at $\frac{1}{16}$ of the previous total, or Rs 4m annually.

Other benefits for which financial values were not assessed are improved opportunities for payment according to quality; savings in farmer waiting time; and better information and access to storage may help farmers to time their sales more favourably.

In Table 3.3 these estimated economic benefits are set out on an annual basis for the 20 years

Table 3.5 Market development costs and benefits, discounted to present value (discount rate 10%)

Year	Capital and operating expenditure		Net incremental benefits	
	Actual	Current value	Actual	Current value
	(Millions of rupees)			
1	200.5	182	—	—
2	202.3	160	—	—
3	202.6	150	—	—
4	103.8	72	—	—
5	103.8	64	—	—
6	4.5	2	113	64
7	3.9	2	127	65
8	2.5	1	135	62
9	2.6	1	142	60
10	2.8	1	149	57
11	2.9	1	156	55
12	3.0	1	165	53
13	3.1	1	173	51
14	3.4	1	182	47
15	3.5	1	191	46
16	3.7	1	200	44
17	3.9	1	210	42
18	4.0	—	222	40
19	4.3	—	232	38
20	4.4	—	242	36
Total	860.5	642	2 639	760

$$\frac{760}{642} = 1.18$$

Table 3.6 Determining the internal rate of return of a market development project

Year	Net benefits and costs	Discounted to current value	
		14%	15%
	(Millions of rupees)		
1	(200.5)	−176	−174
2	(202.3)	−158	−152
3	(171.6)	−115	−112
4	(39.8)	−24	−22
5	(7.8)	−4	−4
		477	464
6	113.5	+57	+49
7	127.3	+54	+48
8	135.3	+44	+47
9	142.6	+43	+38
10	149.1	+40	+35
11	156.5	+39	+34
12	164.6	+34	+31
13	172.9	+31	+28
14	181.5	+29	+25
15	190.1	+27	+23
16	200.1	+25	+21
17	210.0	+23	+19
18	221.6	+21	+18
19	231.7	+19	+16
20	243.2	+18 504	+15 447
Discounted balance		+27	−17

The internal rate of return is about 14.6%

following implementation of the project. They are based on current arrivals of produce, mostly grain, totalling 3 million tonnes. These are expected to increase annually by 5% to reach 6 million tonnes with full development of the project. The total benefit accruing from these various savings and gains is shown in the final column.

The next step is to set the benefits against the costs. This is done in Table 3.4. In the first column the capital outlay is shown, spread over five years. Columns 2 and 3 show the annual increase in operating costs and the land rent applicable. In column 4 the total outlay is carried forward. In column 6 the benefits estimated in Table 3.3 net of

expenditures under the project are shown. For the first five years there is a negative balance; from then on the positive balance increases year by year.

Capital outlays today to bring in returns some years later carry interest costs. They reflect the opportunity cost of not using the capital somewhere else. For a realistic assessment of costs and benefits, therefore, returns in the future must be discounted back to their present value. A table such as that provided in Appendix 1 can be used. The process is illustrated in Table 3.5. Ten per cent is taken as a possible average interest rate over the life of the project. The Rs 149m expected net benefit in the tenth year, for example, has then a current value — to be set against costs incurred now — of only Rs 57m. After conversion to current values the ratio between total outlays and total net benefits is 1 to 1.18. This is the cost benefit ratio.

This ratio can be influenced substantially by the rate of interest used in discounting for current values. However, if the cost benefit ratio of other projects competing for investment funds are assessed on equal terms then this ratio is a fair indicator of relative priority. The social significance of an investment project is an important consideration. In this case some 900 000 farmers stand to benefit — 700 000 of them with less than two hectares of land. Thus the social ranking of this project is high.

Financing agencies take the internal rate of return on a project as one criterion for approval. This avoids the issue of deciding at what rate of interest to discount costs and benefits to current values. A succession of rates are tried until one is found at which the totals of discounted costs and benefits are equal. This rate is called the internal rate of return. The calculation for our market project is shown in Table 3.6: 14% is too low; 15% is too high; the rate is between these figures — about 14.6%. This is satisfactorily above the conventional minimum approval rate of 12%.

Agricultural marketing problems are not always as shown here; they are often interrelated. Those discussed have been singled out to provide a sharper focus on the way marketing can be improved in the tropical countries. It should not, of course, be assumed that there are ready-made solutions for any problems. The intention here is to promote constructive approaches. Difficulties due to lack of capital, lack of good managers and technicians, and adverse organisational and political tradition will necessarily take some time to overcome. Great marketing advances have been achieved in various parts of the Tropics and show what can be done with present resources.

Marketing and production

In all countries, and through all phases of economic development, the pace of advance is quickened as marketing activity increases. At the subsistence level, people must obtain food and satisfy their demands for housing, clothing, tools and all other requirements of living from their own resources. This is irrespective of whether the natural and human environment is suited to all these types of production. Marketing facilities permit concentration on the easiest and most rewarding lines of endeavour. The products of specialisation in one area may then be exchanged for those which are obtained more easily from elsewhere. All parties benefit when the producers of different products are able to sell their goods to each other. They can obtain with part of their own output, more of other goods than they could have produced themselves with the same effort. Thus, improvements in marketing procedure or organisation, which expand trade, raise the level of living of all the people concerned and add to the economic wealth of the community.

Guiding production decisions

A smoothly functioning marketing system indicates, through prices, a consumer preference for one type of product over another, and the economic value attached to that preference. Specific studies of consumer habits and preferences are essential when less familiar or more specialised products enter a development plan. Examples of misjudgements of the market on such grounds are common. In the 1960s consumers were reluctant to buy refrigerated and frozen meat in the Near East and some Southeast Asian cities. This negated investments in processing and transport facilities and blocked programmes to raise incomes from livestock raising. Later, frozen poultry, for example, proved very acceptable. Many officially sponsored programmes to introduce nutritionally valuable foods based on oilseed protein floundered on the rock of consumer resistance.

Logically, market research precedes production planning Production should be planned to meet an assessed demand and price. Developing countries, in particular, cannot afford to support production for which there is no market. Consequently, market studies should begin at the same time as identifying production potentials.

The volume and duration of the work involved in carrying out those market studies that will provide specific guidance, should not be underestimated. Domestic market prospects cannot be based solely on target overall growth rates. Production planners must still make their own estimates of price levels in the light of particular market situations. On international markets the share which a particular producing area can expect to obtain depends on choice of varieties, quality levels, methods of presentation, forms of processing, and other market factors which determine the actual demand for particular lots of produce. Such information can be obtained only by detailed surveys of the wholesale and retail trade in importing countries.

Where production expansion is envisaged, those concerned will normally select that quantity at which marginal revenue will be maximised. This means that determining probable market returns must be undertaken for a range of quantities of the commodities that could be produced. Thus exports of potatoes to the UK from Cyprus have brought steadily increasing returns to the farmers of that country. The quantities produced, however, have been limited by controlled allocations of imported seed.

Assuring a production incentive The agricultural output of tropical countries could be greatly increased by a wider application of scientific methods of farming and of production inputs. This would call, however, for extra effort and cash outlay by many thousands of farm operators. They are only likely to make this outlay if there is a clear prospect of benefit. While adequate incentives at the farm level will not guarantee that all farmers will make the additional efforts needed to increase

production, their absence will certainly mean that such efforts are unlikely to be made. The incentive offered depends on marketing organisation and methods.

There must be specific enterprises which will undertake responsibility for finding foreign or domestic buyers for the various types and qualities of produce. They must be able to arrange assembly from farms; packing and presentation in appropriate containers; grading according to buyers' requirements; transport to buyers' depots or markets which they attend; storage when it is advantageous to time the supply to be put on the market; and processing if this is valuable in assisting conservation, reducing transport costs or opening up new outlets. The enterprises must provide the investment capital needed for fixed facilities, and the working capital to carry purchases from farmers until resale proceeds are received. Implicitly, these enterprises must possess the financial resources; the qualified managerial, sales and technical personnel; the initiative, and willingness to accept business risks which are needed to carry out these tasks efficiently. In export marketing, or substitution for imports in domestic markets, they must be able to match the competence of rival enterprises in other countries. For fresh fruit and vegetables, for example, this requires uniform and precise grading and packing; temperature control in transit; timing and adjustment of total quantities delivered to particular markets; and consistent and thorough sales promotion.

Access on favourable terms to supplies of fertiliser, insecticides and improved seed is particularly important for agricultural development. Likewise, consumer goods of the types preferred for rural living must also be available. With nothing on which to spend the proceeds of additional production, farmers will be less likely to undertake it.

Development of a market economy

To provide a stimulus to agriculture in the tropical countries, marketing systems will have to expand both their coverage and their capacity. Their efficiency must also be sharpened. As this is done, increasing use will be made of productive resources: land, equipment, labour and manage-

ment. More and more, they will be drawn into a market economy. From this flows accelerating economic growth.

Summary of Part A: Analysis

Marketing enables the agricultural producer to step out of a subsistence straitjacket and grow produce for sale. Correspondingly, it permits a large proportion of a country's population to live in cities and buy their food nearby. Marketing also provides an incentive to farmers to grow produce for export. In this way it gives the farmers more income and earns foreign exchange to pay for imports.

We have set out the elements which make up an efficient marketing system. They include functions and services, agencies and channels, the enterprises of which they are composed, and the support frame within which they operate.

Agricultural marketing is complicated by the diverse nature of the products to be handled, and their perishability. A further complication is the scattered nature of agricultural production and, in most tropical countries, the very large number of separate production units. For these reasons, agricultural marketing calls for considerable initiative, decision-making and skill.

Effective marketing structures are generally flexible in operation and allow much scope for local knowledge and experience.

Market conditions are continually changing: large numbers of producers and consumers are intimately concerned, and the interests of these two groups and of the people who earn a living from marketing often appear to conflict. So agricultural marketing problems are frequently in the public eye. Many of these problems are solved by spontaneous action within a flexible economic system. Sometimes, however, there will be a call for government intervention. To handle this well, a government must have its own competent information and policy analysis service at hand, and should not be over influenced by temporary political pressures. A range of such problems has been illustrated from experience in the tropical countries; lines of action have been discussed.

Marketing is vital in ensuring that agricultural products reach consumers in good condition and are presented in a convenient way. In the development of a commercial economy, production itself must be adapted to market requirements. For this reason, research on market outlets is the first step in commercial production. Assurance of a continuing channel to favourable outlets is needed for its continuance and growth.

Issues for discussion on Part A

1 What does 'marketing' involve? What is its role in development?

2 In what ways does the marketing of agricultural products differ from that of most manufactured goods?

3 Which do you think are the most important functions and services in marketing? Why? How would you change this order of importance for different products, e.g. grain, fruit, livestock, milk, eggs, other products?

4 What are the main marketing channels in your area for grain, fresh vegetables, canned fruit or vegetables, meat, eggs, other products? What are the alternative channels between producer and consumer? What is their relative importance in the total movement of the commodity? Are there reasons why this might change soon?

5 Are commission agents important in your country? If so, for what commodities and for what reasons? What is the difference between a commission agent and a broker? Under what conditions is sale through a commission agent of use?

6 What forms of integration in marketing have developed in your country? Can you explain why they have shown up first in these lines of marketing?

7 What types of organised markets are there in your country? How were they established and how are they run now? Some agricultural products are sold in these markets and others not. Can you explain why?

8 How does a 'futures market' operate? Do you think a 'futures market' would be useful in your country? If so, for what products?

9 Is a new wholesale market needed in your capital city? If so, where would you locate it?

10 What are the predominant types of enterprise in your country in the marketing of grain, livestock, vegetables, milk, eggs and fertilisers?

11 Which is the best way to measure marketing efficiency? How can you tell if a monopoly is efficient? Under what conditions do studies of marketing margins provide significant results?

12 What types of enterprises are most prominent in your country in: local assembly; wholesale distribution; processing of agricultural products; retailing to consumers; exporting to other countries? What changes would you recommend? For what reasons?

13 Are marketing cooperatives important in your country? If so, what are their advantages and disadvantages for farmers?

14 What types of marketing parastatal may be distinguished in your country? How does each of these change marketing structure? What are their advantages and limitations? Would you establish new ones? For what reasons?

15 What kind of sales promotion is undertaken for food and agricultural products, fertilisers and pesticides in your country, on domestic markets and on export markets? How could it be improved and who should be responsible for it?

16 What kind of market information is available in your country? How could it be improved? What would these improvements cost?

17 Is any advice in marketing available to farmers, to marketing enterprises, to consumers, in your country? What improvements in this service could you consider practicable and justified? What would they cost?

18 Where can a person who wants to take up marketing as a career obtain training in your country? Is it adapted to his needs? How would you organise it and what curricula would you offer?

19 What are the main marketing problems in your country for rice; maize; fruit; vegetables; beverage crops; livestock; milk; eggs; meat poultry; fibre crops; other products? What solutions would you recommend and how should they be implemented?

20 Are there transport difficulties in your area? What is needed to overcome them? Would the resulting marketing benefits justify the cost?

21 For what products is storage deficient in your country? Where would you locate new storage and who should run it?

22 Are fertilisers and pesticides widely used in your country? How are they distributed? Do small farmers get an adequate service?

23 Are there wide fluctuations in prices for major commodities in your country? Would some stabilisation be advantageous? If so, how would you set about it?

24 Are there potential developments in production in your area that are held back by difficulties in marketing? What are the obstacles? Could they be overcome?

25 Which ministries or departments of your government have responsibilities for marketing of agricultural products and supplies? Is there a recognised unit responsible for initiative and advice in this field? If not, where should it be established?

26 Envisage a new marketing investment such as a grain store offering credit facilities, a milk plant or an abattoir. Identify significant benefits. Assign values to these on the basis of prices prevailing in your country. Using synthetic cost figures if necessary, estimate the cost/benefit ratio of the investment and the internal rate of return.

Part B: Operations

The essence of operating a marketing enterprise is good management. The broad principles of management hold good for food and agricultural marketing as for other business enterprises. They need only to be adapted to take account of specific characteristics of the products handled, of their supply, of the demand for them and the infrastructural environment in which operations will take place. These principles also hold good for different types of marketing enterprises — whether individually owned and operated, transnational, cooperative or parastatal.

Planning marketing operations

The essential starting point for any marketing enterprise is to have a clear idea of the market to be served and a plan of action to service it. A reconnaissance visit to appraise the market, learn about the conditions of entry and identify potential buyers is a 'must' for all new marketing operations.

With the results of such an enquiry, a marketing manager can acquire, select and present produce to meet their requirements, and formulate a sales plan.

Often, people in tropical countries hear of high prices in distant markets for produce that is plentiful in their home area. They are eager to dispatch consignments to these markets. Without first investigating the conditions of sale there, such an action can be very disappointing. High prices for potatoes in Europe one winter attracted a shipload from India. It was refused entry because its condition did not meet the established import standards. The consignors lost both their produce and their outlay on handling and transport.

Market research

The larger the marketing enterprise and the more it has at stake in terms of owner or client commitment, the more important it is that systematic research on the markets open to it are undertaken as a guide to policy. A manager who has grown up in the area where sales are foreseen, who knows the habits and preferences of consumers there, or of buyers who resell in other markets, has important advantages. He may also be limited by what he knows. Specific studies of the nature of consumers' demands and the ways this is reflected in the attitudes of the wholesalers and retailers who serve them can open the way to innovative and more profitable sales policies. In the UK where grapefruit are eaten widely at breakfast, the Israel Citrus Board sells them at a low price, unwrapped, simply stamping the word 'Jaffa' on the skin. In Italy, where grapefruit are appreciated mainly by upper-income consumers who have travelled, they are sold in units of three, with a brand on a plastic wrapper — at a price double that in the UK. This difference in packaging and presentation is *based on market research*.

Such a research programme for agricultural products should cover, for accessible domestic and export outlets, the following:

(a) official regulations and market preferences relating to sanitary requirements, quality standards, containers, inspection, etc.;
(b) quota regulations and levies affecting volume, cost and timing of sales in particular markets;

(c) supply and price trends overall, and for different qualities and forms of presentation, by year and by season, also covering possible substitutes;
(d) sales methods and agencies and respective costs;
(e) prospective consumer demand, and the share that could be obtained, and ways of increasing this.

Inquiry along these lines is designed to answer the following questions: What is the size of the market? What are the predominant consumer preferences? What is the scope for market segmentation, i.e. for separating consumers likely to pay different prices for basically the same product? What are potential bases for such segmentation — quality, packaging, branding, form of presentation, type of retail outlet? Is demand seasonally limited? How would it respond to measures to extend product availability by storage, selection of varieties, modification of planting time? Is demand likely to grow? What are the determining factors? Is demand seasonal or year-round? What financing would be needed to cover shipping costs, delays in obtaining settlement, sales promotion, etc.?

Consumer preference surveys are used increasingly as a guide in the presentation and processing of produce, or to reveal reasons why sales of long-established items are falling off. The services of independent agencies who have specialised in this field can be used to advantage in developing new markets.

Operators of private marketing enterprises are generally free to adapt their policies to match market demand. Managers of farmers' cooperatives and parastatals may be subject to some constraints. One can be a commitment to buy all of the produce that is offered them. This can mean that secondary outlets must be found for produce that does not match the needs of the most favourable markets or exceeds the needs of regular buyers who can be counted to take up similar quantities each season. Preferably, cooperative and parastatal managers should be able to adjust their prices to producers over time and thus direct production towards prevailing market requirements.

Access to capital

If a marketing entrepreneur is to buy produce, transport, store and resell it, he must have enough funds to cover payment for the produce, transport, storage and handling costs until the proceeds of sale come in. This can be a matter of weeks; it can be much longer if produce purchased at the harvest season is held for sale to consumers later in the year. Long-term capital investments in storage, transport and other marketing facilities and equipment have to be made. The salaries of regular staff must also be met.

For many private marketing enterprises, lack of capital can be a continuing disability. Small traders who assemble groundnuts and sorghum in Senegal can often buy only a sack or so at a time; this small quantity must then be sold to provide funds to buy more. Lacking collateral to offer as security, their only source of credit is the wholesaler to whom they resell. Because of the risk involved, the wholesaler's interest charge may be up to 40% on an annual basis.

Haji Mansur of Sidoarjo, near Surabaya in east Java, began rice marketing with working capital from family sources. He was able to acquire a mill, adjacent storage and four trucks with a long-term loan on the basis of a contract to supply a price stabilising agency. With his property and stocks as collateral he could obtain seasonal credit from a commercial bank to buy from farmers and run his mill.

Decision on a site
The location of a marketing enterprise has important implications for its success. Desirable attributes are convenience in obtaining supplies of the produce to be handled; access to a good market for it, directly or via reliable transport means; and prospects of growth.

Haji Mansur set up his rice mill in the centre of Sidoarjo. He began his original rice marketing operations there because it was on family property available to him at no cost. It was convenient for sales to wholesalers in the town. Operating on a larger scale with most of his sales going to the stabilisation agency, he found it much less advantageous. His trucks travelled long distances to get the quantities needed to keep the mill running. He would have been better off located in the centre of the production area alongside a good road leading to the depot of his main customer. Holding onto

his old site also incurred the opportunity cost of not profiting from its value if he sold it for urban development.

Selecting and managing staff
Vital for the development of a marketing enterprise in its early stages are working partners who can be trusted. Often it is a husband and wife team, a father with working sons, or partners who are already friends of mutual confidence, that constitute the operational nucleus. Small private enterprises then take on additional labour as and when they need it.

The terms on which continuing staff are engaged should provide a clear incentive for performance. Salaries and prospects should be attractive so that employees are keen to hold on to their jobs: otherwise they should be paid by results. An employee is likely to work best and develop a favourable sense of initiative if performance objectives for him have been set out clearly and he is consistently supported in their attainment. Adequate training for the responsibilities assigned, and clear definition of his role *vis-à-vis* that of others are also essential.

Cooperative and parastatal enterprises are susceptible to political pressures for the appointment of staff who are not qualified, lack motivation, or are otherwise negative to the successful operation of the enterprise. Difficulty in engaging effective managers in cooperative systems is endemic. Parastatals are also inclined to engage staff in excess of actual needs.

The recommendations of a successful African businessman are to the point:

(a) Seek as a partner the President himself, in the expectation that this will provide protection against pressures from other quarters.
(b) Instead of engaging a product specialist, plant engineer, accountant, purchasing officer and sales manager — with exclusive terms of reference — the operator should do all these jobs himself, together with his brother.
(c) Avoid having to observe government salary scales and fixed working hours. Instead, pay everybody double for the work they do, and thus retain flexibility.

Managing a marketing business

Strategic elements in managing a marketing operation are decisions on what is purchased, at what price and how it is to be sold. Will it be held in store and for how long? What transport, handling and packaging will be involved? How should the enterprise promote its operations? Should it continue along an established path or rather consider new and alternative activities?

Pricing

The role of a marketing manager in setting prices for the products he buys and sells is determined by his market position. In selling, this can range from that of irregular retailer of small lots on a public market to a monopolist who feeds products to the market at a rate designed to maintain a target price.

Illustrating the first position is the woman of Papua New Guinea who sets off to market with a mixed lot of vegetables grown on her own farm and those of neighbours. She has no clear idea as to what they are worth. She asks about prices from people she meets on the way. She starts to sell at the price most often mentioned. If there are no buyers she reduces the price. If she seems likely to dispose of her produce before midday she raises it. In the afternoon, with the prospect of carrying some produce home or giving it away, she cuts her price. Step by step she seeks the best set of prices consistent with disposal of her stock in hand.

The monopoly seller sets his sales price so that he can get most profit. He can supplement his personal knowledge of the market with studies in depth to estimate the elasticity of consumer demand to the price being asked. This information would tell him how much more consumers would buy if the price were reduced and how far sales would drop if the price were raised. Using estimates based on these studies he can then decide what quantity to put on the market in order to maximise returns to his enterprise and the prices at which this would be achieved. This is the position on domestic markets of various parastatal distributors of agricultural inputs and of agricultural output sellers such as the organisation of Mexican tomato growers exporting to the USA. In winter it is empowered to allocate weekly quotas to packing stations in the producing area. Enforcement is by controls at the frontier crossing points and penalties on packing stations that exceed their quota.

Between these two extremes there is a range of intermediate positions. Enterprises offering quantities too small to affect the market in which they sell must generally follow it. They can, however, try to sell part of their supply to special customers at a premium on the basis of freshness or some other attribute of quality or convenience. This is the position of farmers who sell part of their output retail, with the rest going to a wholesaler at whatever price it will fetch.

To be assured of supplies in the future the marketing enterprise buying from farmers must offer them at least as good a price as they can obtain elsewhere. For prices to farmers the price reported on a relevant wholesale market is a common guide. Competition between buyers will have determined a margin between the price at this market and at their own location that reflects transport, handling and transaction costs. Sales work on the basis of the central market price, less this margin. Thus in Paraguay in 1983, farmers could make advance contracts with soybean wholesalers on the basis of a margin of $80.00 per tonne below the price on the Chicago Exchange, even though their soybeans went mainly to Rotterdam. Some farmer cooperatives offered their members a choice of the current price at Chicago or the quoted future price for the following month, or for the month after that, always less the margin.

Parastatal exporters of standard products such as cocoa, coffee and groundnuts tend to follow the established international markets. To let them clear their warehouses for incoming supplies, and reduce their bank borrowings, they sell a large part of their total supply at the current spot price. The rest is sold forward over the months when they can expect conveniently to ship it. For such products the spot and forward prices on the London and New York markets show the best expert opinion.

Many cooperatives follow the practice of paying farmer members a proportion of the expected price for their produce at the time of delivery. The balance is paid later in the year when sales have been completed and the expenses incurred have been deducted from the proceeds. Some parastatals such as the Botswana Livestock Commission also stick to this principle, paying a 'bonus' at the end of the year. Under competition this method of payment can lose business. The delay in payment turns many farmers to private outlets that pay the whole price in cash at the time of purchase, even though the price may be lower, because the buyer carries all the risks in resale.

Purchasing

Marketing begins with producing or acquiring products for sale. In planning production or purchasing, the marketing manager needs to take into account:

(a) The nature of the product. Does he know it well enough to assess its quality and value? Can he pack, handle, transport and hold it for future sales without incurring substantial waste and deterioration?
(b) Financing requirements. Does he have enough of his own capital available or will he have to go to a bank for credit? Will he be able to get enough credit and at what cost?
(c) Probable resale price. Is this a sure price? If it depends on free market determination, is the current trend up or down?
(d) Prospective profit. Most marketing managers incorporate this into a target operating margin which they use in deciding when, and at what price, to buy.

This operating margin is made up of the following:

(i) Direct costs: payments for handling, transport, market charges, sales, etc.
(ii) Overhead costs: office expenses, staff salaries and social contributions, bank charges, depreciation of equipment and facilities. These are estimated per unit of quantity on the basis of recent records.
(iii) Remuneration for management and risk: this is the net income of the operator or his enterprise.

For convenience, marketing enterprises adopt for their operating margin a standard mark-up. This may be 5 to 10% of the purchase price for a wholesaler selling large lots fairly quickly; 25 to 30% for a retailer of perishable produce taking longer to sell, dealing in small lots and carrying the risk of physical wastage and produce remaining unsold; 18% for a supermarket handling a mix of products including many consumer essentials with ample shelf life.

So a manager will buy produce that he thinks he can handle, that he can finance, and that he believes he can sell with the mark-up needed to help his business survive. This will be his standard analysis. If he foresees some risk over the resale price he may reduce the quantity purchased; or he may decide to carry the risk to please a regular supplier and to be sure of satisfying regular buyers.

For processing enterprises, particularly, it is convenient to secure supplies via advance contracts with producers. This lets the processor specify variety, quality, maturity and other standards for his raw material, and time of delivery. He can then operate his plant more efficiently and be sure of satisfying his customers' needs.

Sales

Selling is at the heart of marketing. The owner of a small private marketing enterprise is likely to undertake sales directly. He will draw on his knowledge of the products in which he deals, of the market and his experience of human attitudes in bargaining. If he delegates authority to make decisions on sales it is likely to be to family members whom he feels that he can trust.

Keeping selling within a narrow group of family members holds down overhead costs and permits rapid, flexible decision making. However, it limits the scale of operations. Most joint stock, cooperative and parastatal enterprises need a specialised sales department headed by its own manager. Selecting a suitable person for this key post is crucial. He should have experience of selling in the markets envisaged, organising ability and imagination. He should be open to new ideas and on the look-out for new opportunities.

Appointing agents to sell for a firm at distant locations is a further stage in sales delegation. They must be offered a commission, or a margin that is attractive if they are to put their full weight into selling for the firm. Agents may be exclusive, i.e. the only one supplied with produce to sell in a defined area. Fertisa, the mixed government/private fertiliser company in Ecuador, gave exclusive rights to distribute its products to some 15 wholesalers. These were established firms which could finance transport and stocks. Sales could probably have been increased by developing a more competitive network of distributors. To do this Fertisa would have had to do part of the financing.

Ability to offer short-term credit helps greatly in securing sales. How far an enterprise should go in this direction depends on its cash flow position and its competition. Wholesalers often finance meat and vegetable retailers for a few days: 30 days' credit is common for more durable products, 60 days' for imported fertiliser. Many retailers of agricultural inputs and of food products allow credit to farmers and consumers.

Sales methods should take careful account of buyers' requirements and convenience. Cocoa and coffee are wholesaled by description. Tea and tobacco are offered by auction after buyers have had an opportunity to inspect each lot.

Advertising

Some form of sales promotion is essential if the potential customers of a marketing enterprise are to know about it and what it sells. It can be done through direct contacts in public places or by visits to people at their homes. Signs can be displayed at a point of sale located where potential customers will pass. Advertising can be undertaken by distributing leaflets, insertions in local newspapers and trade journals, announcements on the radio. How best to promote sales and how much to spend on it are continuing issues for the marketing manager. It has always been difficult to assess response to advertising; yet few marketing firms have felt they could do without it.

Promotion on the national television in the UK costs around $1000 per second. This is only justified for products that are branded, like Chiquita bananas and Jaffa oranges, and are sold over the whole area served by the programme. The outlay on such promotion is spread over a large turnover so the cost, which can be 1%, 2% or more of total sales, is still acceptable.

Marketing enterprise promotion should be coordinated with that of other related agencies and services where feasible. Thus mobile promotional vans sponsored by a fertiliser distributor can operate in conjunction with government extension staff in organising field days and on-farm demonstrations. Retailers in the area concerned should have stocks conveniently ready at promotional prices, together with explanatory materials and point-of-sale announcements.

Packaging

The art of packaging is to combine protection of the product with a presentation that helps to sell it, at an acceptable cost. Packaging decisions are based on the requirements of the product, its value, and the market in which it will be sold. For green beans sent by air from Kenya and Senegal, lightweight containers attractive to buyers on European markets are essential. For local markets where consumers are used to accepting produce loose in their own containers and are primarily concerned to buy at the lowest unit price, expenditure on elaborate packaging would be wasted.

Transport

Timely movement of produce from where it is in surplus to where there is strong demand is at the heart of marketing. The concern of the manager is to secure a reliable low cost transport service. To justify investment in a self-owned motor truck, generally there should be pay loads in both directions.

Refrigerated vehicles reduce losses in marketing perishables and maintain quality. They are expensive, however, and a breakdown can mean loss of a whole consignment. Until it is clear that their use is justified by the marketing advantage, simpler methods of product protection may prove more economic. The main supplier of meat from the Sierra of Ecuador to Guayaquil on the coast in the 1980s used an insulated van travelling by night.

Storage

A marketing manager who envisages storing produce until there is a rise in price makes his decision on a realistic assessment of the return that will be forthcoming after covering all costs. These include deterioration in quality and interest on the capital value of the produce, as well as the charge for storage. Such an assessment is illustrated by the following figures for apples under refrigeration in Lebanon.

	$ per tonne
Estimated increase in price over 6 months	60.00
Storage costs	
Rent (or overhead cost for owned facility)	21.00
Storage losses (weight and quality)	23.80
Rent of crates	4.30
Interest (10%) on initial value of stocks	6.20
Total costs	55.30
Net margin	4.70

The difference in price between the harvest and low supply seasons was $60.00 per tonne, but the profit margin in storing until that time was only $4.70 per tonne.

Many small marketing enterprises hold stocks in their houses and outbuildings. Establishment of specialised storage is a long-term investment project, calling for a careful demand assessment. Convenience in location is all-important. Proximity to a mill has the advantage that the mill can be supplied as needed, with no further expenditure on transport. Convenient also for storage are places where a change of transport is obligatory, e.g. at a port or where feeder roads link with a rail line serving a major distant market. Stabilising parastatals that concentrate their storage at central points sometimes forget that this can mean transporting grain back in the direction from which it came earlier in the year.

Ability to offer credit on produce in store is a great advantage. For this a bank is a good partner; also in financing long-term investment in a storage structure. The two major grain stores in Ecuador undertaking storage for farmers or traders on a fee basis are both run by companies in which commercial banks are partners.

Taking on a new activity

From time to time most managers see ways of adding to their marketing business. These can supplement an existing sales line with complementary products, undertake additional functions, e.g. processing or retailing, or extend existing operations by setting up branches or agencies to sell in new domestic or export markets. The decision should be based on the marginal return: that is, profits on the new activity, after covering all costs directly attributable to it, are calculated as a contribution to the general overhead costs of the enterprise, not after a proportion of these overheads have been allocated to the new activity. Use of a worksheet as illustrated in Table 3.7 can be helpful in making estimates. The contribution of a new activity may be small or even negative in the first years: by the third or fourth year it should increase substantially if it is well suited to the enterprise and within the capacity of the personnel available.

Scope for additional activities in conjunction with agricultural marketing is considerable because of the seasonal concentration of many of the major operations and the need to maintain purchasing and supply services in rural areas with a low density of demand.

Combining some processing with the wholesale marketing of farm products is widely advantageous. Greater added value is derived from the same purchasing, financing and sales operations. A manager taking on such an additional activity will need a clear idea as to where it will find its niche and what new ideas and methods it can bring in. He must assess where these could be applied with the best chances of success.

A new rice milling enterprise by a wholesaler in the Philippines started up with the following plan of operation and budget. It proposed to market a differentiated packaged product. It planned to mill 5 tonnes of rice per day for sale to 15 to 20 retailers serving higher income consumers. Gross sales were estimated at $350 000. Some 2 700 tonnes of paddy would be bought from farmers at a price ranging from $4.50 to $5.40 per 50 kg of paddy, depending upon its quality. An average price to farmers of $4.75 in the first year would result in a raw material cost of $256 000. This would leave a gross margin of $94 000. Against this had to be set fixed and variable costs directly related to the processing activity, which were estimated as follows:

	$
Depreciation of equipment (over 5 years)	10 000
Interest on capital	6 250
Salaries	8 750
Power and fuel	4 000
Supplies, packing	5 000
Promotion	2 500
Maintenance	1 250
Miscellaneous	2 250
	40 000

The marketing niche foreseen in this plan was one for milled rice in consumer size packages. In milling alone the main advantage over existing competitors would be in access to new equipment offering perhaps a higher out-turn. Assuming that the market appraisal was correct, failure to achieve the expected target could mean that something was wrong with the firm's business methods, equipment or staffing. This calls for a careful appraisal of these factors. If no significant weaknesses are revealed in the technical efficiency of equipment, access to the market and information on price trends, then attention should be focused on management.

The vital importance of management in marketing is often overlooked by governments seeking to establish cooperative and parastatal enterprises. A marketing organisation may be set up with adequate finance, buildings and equipment, yet it

Table 3.7 Estimating the advantages of taking on a new activity

New activity	Year 1	Year 2	Year 3	Year 4	Year 5
Gross additional income	……………	……………	……………	……………	……………
Less Variable costs	……………	……………	……………	……………	……………
Labour	……………	……………	……………	……………	……………
Transport	……………	……………	……………	……………	……………
Sales	……………	……………	……………	……………	……………
Sub-total	……………	……………	……………	……………	……………
Less Fixed costs relating to activity	……………	……………	……………	……………	……………
Financing of new equipment	……………	……………	……………	……………	……………
Depreciation of new equipment	……………	……………	……………	……………	……………
Continuing salaries	……………	……………	……………	……………	……………
Promotional outlays	……………	……………	……………	……………	……………
Sub-total	……………	……………	……………	……………	……………
Total costs of new activity	……………	……………	……………	……………	……………
Net contribution to general overheads	……………	……………	……………	……………	……………

Fig. 3.17 How could I use a management adviser? What would he do?

will still fail without effective management. A manager is concerned with staff, equipment and money. He must see that all three are used in the right proportions. Labour costs must be in keeping with performance and production. Proper training of staff is essential.

The best sales results are obtained by managers (or salesmen) who know which markets are offering the highest prices for a given type and quality of product; how much a market can absorb without an adverse effect on price; and how to keep sales moving through a range of channels and enterprises. It is essential to develop contacts which provide reliable information on the state of the market and on impending changes. In purchasing, a manager should maintain good relations with growers, because he depends on them for his supplies of raw materials. Good relations with

buyers are also important. Customers should be assisted with their own business wherever it can help future sales (Fig. 3.17).

Business controls

Maintaining accounts

While marketing enterprises extending over several countries have been built up by men who were illiterate, it helps to keep some accounts. At a minimum, a marketing manager should know what he is earning in relation to what he spends and how much he owns in relation to what he owes. For these purposes he should have prepared annually an income and expenditure statement setting out clearly whether he has made a profit or a loss over a defined period and a balance sheet showing his assets and his liabilities at a particular time. Tables 3.8 and 3.9 present such accounts for Haji Mansur's rice milling and wholesaling enterprise in Indonesia. Family enterprises will find such accounts useful as a guide to the progress of their business and to possible financial dangers ahead. These accounts will certainly be needed in approaching a bank for credit and in making statements of income to tax authorities.

Enterprises that are partnerships, joint stock companies, cooperatives and parastatals generally need to produce such accounts for shareholders, cooperative members and responsible departments of government. Table 3.10 is an income and expenditure account for a cotton marketing cooperative. This compares the figures for the current year with those budgeted and those of a previous year. Significant differences call for an explanation. The right hand column shows the unit costs. These are very useful for comparing the results of one society with another. Those with a larger turnover are likely to have lower unit costs since overhead costs are spread over a larger number of units of output. The unit cost can be used as a guide in deciding whether to merge small societies into larger ones, or as justification for a change in the rate of levy.

The cooperative balance sheet (Table 3.11) provides more detail than that used by Mansur because more people are concerned. Current liabilities are set against current assets to show the net assets of the cooperatives. Share capital and reserves are also important elements in the financial status of cooperatives along with joint stock and parastatal enterprises. For Mansur they can be lumped together as 'family investment and retained earnings'. Depreciation rates commonly used are 20% of replacement cost for vehicles and equipment, 10% for buildings and stores.

A produce realisation account (Table 3.12) is prepared for cooperatives to show how their income was derived. It shows what produce the cooperative has collected from its members and delivered to the cooperative union, which acts as its wholesaler. The society levy shown in the produce realisation account is transferred to the income and expenditure account. It is the main source of income of the cooperative.

Table 3.8 Income and expenditure, Haji Mansur's rice mill, 1979

	($)	($)
Income		
Sales to wholesalers	288 000	
Sales to rice marketing board	1 152 000	
Total		1 440 000
Expenditure		
Purchase of paddy	992 000	
Milling costs	16 000	
Interest charges	24 000	
Depreciation	40 000	
Sales, administrative and other expenses	120 000	
Total		1 192 000
Profit		248 000
Taxes		119 040
Profit after taxes		128 960

Table 3.9 Financial statement, Haji Mansur's rice mill at 31 December 1979

Assets	($)	Liabilities	($)
Cash	15 000	Bank overdraft	100 000
Accounts receivable	45 000	Accounts payable	55 000
Stocks	63 000	Accrued liabilities	25 000
Advances to farmers	75 000	Long term loan	80 000
Equipment and vehicles net of depreciation	192 000	Family investment and retained earnings	130 000
Total	$390 000	Total	$398 000

Table 3.10 Cooperative income and expenditure account, year ending 31 December 1985

1984 ($)		Budget ($)	Actual ($)	Per 1 000 kg of deliveries ($)
	Income			
6 506	Levies on produce	7 000	7 700	
1 012	Sundry other income	1 100	1 084	
7 518		8 100	8 784	
	Expenditure			
	Administration:			
1 650	Salaries and wages	1 700	1 672	3.04
110	Staff training	162	134	0.24
35	Subsistence and travel: staff	50	39	0.27
135	Subsistence and travel: committee	150	143	0.26
525	General meeting expenses	550	548	1.00
550	Rent	550	550	1.00
198	Printing and stationery	200	200	0.36
344	Maintenance and repairs	300	56	0.65
18	Insurance	50	20	0.04
376	Audit and supervision fees	380	400	0.73
58	Sundry expenses	60	55	0.10
	Financial:			
52	Bank charges	25	29	0.05
	Provision for doubtful debts		74	0.13
4	Bad debts		16	0.03
1	Cash loss		3	0.01
750	Depreciation	738	738	1.34
4 806	**Total**	4 915	4 977	9.05
2 712	Surplus for the year carried down to Appropriation Account	3 185	3 807	

Table 3.11 Cooperative balance sheet as at December 1985

1984 ($)		Cost ($)	Accumulated depreciation ($)	($)
	Fixed assets			
680	Temporary building	1 062	100	962
690	Furniture	502	124	378
725	Motor vehicles	2 505	626	1 879
2 095		4 069	850	3 219
	Investments			
1 000	100 shares of $10 each in ABC Cooperative Union Ltd			1 000
	Current assets			
250	Stock on hand		225	
192	Debtors after deduction of $14 for doubtful debts		158	
422	ABC Cooperative Union Ltd		406	
598	Bank balance		506	
123	Cash balance		87	
1 590	Total current assets		1 382	
	Less:			
	Current liabilities and provisions			
162	ABC Cooperative Union Ltd		148	
413	Creditors and accrued charges		613	
575	Total current liabilities		761	
1 015	Net current assets			621
4 110	Total net assets			4 840
	Representing:			
2 500	Share capital: 600 shares of $5 each			3 000
541	Statutory reserves			757
1 069	Revenue reserves			1 083
4 110	**Total**			4 840

Table 3.12 Cooperative (cotton marketing) produce realisation account, year ending 31 December 1985

($)		Grade A ($ per kg)	Grade B ($ per kg)	(kg)	($)
75 365	Deliveries to the Union, grade 'A' at	0.148		525 178	77 726
1 661	Deliveries to the Union, grade 'B' at		0.080	24 671	1 974
77 026				549 849	79 700
62 917	Collections from members, grade 'A' at	0.124		525 325	65 140
1 153	Collections from members, grade 'B' at		0.056	24 689	1 383
64 070				550 014	66 523
	Add:				
1 083	Union levy	0.002	0.002		1 100
1 082	Local authority tax	0.002	0.002		1 100
3 248	Union marketing fee	0.006	0.006		3 330
7 579	Society levy transferred to Income and Expenditure Account	0.014	0.014		7 700
77 062				550 014	79 723
−36	Deficit transferred to Appropriation Account (0.03% of collection)			−165	−23
77 026	**Total**	0.148	0.080	549 849	79 700

Table 3.13 Cooperative appropriation account, year ending 31 December 1985

1984 ($)		($)	1984 ($)		($)
2 712	Surplus for the year brought down from Income and Expenditure Account	3 807		**Appropriations**	
	Deduct deficit transferred from		641	Statutory reserve	757
8	Realisation Account	23	814	Members' patronage dividend	1 513
2 704		3 784	1 396	Honoraria to committee men	1 500
	Add balance brought forward from			Surplus unappropriated carried	
1 116	1984	1 059	1 089	forward	1 803
3 820		4 853	3 820		4 853

The surplus for the year is transferred from the income and expenditure account to the appropriation account (Table 3.13). This account shows what the members have decided to do with the surplus earnings of the society. Laws governing cooperative societies usually require that a specific percentage of a society's surplus is put in to a 'statutory reserve fund'. Money may not be withdrawn from this fund except on the authority of the registrar of cooperative societies. The balance may be paid out to members as a patronage dividend, based on the amount of produce they delivered to the society. Also, if the committee have worked well for the society they may be paid an honorarium to cover their expenses. The society for which accounts are shown makes a standard levy to cover its costs, tries to build up its reserves and covers patronage dividends and payments to its committee. From its produce realisation account it can be seen that this resulted in a small deficit ($23.00) on its actual operations. However, the surplus for the year derived from the levy was ample after allowing for this deficit (see Table 3.13) to permit an increased dividend payment to members. An unappropriated surplus of $1 083 was carried forward to the following year.

On accounts such as those presented in these tables are based a number of indicators of the financial health of an enterprise. One is its net worth, i.e. owner's capital after deduction of indebtedness. Another is the current ratio, which is

$$\frac{\text{current assets}}{\text{current liabilities}}$$

Generally acceptable is a current ratio of 1.6 to 2.0. This is an indicator of adequate working capital. If it fails to keep pace with increases in sales turnover, a business is said to be over-trading. If the reverse applies it is said to be under-trading, i.e. its assets are not fully employed. Either over- or under-trading can be dangerous and can lead to a serious financial situation, possibly ending in liquidation. The liquidity ratio, which is

$$\frac{\text{liquid assets}}{\text{current liabilities}}$$

shows the ability of an enterprise to meet its immediate obligations. Liquid assets include cash and items that can be immediately converted into cash. Current liabilities include all unpaid short term commitments.

Another critical ratio is the rate of earnings on the capital invested. If for some time this is lower than that available elsewhere, the owners of the capital will be dissatisfied and be inclined to withdraw it.

A strong cash flow position gives a manager scope for initiative and movement. A commonly used indicator of this is the ratio

$$\frac{\text{net income to shareholders + depreciation allowances + other income net of taxes}}{\text{capital expenditures + change in inventories + dividend or interest commitments on capital}}$$

A ratio of more than 1.0 indicates a strong cash flow and high capacity to take on new activities and make new investments.

Keeping watch on costs

The low operating costs of many family marketing enterprises stem from the direct relationship between outlays on services and the owner's pocket. The more use he can make of family labour and of his own resources such as his house, outbuildings and a vehicle perhaps, the more he keeps for himself.

Under the pressure of handling a seasonal product, however, a larger scale operator will have to engage whatever services are necessary to carry out the operation. Preferably such needs should be foreseen in advance, and the costs of using alternative suppliers appraised against their quality, reliability and timeliness. When the marketing season is over, the manager can do his cost accounting, setting out the supplies and services purchased and analysing their impact on the profitability of his operation.

This type of cost control is just as relevant to parastatal marketing operations as it is to private firms and cooperatives. Comparing the current cost of standard operations per tonne of produce handled with those of previous years is one of the efficiency measures available to a monopoly enterprise. Thus the ocean freight loss is a strategic indicator for an export marketing board. A rise above the normal suggests pilferage of cargo during port loading. A rise in the average turn-around time of vessels in port implies poor organisation of transport or handling equipment and crews. A rise in administration and other overhead costs per tonne could reflect reduced handlings because of a poor harvest; otherwise it would point to a need to simplify procedures, combine personnel responsibilities and reduce total staff employed. To permit such analyses, expenditures on major operating functions — transport, packaging, storage, port handling — should be accounted for separately, not lumped together under such headings as labour, services, etc.

Currency risks
Sudden changes in exchange rates can affect dramatically a marketing enterprise engaged in exporting agricultural products or distributing supplies that are imported. If a change in exchange rates is anticipated, the operator will do well to budget his outlays on replacements at the rate foreseen for the future. This will be the rate used by traders in the 'black' (unofficial) market.

High rates of inflation are common in many countries. The manager of a marketing enterprise must be aware of their implications. Selling on the basis of a 10% margin to cover costs and profit will leave him in deficit if the currency has devalued 10% in the meantime. To maintain his income in real terms his margin must be costs, plus target income, plus an allowance to cover the expected degree of inflation! An enterprise distributing fertiliser in Brazil in 1983 added a 10% margin to its buying prices to cover its own costs and profit, then a further 50% to cover expected inflation. Depreciation allowances should also be based on the cost of replacement at current prices, not on past costs of purchase or construction.

Insurance
Agricultural marketing enterprises face a wide range of risks. They include losses of produce in storage or transit, misuse of funds by responsible officers and price changes due to events over which the enterprise has no control.

Insurance against some of these risks can be had from national agencies. A cooperative can insure against the disappearance of a manager with its funds by requiring that he take out a bond for $5 000 or $50 000, according to an estimate of the amounts at risk. A firm undertaking storage for others can be required to obtain insurance against loss due to fire, its own negligence, etc. Insurance is available against losses of produce shipped on consignment due to delays in transit and mishandling by the transporter or consignee. Where the risks of accidents, illness, etc. sustained by employees or users of marketing enterprise facilities are substantial, insurance against them should be obtained annually as a matter of course.

Protection against losses on stocks or forward contracts due to price changes can be secured by hedging on a futures market where one is available for the commodity concerned. Government policy and foreign exchange controls may limit access to such markets. However, sales agreements can be related to prices on recognised forward markets as illustrated for soybeans in Paraguay.

Accounting machines and micro-computers
Marketing and farm supply enterprises will find such equipment helpful in conducting and controlling their business. Common uses according to the nature and complexity of the operation are to:

(a) prepare and address standard letters to potential customers;
(b) maintain and provide quick access to stock inventories at a number of depots or branches;
(c) maintain and analyse sales and payment records, programme sales forward and provide financial management information;
(d) maintain records of staff salaries and social contributions, make tax deductions and prepare salary cheques, where applicable.

Computers are a great help in solving problems involving simultaneous equations of input and price variables. Thus a feed supply enterprise can determine quickly the lowest cost combination of ingredients to maintain a particular nutritional formula. A fertiliser distributor can assess where best to locate sales depots on the basis of demand patterns and transport costs.

Assessing performance

Commonly accepted indicators of performance are profitability, return on investment, market standing, quality of service, innovativeness and social responsibility.

Profitability

At the end of the year the marketing enterprise should achieve a net profit after allowing for all costs. How big that net balance should be will depend on the attitude of the owner. A private operator will expect it to provide a profit at least equal to what he could earn in alternative occupations open to him. If he lives in an environment of low wages and high unemployment he may accept a very low net income for lack of an alternative. For example, this is the position of many street retailers.

The transnational, with other sources of income, may be prepared to take a long-term view on profitability. It may accept low earnings on some activities in the hope of building up a favourable public image. More characteristic, probably, is the action of Gulf and Western Inc. It sold its holdings in the Dominican Republic in 1984 when low sugar prices and high taxes meant that they contributed less to its earnings than its investments elsewhere.

A marketing or input supply cooperative may be satisfied with a very small profit. Its main concern is to serve its members by providing a favourable outlet for their produce and/or supplying inputs conveniently at low prices. An income that covers its costs and maintains its reserves may be judged sufficient.

For a parastatal enterprise, profitability may have still lower priority. Stabilising the market for producers and consumers, earning foreign exchange for the national economy and redistributing income in accordance with concepts of equity, can be prior considerations. However, unless the government concerned is in a position to provide subsidies, a parastatal, like a cooperative, *must cover its costs*.

Return on investment

An adequate return on the capital employed in a marketing enterprise is important where the sums involved are substantial and have either been borrowed by private owners or could be used by them in some other income-earning investment. For owner operators the return on capital includes remuneration of their own labour and management skills. Enterprises employing a manager would charge his salary as a cost and arrive at a net return on capital invested. *The criterion for most investors is that the return should be at least as high as could be obtained from other available investment opportunities*.

The risk of losing the investment must also be taken into account. If a safe government bond pays 5% interest net of inflation, i.e. a *real* interest rate of 5%, then a private business investment should pay substantially more. For a transnational investing in a country where it faces political, exchange rate and other risks additional to those of a familiar marketing business, a return of 20% (real) on external capital invested could be a normal target rate.

Returns on capital employed receive less attention in parastatals. Their original capital may have been provided from public sources without the need to pay interest. Some governments charge interest on 'new' capital at a concessional rate and expect the parastatal to obtain bank finance for its purchases and stocks; they help in this by providing a guarantee. While a marketing parastatal may well be justified on service and social grounds, it is appropriate, nevertheless, that it accounts, at market rates, for the capital it employs. The advantages it offers may then be set against its full cost.

Market standing

Market share, or market standing, is another objective measure of an enterprise's performance. If it has a 20% share of total sales of a certain product or products as against 12% some years ago, then it has performed well. A declining share would imply the reverse. This measure can be applied to most marketing enterprises including parastatal monopolies where they compete on export markets.

The market standing of a firm is high if its share of the market is at the higher income end, and if it has a reputation for quality produce and for strict reliability in its dealings. It is unwise, however, to rest on such a reputation for long. An economic recession or other adverse shift in the market may find it unable to match more innovative or cost-conscious competitors.

Quality of services

This is not easily measured, but it is well understood by the clients of a marketing enterprise. A rural assembly buyer will be liked by farmers if he pays them promptly, uses correct measures, does not keep them waiting and is generally polite. A fertiliser distributor would be providing good service if he could make available for farmers the types and quantities of fertiliser they want at the *time* they want them, if he could explain clearly how they should be used and could arrange for sales on credit.

Innovativeness

A readiness and capacity to introduce new techniques, to adopt new forms of organisation and to develop new markets are all aspects of innovativeness, which is important if there is to be progress in marketing in a particular sector of agriculture.

New techniques are quickly taken up after they have been shown to be effective under prevailing conditions. Cassava chips became the main foreign exchange earner of Thailand in a decade of development of new technologies and markets by European transnationals and their local partners.

Social responsibility

Consideration for the welfare of the people with which it deals is also a criterion of a marketing enterprise's performance. Often, their longer-term interests coincide. An enterprise buying produce from farmers must treat them fairly well if it is to have their business in the following year. It cannot overcharge farmers using its supplies for long or they will find another supplier or change their production pattern. Too relaxed an attitude, on the part of an assembly cooperative for example, over quality control, may not help the growers concerned. It can mean that the eventual buyer is dissatisfied with the produce coming from the cooperative, and the cooperative loses his business.

An equity goal in some parastatal marketing is to pay the same price to all producers, irrespective of their distance from the eventual market and the transport costs involved. This is unfair to the farmers who are conveniently placed; they receive lower prices than they should. It also raises the costs of the enterprise as a whole. Thus against a high performance on equity must be set a lower rating for economic efficiency. Striking an appropriate balance between competing criteria of performance is the test of a good marketing system.

Summary of Part B: Operations

For a marketing business to succeed, a clear plan of action based on a thorough, up-to-date knowledge of the market is needed. Systematic market research can provide valuable leads for sales policy, packaging and presentation. The place of business should be convenient for transport, communications and support services. Access to a flexible source of finance is vital for a business that is to handle farm output concentrated seasonally and subject to considerable variation in supply.

Quality of management is vital. The manager must respond to perishability in the product handled, to prices often changing from day to day and to specific transport, packaging, storage and market requirements. In buying and selling he must maintain an operating margin that covers expected costs and an allowance for profit. At the same time, suppliers and customers must be served well and promptly.

When considering taking on a new activity, the contribution it will make to the overhead costs of the ongoing operation is the main criterion. We have provided formats and models to help the reader to work this out for himself, and to prepare the financial statements that are a guide to the operator on the state of his business, as well as to banks, members of cooperatives and the government (in the case of parastatals). These statements also permit the appraiser to calculate financial ratios that are convenient in assessing the financial health of an enterprise. In many situations, use of accounting machines and a mini-computer can be a great help in maintaining business controls and keeping watch on inventories and costs.

Efficiency criteria for a marketing business include profitability, return on the capital employed, market standing, quality of service and readiness to take up new ideas and methods. Social considerations are also important, both to the private marketing enterprise and to cooperatives and parastatals. A good manager keeps them to the forefront along with the other criteria of effective performance.

Issues for discussion

1 Prepare, as manager of a marketing enterprise, operating plans for three agricultural products of your country (a) on domestic markets and (b) on export markets. Assess the scope for promotion by various methods. On what data do you base your recommendations?

2 In what ways can managers of cooperative and parastatals get signals on market requirements? How can they transmit these signals to producers? Give some examples.

3 Find out from informed people, direct enquiry, etc. how a rural assembler of grain, a vegetable wholesaler, a retail butcher, a fertiliser distributor, in your country got their fixed and working capital, and on what terms. Compare how private, cooperative and parastatal enterprises get their money to operate.

4 For some marketing enterprises you know, prepare analyses of their main and supplementary business sites. What factors determined their choice? Are there disadvantages now?

5 For what products and through which marketing channels are farmers in your country paid (a) partially in advance, (b) in cash at time of sale, and (c) wholly or partially some time later? Prepare profiles of these arrangements and assess the balance of advantage and disadvantage and the alternatives open to the farmers concerned.

6 What are the main physical characteristics of paddy and rice, potatoes, sheep and their meat, urea, to be taken into account when marketing them? What are the implications for you as a marketing expert?

7 Prepare, for your country, estimates of prevailing operating margins or mark-ups in the main product marketing channels. What costs and profit allowances do they cover?

8 Appraise the sales promotion now being undertaken by enterprises marketing fertiliser, seasonal fruit, basic foods such as cassava. What improvements would you suggest? Consider the financial implications.

9 Examine the following proposals for additional activities: (a) a farmer setting up a retail sales point by the side of a main road, (b) a fruit and vegetable wholesaler acquiring a refrigerated store, and (c) a rural assembler of grains and pulses accepting an agency for the distribution of fertilisers. Identify the main management issues. Construct a set of figures for Table 3.7 for each situation.

10 What can each of the financial ratios discussed in this chapter tell you about a marketing business? Calculate such ratios for the rice marketing enterprises and cotton marketing cooperative for which financial data are provided, supplementing these data with synthetic figures where necessary.

11 Assess the performance of some agricultural marketing and input supply enterprises for which you can obtain information.

Further reading

Abbott, J. C. (1987) *Agricultural marketing enterprises for the developing world*, Cambridge University Press, Cambridge.

Abbott, J. C. *et al.* (1984) *Marketing improvement in the developing world*, FAO, Rome.

Arbin, K. *et al.* (eds.) (1984) *Marketing boards in tropical Africa*, Routledge and Kegan Paul, London.

Bauer, P. T. (1963) *West African trade*, Routledge and Kegan Paul, London.

COPAC (1984) *Commodity marketing through cooperatives — some experiences from Africa and Asia and some lessons for the future*, COPAC Secretariat, FAO, Rome.

FAO Marketing Guide Series: No. 1 *Marketing problems and improved programmes* (1973). No. 2 *Marketing fruit and vegetables* (1970). No. 3 *Marketing livestock and meat* (1977). No. 4 *Marketing eggs and poultry* (1961). No. 5 *Agricultural marketing boards: their establishment and operation* (1966). No. 6 *Rice marketing* (1972). No. 7 *Fertiliser marketing* (1977). FAO, Rome.

Harper, M. and **Kavura, R.** (1982) *The private marketing entrepreneur and rural development*, FAO, Rome.

International Trade Centre: Advisory manuals on export markets for specific products and on export marketing procedures, ITC/GATT, Geneva.

Jones, S. F. (1985) *Marketing research for agriculture and agribusiness in developing countries: courses, trading and literature*, Tropical Development and Research Institute, London.

Jones, W. O. (1972) *Marketing staple food crops in tropical Africa*, Cornell University Press, Ithaca.

Kaynak, F. (ed.) (1986) *World food marketing systems*, Butterworth, London.

Kindra, G. S. (ed.) (1984) *Marketing in developing countries*, Croom Helm, London.

Kotler, P. (1984) *Marketing management: analysis, planning and control*, Prentice Hall Inc., Englewood Cliffs, N.J.

Van der Laan, H. B. (1984) *The Lebanese traders in Sierra Leone*, Mouton, Hague.

4 Farm management

In this chapter we deal with the management of farms.

The role and scope of formal farm management

The size and type of a farm may range from a small subsistence plot of less than one hectare to a commune or state farm comprising all the land of several villagers. They may be operated by a tenant, by an owner, or by a manager employed by a cooperative or a state farm or an absentee owner. Even so, to each type, the same principles of farm management economics and the techniques which are based on these principles, apply, though with varying degrees of emphasis.

Meaning of farm management
Our purpose in this chapter is to show how the principles and techniques can assist the farm adviser, the farmer or the farm manager, regardless of the farm size and amount of capital and resources available. Two major tasks facing today's farm managers are:

(a) how best to incorporate new technology into the farming enterprise;
(b) how to be sufficiently flexible, mentally and financially, to adjust the management of resources to meet changing costs and prices and varying climatic conditions.

The principles and techniques
The management principles and techniques outlined in this chapter should help farmers meet these two challenges with some success. At the same time it is recognised that farm management economics is only one of a number of disciplines, each of which has an important effect on the success of a farm operation.

The usefulness of farm management
There are real advantages in using the farm management approach along with new technical advances and capital. There is a wide contrast in net farm income per hectare between those farms where this approach is used and those where it is not. The gap between them becomes wider each year (Fig. 4.1). During the last ten years, the 'management' or 'whole farm' approach to raising productivity has been shown to work in practice. Some dramatic improvements have been made on farms which have used advice from management specialists to assist their technical and economic planning. Increases in profit of up to 20% have not been uncommon. Most farmers who have used management advice have increased profit relative to farmers who have not done so.

Fig. 4.1 Upper Lofa region, Liberia
(a) Rice grown by a farmer who has adapted management principles to local conditions
(b) Upland rice grown following traditional practice.
(Courtesy of P. A. Ryhanen)

What does farm 'profit' mean?

Makeham and Malcolm, in their book *The economics of tropical farm management* (Cambridge University Press, 1986) defined 'profit' as follows:

> If you asked most farmers: 'How much profit did you make last year?' they would express their answer in terms of cash. The commonest answer would be 'I had only $300 at the start of the year, now I have got $700, so I suppose I made $400 "profit".' He has kept his family for the year, maybe bought an extra couple of goats, pigs, or cows, got a $200 loan from the bank which he does not have to pay back until next year, won some bets, married a second wife, and sold an old bicycle. Accountants and economists would shudder at his definition of profit—nonetheless, the $400 gain is real to him; in his terms, it is 'profit'.

There are almost as many definitions as there are definers of profit. For example, one person may define farm profit as the sum of:

(a) the difference between the cash held by the farmer at the start and the end of the year;
(b) the extra grain or animals on hand at the end of the year; and
(c) the increase in value, over the year, of the assets the farmer owns, e.g. house, machinery and land.

Another person may use the rules of the local stock exchange in reporting the results of a year's operations. A third person may follow a definition conjured up by the particular school of economics of which he is a devotee, and so on.

When speaking of profit, most people have some notion of the money left over from income, after all the costs which were involved in earning the income have been deducted. Profit usually refers to some surplus or excess of income over costs (the net gain from a production process). To us, profit is the difference between the gross income and the operating costs. The operating costs are the sum of all the variable costs and the operating overhead (not total overhead) costs. Put another way, it is the total gross margin minus the operating overheads (see later for definitions of these terms).

Why do some farms perform poorly?

When the reasons for the poor financial performance of a farm are analysed, it is often found that:

(a) activities (e.g. crop and animal production) are not being carried out in the best way;
(b) different activities are not suitably coordinated;
(c) wrong activities are being conducted;
(d) new opportunities are not being exploited.

An adviser can sometimes indicate to a farmer the cost, in terms of lost or unrealised income, of the present way of organising and managing his farm. This will frequently stimulate the farmer to take a much keener interest in the technical aspects of how he carries out his farming activities. It may also arouse his interest in new activities which can increase his profit.

Different views of farm management

Most people who are responsible for running farms see farm management as the day-to-day problems of organising and of making decisions about practical and technical matters. Jobs must be done well and and on time. It is vital that the mechanical, husbandry and labour operations, which are fundamental to the smooth running of any farm enterprise, are carried out efficiently. A successful farm operator should be able to perform the numerous, varied and testing practical tasks, and be able to organise and motivate his labour force, yet he must be flexible enough to deal efficiently with rapid changes in seasonal conditions, prices and costs.

A farm operator must also apply systematic controls to check that production is proceeding as planned. Milk yields, egg production or liveweight gain, for example, must be tested regularly to ensure maintenance of expected livestock performance. Variations in production should be analysed carefully to ascertain the causes. It is not, however, the purpose of this chapter to give details of planting crops, maintaining pastures, managing labour and caring for livestock. These can be found in specialised agricultural books, and in leaflets issued by agricultural extension services and farm input suppliers.

The disciplines which have provided the most valuable recent insights into farm management have been economics, mathematics and sociology.

Some of their principles have been applied to agriculture because progressive farmers, and their advisers and financiers, have recognised the importance of the business aspect of farming. They have helped so much in the management of other kinds of business that farm economists have been quick to adapt their ideas to the business of farming.

Some people regard farming primarily as a way of life. Others, and this includes the vast majority of farmers in many tropical countries, are obliged to consume most of what they grow simply to feed and clothe themselves and their children. Nevertheless, the principles and techniques discussed in this chapter can help both groups of people to run their farms more efficiently, even though the economist's idea of profit means little to some of them.

Resource management

Farmers, in an economic sense, are resource managers who endeavour to manipulate their land, capital and other resources to achieve certain ends. These ends or goals vary with each farmer's responsibilities and sometimes also with his ambitions for himself and his family. Common goals are likely to include:

(a) assuring food supplies and other living requirements for himself and family;
(b) achieving independence from debt and reaching a personal level of living on a par with his community;
(c) obtaining a satisfactory income for the cooperative or other body which employs him;
(d) improving the physical appearance of the farm for which he is responsible.

Capital involved in farming

In some tropical countries the land does not belong to an individual farmer but to the tribe, the community, cooperative or government department or corporation. In these cases, the major resources or assets which a farmer owns are his money, his livestock, implements and other farm equipment, and perhaps his house. Where there is a land market, the value of the land owned by the farmer is an additional resource. Often this is a very valuable asset.

The resources which are owned minus the total of his debts, have a value which is known as the farmer's capital or his equity. The farmer who takes a commercial view of the resources he controls will seek:

(a) to obtain the greatest annual profit from his resources;
(b) to obtain the maximum annual increase in the value of his capital, i.e. to make capital gains.

For a semi-subsistence farmer, whose major resource is the family labour force, the first interest is to produce enough food to feed his family, with the minimum risk. Second, he would like some cash income. Third, he needs savings which are easily convertible into cash or food in times of adversity. Capital gains are hardly relevant to his situation.

Decision-making

Farm management, as a formal discipline, is concerned with helping the farm manager to make sound decisions. Decision-making usually involves choosing between alternatives in the light of the decision-maker's goals. The decision-making process has six generally recognised steps:

(a) having ideas and recognising problems;
(b) making observations, collecting facts;
(c) analysing observations and testing alternative solutions to the problem;
(d) making the decision;
(e) acting on the decision;
(f) taking the responsibility for the decision.

This farm management section of our text aims to help the farmer to make better decisions based on these steps of perceiving problems, collecting information and analysing possible solutions. What should I produce? What method of production should I use? What capital do I need? Should I borrow? Answering these questions requires an understanding of economic principles, management techniques, finance and technology. Decisions often have to be made under conditions of change and uncertainty.

We will illustrate some of the processes and problems of decision-making by listing the steps which the owner of a drought- or flood-afflicted farm should go through when he is deciding on a recovery programme. These steps would probably run as follows.

(a) Calculate how much money he needs to meet loan repayments, short term working capital and current overhead costs (including living and schooling costs).

(b) Assess whether this income can be obtained with his present activities, assuming 'average' seasons and prices.

(c) Determine the technical and capital inputs needed to increase his income where present activities do not provide enough to meet commitments. More intensive farming usually calls for more capital, and this implies increased repayment and interest costs on loans.

(d) Specify details of the broad plan:
- resources and amounts of extra funds needed;
- technical basis of the programmes;
- a development budget containing loadings for risk;
- the farmer's equity position (total assets minus debts) before, during and at the end of the plan;
- the likelihood of his equity being reduced to dangerous levels by another disaster or personal illness;
- terms of loan repayment: under-borrowing, or over-stringent repayment terms may thwart the successful achievement of the plan.

(e) Consider the alternatives if attainable revenue falls short of essential minimum; total or partial sale of assets; a partnership with an investor while continuing to manage the farm; doing nothing and hoping for the best (e.g. a large price increase for products).

The programme calls for a fairly high level of budgeting and technical skills, and the penalty for wrong decisions may be high. Where can these skills be best obtained? Should the farmer rely on his own experience or should he obtain advice from an outsider? State advisory services, a specialised agricultural bank, or a farm management specialist may be of help. At least two of these could probably help him in making a sound decision.

Application to various types of farm
The problems faced by the various different types of farm differ in many important respects: the cattle farmer, the fruit producer, a cash crop farmer, dairyman or chicken raiser each has his own particular problems. Many farmers combine advantageously several different lines of production but four basic farm types may be distinguished:

(a) those where animals and animal products are produced;

(b) those where crops are produced by annual cultivation; the produce may be eaten during growth, e.g. fodder sorghum, or harvested and sold, e.g sorghum and cotton, or harvested and kept as food, e.g. maize;

(c) those concerned with perennial plants: tree fruits such as citrus and bananas, coffee or rubber plantations, perennial seed and hay crops, where there is a flow or income over a long period, and frequently a long time between initial investment and first pay-off, but a need to replant only at relatively long intervals;

(d) farms with a mixture of several of these activities.

Although the diversity of farm types is wide, the principles and technqiues of farm management economics apply with varying degrees of relevance to all of them. This includes the shifting cultivator who moves to new land when existing plots lose fertility under continuous cropping.

Subsistence and semi-subsistence farms
Over large parts of many tropical countries the agricultural activities noted above are carried out on small subsistence and semi-subsistence farms. The principles of management and decision-making also apply, with necessary adaptations, to semi-subsistence farms, where there is an element of cash income. Some of these principles apply also to subsistence farms.

The main features of semi-subsistence farms are:

(a) They are generally of small size.

(b) There is very low reliance on mechanical power or fertilisers.

(c) There is a need to select crop and animal activities, including hunting and collecting the products of wild plants, to supply the basic nutrient needs of the farm household, and where possible, a surplus for barter or sale. Traditional methods of achieving these two ends have been formed by a long process of trial and error and are often quite ingenious. However, increased population pressure has forced many tropical farmers to modify their traditional forms of land use, e.g. by reducing the period of bush fallow or increasing the proportion of starchy crops at the expense of high protein foods. There is thus an increased need for different production techniques, better planning and new forms of dietary supplements to ensure an adequate and nutritionally balanced food supply for the household.

(d) There is a reluctance to accept new practices which involve more risk although they offer prospects of more and/or better food and a higher cash income.

For the semi-subsistence farmer, the failure of one of the activities upon which he depends for the provision of an important share of his household's diet, can be calamitous. The small or medium-sized commercial farm operator can afford to take more risks and so be more innovative.

(e) Because even traditional activities carry some risks, the subsistence farmer tends not to put his savings into long term fixed-capital investments such as buildings and land improvements. He cannot turn these investments into cash in the event of bad seasons and/or prices. He prefers to keep his savings in 'liquid' assets such as cattle, precious metals, and jewellery for his womenfolk. These can be converted readily into cash.

(f) There is a relatively low proportion of cash sales to total 'income' of the farm household. The total or gross 'income' has four components: cash sales; cash income from off-farm employment; the market value of farm products consumed by the household; and payment in kind, e.g. food received for services performed.

An example of the breakdown of 'income' for a semi-subsistence tropical farm household is as follows:

	Income ($)
Cash sales	180
Cash income from off-farm work	80
Value of home consumed products	410
Payments in kind	30
Total 'income' for household	700

(g) Cash expenditure on direct farm inputs is small in relation to the value of the labour inputs used. Actual cash payments may be less than half of the value of the family used, e.g. $100 as against $220 for the kind of farm just illustrated. In addition to payment for inputs such as fertiliser, pesticides, tools, contract services, and interest on loans, cash is also used for overhead and personal expenses. These will include schooling, rent, taxes, and possibly savings and investment. For example from $260 cash income, $100 may be spent on farm inputs, leaving $160 for meeting overheads, personal expenses, investments and savings, etc.

The other type of expenditure incurred by many such households is 'payment in kind', where farm products are delivered for services rendered, taxes or as 'tribute' to community leaders.

Problems and decisions

Some of the main types of decisions and problems facing semi-subsistence households which can be helped by applying the concepts of farm management economics are how to:

(a) use limited resources, e.g. family labour, outside labour, borrowed money and cash, to best effect;
(b) plan and budget expected food supply and cash income for the maximum benefit of the household;
(c) plan in advance alternative courses of action in the event of the budgeted food and cash plan not working out as expected;
(d) select the best combination of activities, both on and off the farm, to produce the food supply and cash income needed to cover essential household needs;
(e) choose between risky alternatives;
(f) plan a crop rotation;
(g) minimise the chance of being seriously harmed by adverse seasons or prices;
(h) estimate available resources to overcome: shortages of labour for clearing, sowing, or harvesting, lack of feed for animals during the dry season of the year or a poor family diet.

The human factor in farm management

In the following pages, considerable emphasis will be given to planning, analysis and budgeting.

However, it is vital to stress the importance of effective communication between the farm manager and his workers. Lack of proper understanding can stop the best of plans from being achieved.

Effective communication

When a farmer employs labour, the quality of field operations can be greatly reduced if the workers are dissatisfied or lack motivation. Similarly, if a farmer or farm manager tries to introduce new activities or projects into the farm, the expected increase in profits may never be realised because the workers prevent the programme from working properly. This may be because they do not understand the reasons for its introduction, or because they feel that the farmer is going to get extra benefits, whilst they gain nothing. Sometimes workers do not have the necessary skills to cope with new programmes. This problem requires training linked with appropriate wage rates.

In many cases where workers are resentful or lack motivation, the main cause is that there is no effective two-way communication of ideas and aspirations. The farmer sees things from one point of view, the workers from another. The two parties have different 'frames of reference'.

It is around points of common interest that effective two-way communication can occur. Where such communication exists, there is a greater chance of reaching a suitable compromise.

Once the farmer or farm manager understands the value of good communications in helping him achieve his financial and social goals, he can choose from the range of communication techniques available, the ones that are most relevant to his situation.

Assigning responsibility

One way of bringing the frames of reference of farmer and worker closer together is to give the worker responsibility. This may be responsibility for a particular segment of the work and the right to make many of the detailed decisions about how it is to be done. The farm manager must tolerate some mistakes in the interest of developing the worker and establishing a better rapport.

When the worker begins to refer to 'our cows' rather than 'your cows' the farmer knows he has

succeeded in closing the gap between their respective frames of reference. Once this has occurred, the prospect for improving communications and the performance of the worker, greatly increases.

Small discussion groups

The common techniques such as charts, graphs, pictures and, where appropriate, the written word, can all aid the communication process. But generally none of them are as effective, on both small and large farms, as the small discussion group.

Whenever a problem involving the cooperation and performance of the workers arises, or when a new activity is being introduced, a small informal discussion between farmer and workers is useful.

Fig. 4.2 Communications: 'We are holding one of those informal discussion groups.'

It is best to confine each discussion to a few specific points, such as: introduction of a new crop; incentives for good field performance by workers; methods of reducing the costs of repairs to machinery; safety precautions with machinery and chemicals; or techniques for improving the yield of a particular crop or animal activity.

The discussion group can be used for sharing, e.g. pooling knowledge about keeping cattle healthy; for explaining, e.g. why it is necessary to work long hours to get the crop planted in seven days; for resolving, e.g. the amount of money the workers should pay for the rice that they consume; and for learning, e.g. how to use a new spray.

Provided such groups are led skilfully, that there is no 'talking down' and that the topics discussed are of real interest to the workers, they can result in a more efficient and contented work force and a more profitable farm.

Even where authority is traditionally lodged in the leader of the family, tribe or community, as it is in many semi-subsistence farming areas, there is still the need for individuals to know 'why'. Thus any measures which can be taken by leaders to reduce conflict and increase understanding are likely to lead to better group performance. For greater effectiveness they must recognise existing social structures, and manoeuvre within the framework of the surrounding culture and traditions.

Key concepts in farm management

Space does not permit a detailed application of management techniques to each of the four basic farm types described on p. 87. The approach followed here will be to explain the key concepts which underlie farm management. Where appropriate, the relevant farm management accounting techniques will be discussed with each concept.

It is hoped that these concepts will help managers of all four types of farm make sound decisions about their operations, use of resources and investment programmes.

The following concepts will be discussed:

(a) Cash flows
(b) Costs and receipts
(c) Gross margins
(d) Farm profits and profit budgets

(e) Return on capital
(f) Decision-making
(g) Financial basis for decisions on crop and animal production
(h) How to decide whether to adopt a new activity
(i) Taking account of variability
(j) Discounting and productive values
(k) Principles of equimarginal returns and substitution
(l) Use of farm accounts and records.

Part A: Analysis

Cash flows

The annual net cash flow or receipt of money is very important for most commercial farmers. For the semi-subsistence farmer, a budget showing the 'net food flow', i.e. the expected supply and demand for food, needs to be drawn up before a cash flow budget can be constructed. Both budgets stimulate farmers to make plans. The cash flow is found simply by subtracting the money spent from the money received, over the whole year. Often farmers find it useful to calculate cash flows on a monthly or quarterly basis. They may do this when they are budgeting next year's programme, or when comparing this year's actual results with the expected results set out in the budget which they prepared before the start of the year.

When a farmer is planning either next year's programme, or a longer term project which perhaps involves investing borrowed capital, the things he wants to know are:

(a) How much money or food the programme is likely to produce and how much the programme will cost.
(b) When he will receive the money or the food and when he will need money or food.
(c) If the amount of money or food he expects to receive in a given period does not cover the amount he will need, the farmer will want to know how he can make up the difference. Will the bank provide a loan? Does the farmer have any savings? Does he have any stored reserves?
(d) How much money he will be able to save in say one, two and five years' time if he undertakes this programme.

90

Cash flow budgets

These are designed to help the farmer to plan his future activities, either on a short term (one year) or a medium term (four to five years) basis. Cash flow budgets are also used to provide continuous feedback or monitoring during the period of the programme. The farmer will be able to compare his actual cash income and costs with the estimates he made when drawing up the budget. If the actual results differ greatly from the target results, then he can try to take steps to modify the situation before any serious harm results.

The main feature of a cash flow budget is that it focuses specifically on cash. For example, borrowing from the bank is regarded as cash received. Worksheet 1 shows a cash flow budget for the first quarter of a one-year period. The figures are hypothetical.

Worksheet 1: Cash flow budget for the first quarter of one year

	1st quarter ($)	2nd quarter ($)	3rd quarter ($)	4th quarter ($)	Yearly total ($)
Receipts					
Sales:					
crops	500				2 000
livestock and products	200				500
Loans to be received	800				2 000
Other receipts	30				200
Total receipts (A)	1 530				4 700
Payments					
Machinery cash costs	100				250
Variable production costs (excluding machinery)	150				650
Marketing costs	30				100
Overhead costs	70				400
Living costs	250				1 000
Machinery replacement					
Interest	100				250
New capital investment	150				500
Taxes	20				150
Other	30				200
Total payments before loans (B)	900				3 500
Net cash flow (A–B) (before loan repayment)	+630				+1200
Loan repayment	700				1 000
Bank balance at end of period:					
Credit					+200
Debit	−70				

Comparison of actual against budgeted results

To help the farmer or manager check the actual financial progress of his plan against the expected or budgeted outcome, a tabulation as in Worksheet 2 is useful. For each quarter it shows the following:

Worksheet 2: Quarterly comparison of actual against budgeted figures

	Actual this quarter ($)	Budget this quarter ($)	Total actual to date for year ($)	Budget for year ($)	Difference: budget for year and total actual to date ($)
Receipts					
Sales: crops	400	500	400	2 000	1 600
livestock and products	250	200	250	500	250
Loans to be received	870	800	870	2 000	1 130
Other receipts	20	30	20	. 200	180
Total receipts (A)	1 540	1 530	1 540	4 700	3 160
Payments					
Machinery cash costs	120	100	120	250	130
Variable production costs (excluding machinery)	100	150	100	650	550
Marketing costs	30	30	30	100	70
Overhead costs	70	70	70	400	330
Living costs	300	250	300	1 000	700
Machinery replacement					
Interest	110	100	110	250	140
New capital investment	100	150	100	500	400
Taxes	25	20	25	150	125
Other	25	. 30	25	200	175
Total payments (B) (before loan repayment)	880	900	880	3 500	2 620
Net cash flow (A–B) (before loan repayment)	+600	+630	+660	+1 200	+540
Loan repayment	660	900	660	1 000	340
Bank balance at end of period:					
Credit				+200	+200
Debit		70			

(a) actual receipts and payments;
(b) budgeted or estimated receipts and payments;
(c) the total for the year so far, of actual receipts and payments:
(d) the total yearly budget of receipts and payments;
(e) the difference between the total yearly budgeted figure and the actual amount of money received and paid so far, for the year.

Cash development budget

The next type of cash budget deals with a medium term development which requires the investment of borrowed capital with a pay-off over several years. Worksheet 3 brings out the main principles of cash development budgeting, which can be applied to any individual situation.

It is assumed here that the physical programme has already been planned. The cash flow budget simply tests whether the plan is economically feasible. Often, it is necessary to test three or four plans before making a final decision on the best programme.

In Worksheet 3 the planning period is one year. Many farmers, managers and bankers are more interested in monthly or quarterly cash flows. In

Worksheet 3: Total cash flow budget of a farm on which a development programme is proposed

	Year 1 ($)	Year 2 ($)	Year 3 ($)	Year 4 ($)	Year 5 ($)
Cash receipts					
Sales of farm products	2 000	3 000	4 500	5 000	5 500
Loans to be received	8 700	1 500			
Other receipts	500	300	600	500	500
Total receipts (A)	11 200	4 800	5 100	5 500	6 000
Cash payments					
Variable costs	500	750	1 000	1 250	1 500
Overhead costs	1 000	1 100	1 200	1 300	1 400
New capital investment	8 000	1 000	500		
Interest	400	500	500	450	400
Living costs	1 000	1 100	1 200	1 300	1 300
Taxes	300	350	400	500	550
Total payments (B) (before loan repayment)	11 200	4 800	4 800	4 800	5 150
Net cash flow (A–B) (before loan repayment)			+300	+700	+850
Loan repayment			300	700	850
Bank balance at end of year:					
Credit					
Debit	8 700	10 200	9 900	9 200	8 350

such cases, cash flow sheets with the requisite breakdown can be prepared.

It will be seen that no repayments can be made on the loans during the first two years. In fact, the level of debt increases, as shown under the bank balance. This is a fairly typical situation in a development programme. It shows the need for both banker and farmer to appreciate the likely pattern of cash flow if a development programme is to be properly financed. Many development programmes fail because the banker does not provide sufficient credit in the early years.

Over the five-year period there is only a small reduction in debt. The rate of reduction of debt over the next five-year period would be faster.

Food and cash flow budget

On semi-subsistence farms, the proportion of crops, animals or animal products consumed by the household usually exceeds the proportion sold. For such a farm the equivalent of the cash flow budget of the commercial farm is the 'food and cash flow budget'. It has exactly the same purposes as the cash flow budget:

(a) to indicate the likely balance between supply and demand of the items in which the farmer is most interested;

(b) to allow the farmer to plan measures to overcome periods of deficiency. Examples of seasonal food and cash flow budgets are illustrated in Worksheets 4 and 5.

Worksheet 4: Food and cash flow budget for a semi-subsistence farm

| | 1st Season (kg) | | | 2nd Season (kg) | | | 3rd Season (kg) | | |
	supply	demand	difference	supply	demand	difference	supply	demand	difference
Grain crops	100	160	−60	100	170	−70	300	180	+120
Root crops	400	200	+200	100	190	−90	200	200	
Vegetables	200	100	+100	250	150	+100	400	200	+200
Tree crops	100	150	−50	300	150	+150	20	150	−130
Animal products	20	30	−10	20	30	−10	45	35	+10
Overall adequacy of food supply for household needs	adequate: *can substitute some roots for grain*			inadequate: *little room for substitution*			adequate: *small amount of substitution*		
Proposed plan of action on basis of budget	Sell some surplus roots			Buy grain and meat Try to raise more animals by this time Hunt Borrow money Seek more off-farm work			Store some surplus grain Sell surplus grain and vegetables		

Season	Expected cash receipts for surplus products ($)	Expected cash payments for deficient products ($)	Difference ($)	
			+	−
1	25	60	25	
2				60
3	130		130	

Worksheet 5: Cash receipts and payments budget for a semi-subsistence farm

	1st Season ($)	2nd Season ($)	3rd Season ($)
Cash receipts			
Crops, animals and animal products	25		130
Off-farm work	15	18	10
Other cash receipts (not loans)	5		3
Essential loans needed		78	
Total cash receipts (A)	45	96	143
Cash payments			
Farm expenses	12	15	25
Family	20	80	30
Interest and taxes	4	6	3
Other cash payments		4	
Total cash payments before repaying loans (B)	36	105	58
Net cash flow before loan repayments (A–B)	9	−9	85
Money available to repay loans (if necessary)	9		85
Money:			
Owed		78	
Saved	9		8

Costs and receipts

Apart from the value of cash flow figures it is also important, especially for planning purposes, that a farmer or farm manager understands the nature of all the different types of costs and receipts in his farm business. Not all costs and incomes are of the same type. For instance, $50 spent on clothing has no effect on farm profit, but $50 spent on fertiliser has. Similarly, income from sales of a crop is of a different nature from income received from the sale of a machine that is no longer needed. It is helpful to understand such differences because they are important when planning future farm activities. A brief explanation of each main type of cost and receipt will be given here.

Five main kinds of farm costs are: variable, overhead, finance, capital and personal costs.

Variable costs

These are also known as direct costs. As the name implies they are costs which vary as the size and/or level of output of an activity varies. For example, if the area under maize is increased by 50% then seed, fertiliser, and labour inputs will also increase, though not necessarily increasing costs by 50%. Sometimes, for example, labour may be available without extra charge. If cattle numbers are doubled, variable costs such as feed, and veterinary fees will also double approximately.

Typical examples of variable costs are:

fertiliser	seasonal labour
seed	fuel and oil
bought feed	repairs to machinery and plant
sprays	insurance on animals and crops
animal replacements	irrigation running costs

Variable costs are directly associated with the level of intensity of each activity, but may also determine the yield or level of output of the activity. Thus with crops, the amounts and kinds of fertiliser, seed, spray and cultivation largely control the crop yield. Similarly, with animal activities, the level and type of feed, and the types of 'medicines' used have a major effect on the productivity of any given type of animal.

Very little output would occur on commercial farms unless money was spent on variable cost items. Conversely, even though a large amount of money is spent on overhead costs (see below), most of this has little effect on the level of crop yield or animal production, because overhead costs are, by definition, not related to a specific activity.

The reason for identifying the variable costs of an activity is to give the farmer an idea of the size of the change in costs which will occur if he expands or contracts one or more activities. For example, if he decides to decrease the area of cotton and increase the area of maize, the variable costs will change, but the overhead costs are likely to remain about the same. Knowing the likely variable costs and gross income, the farmer is in a position to make a quick assessment of the merit of making a change in activities.

Overhead costs

Sometimes known as fixed costs, these are costs which, within limits, do not change when the level of the activity changes. Thus an increase of 20% in the area of a crop, or in the number of animals, is not likely to lead to a rise in overhead costs. An increase as great as 100%, would, however, increase overheads.

On most farms, the overhead costs do not change very much as the level or mixture of activities changes, except of course for increases due to rising costs.

Three types of overheads are generally recognised: total, operating and activity overheads.

Total overheads These include:

(a) essential living expenses of the farmer;
(b) wages and food for permanent workers;
(c) loan interest and repayments;
(d) replacement of capital items such as plant, machinery, buildings, etc.;

(e) all taxes;
(f) repairs to water supply, roads and structures;
(g) insurances on employees, fixed structures and plant;
(h) travel and other business expenses.

Sometimes the wages of permanent workers are allocated among the different activities and treated as activity variable costs. This procedure can be a waste of time as it provides little additional information for planning purposes.

The main advantages in the farmer knowing the level of total overheads is that they are the unavoidable costs which must be met each year. This makes clear the minimum total gross margin (gross income less variable costs — see pp. 102–105) he must achieve for all the farm activities he is planning. If the expected total gross margin from his present type and intensity of activities is not enough to cover the total overhead costs, he should modify his plans to produce a programme which will cover them. Otherwise his debts will increase, perhaps to a dangerous level.

The total gross margin is normally the only source, other than additional borrowing, from which the overhead costs can be met.

Operating overheads These are used in calculating the true profit in an accounting sense. They are the overheads associated with the annual business operations of the farm. For accounting purposes, we do not include repayments of loans, interest, living expenses, or income tax in operating overheads. However an 'operator's allowance' for the work done by the operator is included. Also considered is the decline in value or depreciation of all capital items such as tractors, rather than the actual cost of replacement.

The main components of operating overheads are itemised here:

(a) 'operator's allowance';
(b) depreciation of capital items such as buildings and machines;
(c) wages of permanent workers;
(d) taxes but not income tax;
(e) repairs to water supply, roads, buildings and structures;
(f) insurance on employees, fixed structures, plant and buildings;

(g) telephone and business expenses.

Operating overheads + total variable costs = total operating costs

Activity overheads These costs are those which would not be incurred if the activity was terminated. An example would be depreciation on equipment used for a particular crop, assuming it could be sold. In most analyses, however, activity overheads are simply included in operating overheads.

There are some costs which are partly overheads and partly variable costs. Machinery depreciation, for example, has both an age component (the machine loses value as it ages) and a use component (the more the machine is used, the greater the loss in value). Strictly speaking, the cost will be an overhead if it is not directly associated with just one particular activity but affects the general running of the business.

Finance costs

These cover the annual interest paid on borrowed money, and the repayments made on loans. When hire purchase is used, the payments include interest, loan repayment and often some insurance costs lumped together in one sum.

Capital costs

Typical items of capital expenditure are new buildings, machinery, land purchase, land clearing, water supply, extra livestock and planting of palm oil, rubber, cocoa or fruit trees. Funds spent on capital items should, but do not always, increase the productive potential and asset value of the property, i.e. $1 000 spent on a capital item may add only $700 to the market value of the farm.

Most capital items lose value, or depreciate over time, and a depreciation allowance should be deducted from gross income each year so that the item can be replaced at the end of its useful life.

The simplest way of calculating depreciation is to use the 'straight line' method, which assumes that an item loses value by the same amount each year. However, in many countries the cost of many working capital items such as breeding stock, irrigation equipment, and farm machinery tends to increase both in money and in real terms as time

Fig. 4.3 'According to this book, I must write you off altogether by the end of this year.'

passes. So it is best, from a management and planning point of view, to use expected replacement cost, rather than purchase price, as the amount which should be depreciated. As an example:

	Cost ($)
Purchase price	2 100
Expected net replacement price	2 800
Expected life: 7 years	
Annual depreciation $ $\dfrac{2\ 800}{7}$	400

(Not $300 which would be the figure if purchase price was used.)

97

Where there is a resale market the salvage value of the piece of equipment, etc. can be taken into account.

It is important that the smaller farmer understands the need to make allowance for replacement of capital resources such as work animals or tractors. Otherwise, when their working life is over he may not be able to find the money needed. Normally, replacement funds are used in the farm business because the financial return on them is likely to be higher there than if the funds are deposited in a bank, for example. However, such funds should be easily available either directly, or as items acceptable as a security for borrowing when the time of replacement falls due (Fig. 4.3).

Personal costs

Purchased food, clothing, medical expenses, school fees and family travelling costs are considered as personal costs. In certain cases, some of them are directly related to the level of output of the farm. For example, an ill or under-nourished farmer is not likely to have a high work output and money spent on food or medicines is likely to have a direct effect on total farm output. However, in many other instances, e.g. schooling and clothing, such an effect is hard to measure. The minimum total living or personal costs of the farmer are normally included in the total overheads when budgeting for family farms, as they are one of the most important and unavoidable items in total farm costs (Fig. 4.4).

Relation between costs, income and operating profit

Spending $500 on a capital item has a different effect on the operating profit of the farm from spending $500 on overhead costs. Capital investments occur at irregular intervals and usually add to the productive resources and the long-term profitability of the farm. Overheads are annual, largely unavoidable costs which do not contribute to income in the short term, though they are an essential prerequisite to the ability to earn income, e.g. non-payment of taxes could lead to forced sale of the farm.

Similarly $500 spent on a variable input such as improved seed or fertiliser can have a big effect on

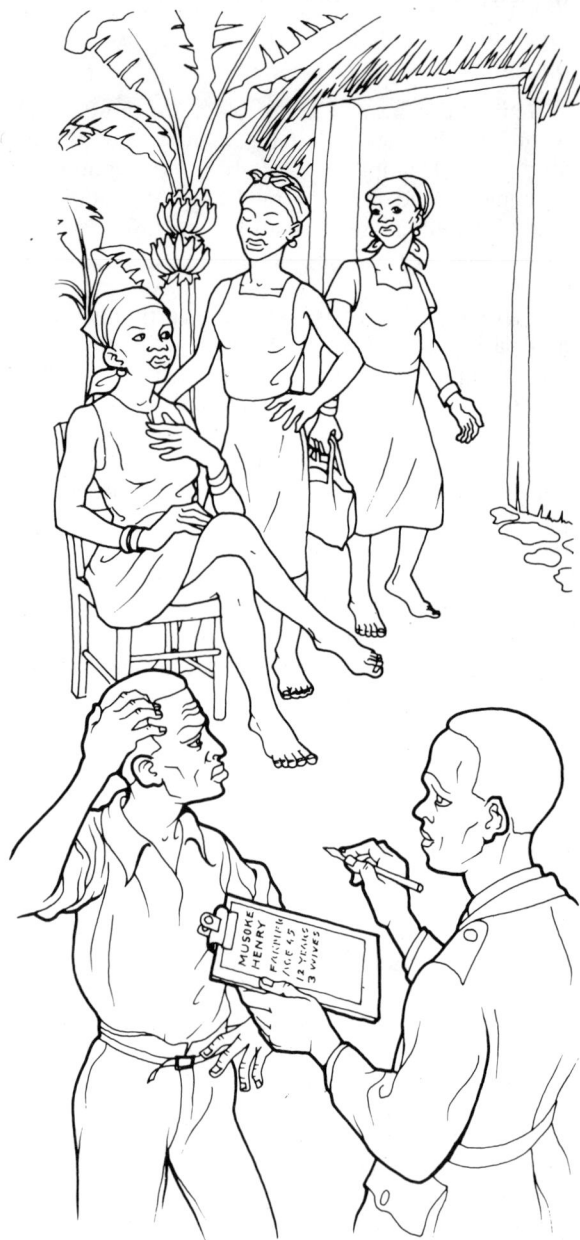

Fig. 4.4 Costs or capital? 'What about your wives? Do they come under Personal Costs or Farmer's Capital?'

revenue earned; $500 of personal expenditure produces no farm income at all even though that adds to the owner's satisfaction or improves his way of life.

Fig. 4.5 is presented to help show the relative effects of overhead and variable costs on income and operating profit. The operating profit is the difference between the gross income and the operating costs. Note that overhead costs are not allocated to the activity. We imply here that a certain 'break even' profit (after deducting variable costs from gross income) is necessary if total farm overheads per hectare are to be met.

Assume that a farmer is applying fertiliser (a variable cost input) to a hectare of crop. As the operating overhead costs per hectare are $6, the first $6 spent produce no income since they are used to meet overheads. The first dollar spent on fertiliser produces $3 of income, the next dollar produces $2.90, and so on. Table 4.1 shows the operating profit obtained by applying extra units of fertiliser. It is necessary to apply $4 worth of fertiliser before a profit is made.

Money spent on variable costs can reduce losses For a short period, it can be worthwhile to continue production even though the total costs exceed the total returns, as Fig. 4.6 shows. The unavoidable overhead costs are $150. If the farm produces $150 worth of produce, the total costs will be $150 for overheads plus $100 for variable costs; total $250.

While this means a loss of $100, the loss would be greater, i.e. $150, if the farmer did not produce anything. The farmer is $50 better off, even though he has produced at a loss. Of course, he cannot carry on like this for ever. This approach is only valid if gross income exceeds variable costs. If the opposite were true, though this would be unlikely even in a temporary depression, the farmer would soon be out of business.

Farm receipts

The main source of income is normally from the sale of crops and animals. There can also be non-cash income resulting from an inventory change, e.g. extra stocks or animals on hand at the end of the trading year, or from farm products consumed in the home.

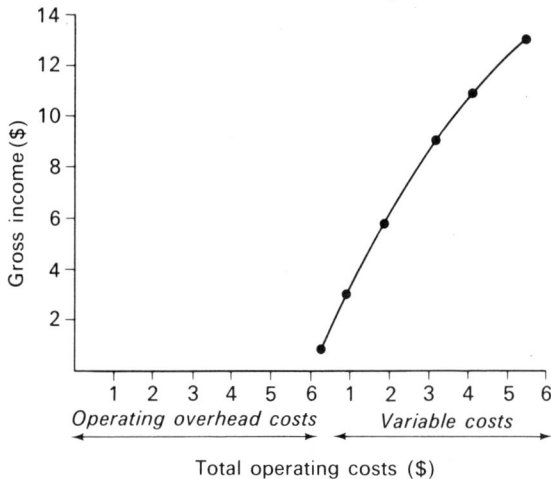

Fig. 4.5 Contribution of variable costs to gross income

Table 4.1 The contribution of variable costs to net profit

Operating over head cost ($) 1	Variable cost ($) 2	Total operating cost ($) 3(1 + 2)	Gross income ($) 4	Operating profit ($) 5(4 − 3)
6	1	7	3.00	−4.00
6	2	8	5.90	−2.10
6	3	9	8.70	−0.30
6	4	10	11.20	+1.20
6	5	11	13.40	−2.40

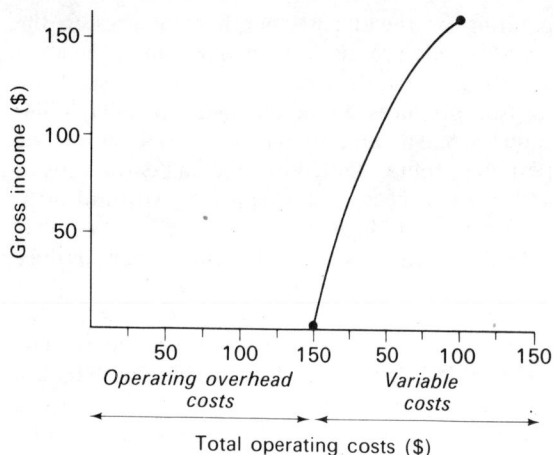

Fig. 4.6 Production during a temporary depression

For example, take two farms of comparable size and efficiency which each produce 5 000 kg of grain worth 5 cents per kg. The two farmers use the crops as follows:

	Farm A	Farm B
Sold	5 000 kg	3 000 kg
Kept	—	2 000 kg
Total	5 000 kg	5 000 kg

Even though the cash income from Farm A is 5 000 × 5 cents, and from Farm B 3 000 × 5 cents, most economists would say that the true yearly income of both farms is 5 000 × 5 cents. Grain kept in store is valued at the original selling price of grain of similar quality. If, upon later sale, the actual price obtained differs from that shown as the value of inventory, the difference is recorded in the next year's accounts as a profit or loss on storage.

If there is a decrease in value of inventory over the year, the amount of decrease is deducted from the sales to give the true income. Thus:

	Value ($)
Value of inventory at start of year	500
Value of inventory at end of year	200
Change in value of inventory over year	−300
Value of current year's production	1 100
Cash sales of crop during year	1 400
True income for year ($1 400 − $300)	1 100

Inventories can also be valued at the cost of production, but in farming this is difficult to assess.

The value of produce consumed by the farmer and his family is also counted as part of farm income. It is income in 'kind', not in cash. It is usual to count only those items which have a market value. For instance, produce which was unsaleable because it had suffered some damage or because there was no market for it would not be counted.

When a farmer is a member of a cooperative society he will often receive annual dividends and rebates on purchases. These are accounted for under annual farm income.

When a capital item such as land or machinery is sold, the money received is not part of the annual farm operating income. It is treated as part of the total receipts for the year.

Money received from non-farm sources such as gifts from relatives, sales of handicrafts or work done elsewhere is not part of farm operating income. It is classed as personal receipts.

Whilst a loan brings money to the farm business, it is not counted as part of the income produced by the farm.

Diminishing returns

In any biological system, such as an agricultural activity, there is a relationship between inputs and outputs. Where there is a fixed level of a resource, such as land, output can be increased only by adding more variable inputs to the fixed resource. Fertiliser, seed, and labour are variable inputs that can be combined with land to raise output. Similarly, in livestock feeding, various levels of feed can be applied to the fixed resource, which in this case is the animal. This principle is illustrated in Table 4.2.

Here land is the fixed resource. As fertiliser application is increased the total returns also increase at first but, ultimately, decline to a point where no extra return is obtained for extra fertiliser (at 6 units per hectare). Up to this point, total crop yield per hectare increases at a decreasing rate, i.e. there is a diminishing marginal return per unit of extra fertiliser. The law of diminishing returns states that if the inputs of one factor are increased while the use of other factors is held constant then the marginal (and average) return per unit of the variable factor will eventually decline.

Table 4.2 Total and marginal crop yield per hectare with applications of fertiliser

Units of fertiliser	Total crop yield (tonnes per ha)	Marginal crop yield (tonnes per ha)
1	1.0	0.9
2	1.9	0.7
3	2.6	0.3
4	2.9	0.1
5	3.0	−0.1
6	2.9	−0.2
7	2.7	

The word 'marginal' is the economist's synonym for 'added' or 'extra' or 'incremental'. For example, the marginal cost of fertiliser is the cost of an extra unit of fertiliser.

As one aim of the farm business is to make a profit, every production process needs to be considered in the framework of costs and returns. The diminishing returns principle implies that if overheads remain constant, it is profitable to increase the level of production so long as the marginal return is greater than the marginal cost. This is a technical way of saying that it is profitable to spend 3 cents for a return of 3.1 cents, but not for a return of 2.9 cents. Marginal cost takes changes in overheads into account. It is made up of two parts: marginal fixed cost and marginal variable cost.

Table 4.3 shows an application of the principle of maximising profits by applying fertiliser up to the point where unit factor cost and marginal returns are approximately equal. Total costs rise by $5 per hectare for each unit applied (column 2). Column 3 shows the total variable fertiliser costs. As overhead costs per hectare remain constant, the total costs, overheads and fertiliser, are as shown in column 5. The total yield (column 6) gives rise to the total receipts, i.e. net of harvest and other costs in column 7. The marginal return (column 8) is the difference between total net receipts as the level of fertiliser is increased, whilst column 9 shows the net profit or loss per hectare.

The main conclusions from Table 4.3 are:

(a) The point of maximum profit is at 4 units of fertiliser ($57). If 5 units are used, the extra cost is $5 but the extra or marginal return is only $3, giving a total profit of only $55. Thus the point of maximum profit has been passed. Marginal returns are less than marginal costs at 5 units of fertiliser, with overheads remaining constant.

(b) Because inputs have a cost, it is only very rarely that the point of maximum physical production (at 5 units of fertiliser) is the point of maximum profitable production (4 units), but the two points may be quite close together.

Table 4.3 Profit from applying different levels of fertiliser to a crop (measured per hectare)

Units of fertiliser	Extra or marginal variable cost ($)	Cumulative variable cost ($)	Overhead cost ($)	Total cost ($)	Total yield (tonnes)	Total net receipts ($)	Marginal return ($)	Profit or loss ($)
1	2	3	4	5	6	7	8	9
1	5	5	10	15	1.0	30		15
2	5	10	10	20	1.9	57	27	37
3	5	15	10	25	2.6	78	21	53
4	5	20	10	30	2.9	87	9	57
5	5	25	10	35	3.0	90	3	55
6	5	30	10	40	2.9	87	−3	47

Note: The marginal return per hectare is shown as falling between the lines specifying the amount of fertiliser applied. Thus, in going from 1 to 2 units, the extra return due to the additional unit of fertiliser is $27.

People often equate maximum yields with maximum profits, but the principle of profit maximisation illustrated above shows that this is usually erroneous.

Gross margins

The gross margin on a farm activity is the difference between the gross income earned and the variable costs incurred. For a farm undertaking several different activities the total gross margin is the sum of the gross margin on each activity.

In any one year, total gross margins should not be less than overheads if the farmer is to avoid extra borrowing.

The gross margins per hectare of crops and per head of livestock are widely used for comparative analysis of activities on one farm, and between farms in similar environments. For example, if the gross margin on one farmer's maize crop is $40 per hectare, and the average gross margin on a neighbouring farm is $55, then he should look for the technical explanation of the poorer performance.

Valid comparisons can, of course, only be made in terms of a production unit common to all the farms of activities being compared. This unit can be the land area, if the land used by each activity is equally suitable. It could also be per hour of labour during a critical period (such as planting, weeding or harvesting); or per $100 of annual working funds or capital invested; also, per head of livestock. In tropical countries where the family labour available, or the village labour in the case of a cooperative enterprise, is regarded as a fixed factor, labour may be the most appropriate basis for comparison. Note that the gross margin technique assumes a linear relationship as the activity is expanded, i.e. if the hectarage of maize is doubled, we assume that the gross margin for the extra hectares will be the same as for the original area. This is not always so, as there can be a diminishing returns effect as the activity is expanded. While in many cases it is reasonable to assume a linear relationship when planning to increase the area, the farmer and/or his adviser should keep the possibility of diminishing returns in mind as the activity is expanded.

Use of gross margins

For simple changes in activities, if one activity has a gross margin of $20 per hectare on a particular soil type, and another has a gross margin of $40 per hectare, then, provided certain qualifications (which will be discussed) are met, the activity with the gross margin of $40 should replace the one with $20.

Gross margins are also a useful first step in deciding on the best combination of activities on a farm. The procedure here is to select the highest gross margin per unit of the most common limiting resource (hectare of land, $100 of capital, rotation, man hour or man week of labour), and expand it until some other restraint is met.

Then the activity with the highest gross margin of all the remaining available activities is introduced until it too meets a restraint, and so on.

For example, a limiting resource on the farm might be arable land, though on small farms, the first restraint may be seasonal labour. Vegetables are selected first and expanded until the hectares planted are such that the vegetable activity meets the restraint of, say, a lack of reliable seasonal labour to harvest the crop quickly enough to avoid loss of yield and/or quality. So a crop activity with a different harvest period should then be introduced. (Similarly there may be a lack of labour for weeding.)

The activity which should be selected is that which has the highest expected gross margin of the alternative crops which it is feasible to plant at this time. We will assume that maize is the crop which meets this criterion, though the maize gross margin per hectare may be less than for vegetables. The maize will then be planted on as much of the remaining arable land as is possible until the next restraint is met.

We next assume that at the time of the year when he is planting maize the farmer draws near to the limit of the next restraint—working funds. So he plants as many hectares of maize as his working funds will allow, and waits until he gets more working funds perhaps from the sale of his vegetables. With these funds he is able to plant the remainder of his arable land with that crop from the range of crops which can be now grown at this time of year which has the highest expected gross margin. The procedure can be repeated with the animal activities on the non-arable land until all the available resources are used to the limits of the restraints imposed on their use.

We noted above that the use of gross margins was a useful first step in planning the best combinations of activities on a farm. In practice, it is probably the most commonly used technique for planning activity mixes. A more sophisticated approach is to use substitution ratios. These are discussed later in this chapter.

The use of gross margins is a simple and quick method of planning changes in activities, activity mixes, or analysing a farm business. There is usually no need to consider overheads, and the sensitivity of the proposed change to possible variations in yield, prices or costs can be readily tested.

Application to semi-subsistence farms

In planning the food supply on semi-subsistence farms, where there is a relatively low cash input, the main objective is to produce an adequate diet for the household. Thus the contribution which the main activities make to the total food supply are often more important than the size of the gross margin. Of course, if one or two crops have very high gross margins, it may be best to grow them for sale and buy some food. Given that most of the activities are concerned with food supply rather than cash sale, then activities should be chosen on the basis of the starch, protein and vitamins they will supply at different times of the year.

Although 'food supply' has thus supplanted the 'gross margin' of the commercial farm as an objective, exactly the same principles in choosing activities and activity mixes can be applied. Thus the semi-subsistence farmer should identify the activity with the safest, highest expected 'food supply' and expand that first until it meets a restraint. Then the next best activity is expanded to the point where it in turn meets a restraint and so on.

On semi-subsistence farms, there can be many restraints, e.g. labour restraints, both in numbers and skills at various critical times of the year; money restraints for essential cash inputs; and also rotation restraints where the land must be fallowed after a certain period of cropping. If one of these

is the major restraint then that should be used as the starting point for gross margin analysis instead of land, for example.

Precautions when using gross margins

Some care needs to be taken where using gross margins as a basis for planning. For example, it is frequently found that cash crops show the highest gross margin per hectare. But before the crop area is increased it is necessary to know:

(a) the maximum area that can be grown with present soil type, hectarage, machinery, labour and working capital;
(b) the technical limit of expansion, e.g. under a legume and crop rotation system it may only be possible to cash crop a particular field for three years out of six.

There are obvious physical and financial limits to expansion such as availability of suitable land, shortage of both labour in peak periods and of credit. In parts of West Africa, for example, the availability of women to undertake the planting and harvesting, has set a limit to the planting of rice.

It is very important to investigate the technical efficiency of present practices before gross margins are used as a basis for changes. If the gross margin for a crop is $20 per hectare, and the district average is $40, it may be desirable to replace this crop with some other activity whose gross margin is, say, $30. Such a decision should however be preceded by a check to see if the gross margin of the first crop activity could be raised more easily by better use of fertilisers and pesticides; by greater attention to performing operations on time; or by better field management.

Other circumstances under which it would not be wise to adopt the activity with the highest gross margin would be where suitable labour to handle the activity was not available or where capital was limited. To illustrate this latter limitation, let us take a farmer who has access to only $600 credit and who has to decide between two activities A and B with the conditions indicated below:

	Activity A ($ per ha)	Activity B ($ per ha)
Gross margin	30	20
Capital needed	60	30

If he adopts activity A, the farmer needs to invest $60 for every hectare. Since he has access to only $600 of credit for capital investment, he can only have $\frac{600}{60}$ or 10 hectares of activity A. This will give him an annual gross margin of 10 × $30 or $300. If he adopts activity B, he can have $\frac{600}{30}$ or 20 hectares of this activity. This will produce an annual total gross margin of 20 × $20, or $400.

Thus, where capital is limited, it is necessary to consider both the gross margin and the capital investment needed per hectare before deciding which activity to choose.

Calculation of gross margins for crop and animal activities

Variable costs of crop activities are made up mainly of:

(a) pre-harvest or growing costs: seed, fertiliser, water, extra labour, sprays, direct machinery costs (fuel, oil, repairs);
(b) harvest costs: extra labour, direct machinery costs, bags, etc.;
(c) marketing costs: direct costs of storage, processing, transport and selling.

How to allocate the wages of permanent workers and depreciation of machinery plant and buildings directly involved in the activity is a vexed question. If it would lead to better decisions about which crop activities should be chosen, then these costs should be allocated. In many cases, however, the wages of permanent workers and depreciation of machines, etc. are costs which must be met and remain roughly the same, regardless of the activity mixes chosen. So they need not be considered in deriving activity gross margins for use in planning.

The income of a cropping activity is made up of crop sales, inventory changes, and the value of food and fibre used by the farm household. The calculation is illustrated in Table 4.4.

The main components of the variable costs of any animal activity are:

(a) feed, including maintenance costs of improved pastures, and the costs of forage crops, hay, straw,

Table 4.4 Calculation of gross margin per hectare of cash crop

	Amount ($)
Income:	
sales of crop	75.00
Variable costs:	
seed	2.50
fertiliser	5.00
additional labour	9.00
repairs and maintenance of machinery	6.00
fuel and oil	2.00
sprays	2.50
insurance	2.50
transport to market	11.00
selling costs	6.00
Total	46.50
Total gross margin	28.50

silage, purchased feed, home grown grains, payments for grazing, as well as direct labour costs;
(b) husbandry, i.e. medicines, cleaning materials for milking sheds, labour and veterinary services;
(c) marketing, i.e. transport, processing and selling;
(d) breeding and replacement stock where not reared on the farm.

In many livestock activities, the value of the flock or herd may change due to a change in numbers and this is an important part of the yearly profit. Thus the value of the animals at the start of the year must be compared with their value at the end of the year to obtain a correct measure of the activity gross margin.

A calculation of the gross margin of an animal activity is shown in Table 4.5. Table 4.6 is a more detailed illustration of this calculation.

Table 4.5 Calculation of gross margin of an animal activity

Value of stock at beginning of year	Cost of animals bought	Cost of: (a) feed (b) husbandry (c) marketing	Total of initial value + all costs
1	2	3	1 + 2 + 3 = A
Value of stock at end of year	Sales of animals and animal products	Sales of by-products (e.g. manure)	Total of end of year value and sales
1	2	3	1 + 2 + 3 = B

$$B - \left(A + \begin{array}{l} \text{Depreciation of structures and} \\ \text{equipment associated with activity} \end{array} \right) = \text{Gross margin}$$

Table 4.6 Calculation of gross margin per head for a milking cow

	Amount ($)	
Income:		
milk sales	150.00	
calf sales	10.00	
Total gross income		160.00
Variable costs:		
feed costs	30.00	
marketing and transport	5.00	
cow replacement	6.00	
bull replacement	6.00	
milking shed costs	5.00	
medicines	3.00	
labour	20.00	
Total variable costs		75.00
Gross margin per cow		85.00

Note: Many of these figures will have to be estimated from records for the herd as a whole.

Farm profits, profit budgets and financial statements

The word 'profit' has different meanings for different people. To some, it means the amount of money left in the bank at the end of the year's farming operations. To others, it means cash receipts less cash costs, whilst other people may use various accountancy definitions.

Here we will refer to profit as 'operating profit' and define it in the manner used by modern farm management accountants. For our purposes profit is the gross income from the annual farming operations minus total operating costs. Total operating costs are made up of total variable costs plus operating overheads.

The operating profit can be calculated in two ways:

(a) subtracting total operating costs from gross income;
(b) subtracting the operating overheads from the total gross margin.

The total gross margin is calculated as the gross income minus the total variable costs.

The amount of money which is left over at the end of the year after all costs have been paid is known as the annual surplus (or deficit). The annual surplus can also be calculated by subtracting from the operating profit any living or school expenses in excess of the operator's allowance, income tax, interest paid, loan repayments and any new capital investment made. Then the total (i.e. not operating) overheads plus new capital investment is subtracted from the total gross margin.

Table 4.7 Calculation of annual surplus (deficit)

	Amount ($)	
Activity gross margins:		
crop A	200	
crop B	500	
dairy	160	
beef	100	
sheep	140	
other activities	20	
Total gross margin		1 120
Less operating overheads		700
Operating profit		420
Total capital of farm = $6 000		
Percentage return on capital		
$= \dfrac{420}{6\,000} = 7\%$		
Disposal of operating profit		
living expenses above operator's allowance	100	
income tax	70	
interest	60	
loan repayment	100	
new capital investment	50	
Total operating profit disposed of		380
Annual surplus		+40

Table 4.7 illustrates the calculation of the annual surplus (or deficit) for a small mixed farm.

This table shows both the true profit of the business and how it is disposed of. However, it does not reconcile with the bank statement because the gross margin for the animal activities usually contains an allowance for depreciation. Thus livestock may be replaced only every four years, yet an allowance is set aside each year so that funds are available for replacing the stock when they are old. A similar depreciation is made for plant and machinery. Inventory changes are added to, or subtracted from stock values. Thus if two calves worth $50 each are retained, instead of sold, the farm has extra livestock capital of $100. These do not show on the bank statement as cash paid in.

Profit budgets

In the section on cash flows a model cash budget was shown. It is also useful to draw up an annual operating profit budget. The following five worksheets show how to do this.

Worksheet 6 contains an estimate of gross margin of two activities under three assumptions: 'most likely', 'pessimistic', 'optimistic'. The farmer then estimates on the basis of all the evidence available to him the percentage chance of each of these three gross margins occurring.

Worksheet 6: Range of possible gross margins

	A ($)	B ($)	Chance (%)
'Most likely' gross income	500	200	
'Most likely' variable costs	300	60	
'Most likely' gross margin	200	140	60
Pessimistic gross margin	50	40	15
Optimistic gross margin	350	220	25

In Worksheet 7 the total operating profit from all activities put together is estimated under the three assumptions. This is based partly on the information in Worksheet 6. It is not likely that every activity on the farm will, for example, have a pessimistic outcome in the one year, although this is possible. It can also happen that the operating overheads could be higher or lower than the 'most likely' estimates. Thus the manager, after taking local climatic, field and market conditions into account, should assign values and percentage chances to three possible operating profits. If he just takes the totals from Worksheet 6, and does not modify them as suggested above, then his figures in Worksheet 7 are likely to be misleading.

Worksheet 7: Range of possible total operating profits

	'Most likely' ($)	Pessimistic ($)	Optimistic ($)
Total gross margin	1 000	600	1 300
Operating overheads	600	600	500
Operating profit	400	0	800
Per cent chance	65	10	25

Worksheet 8: Proposed use of 'most likely' operating profit

	Amount ($)	
'Most likely' operating profit		400
Less profit to be spent on:		
living and schooling costs in excess of operator's allowance	100	
interest	50	
loan repayments	100	
capital investment in development	40	
tax	20	
social welfare and amenities	40	
other	20	
Total profit to be used		370
Surplus (or deficit)		+30

The proposed manner of spending the expected, or 'most likely' operating profit, is set out in Worksheet 8. This profit can be used to pay for extra living, schooling and personal costs above those met by the arbitrary operator's allowance. Tax has often to be paid from profits as well as interest payments, loan repayments, development costs (other than those paid for from new loans) and sometimes welfare measures for workers or villagers.

The major purpose of Worksheets 9 and 10 is to help the farmer or manager to think in advance about alternative strategies in the event of profits being smaller or greater than expected. The sheets have space for the farmer to state the course of action proposed by him under three possible outcomes. Such steps in the case of a pessimistic outcome could include obtaining longer term loans or reducing development and personal expenditure. Where profits are higher than expected plans could include an expanded rate of development or, particularly for collective farms, increased contributions to social welfare.

Worksheet 9: Proposed plan of action if profit is less than the 'most likely' profit

	Amount ($)
'Most likely' operating profit	400
'Pessimistic' operating profit	0
Deficiency	400

What action may be taken if actual profit is less than the 'most likely' profit by the amount shown above:

(a)   Borrow money from relatives

(b)   Try to obtain off-farm work

Worksheet 10: Proposed plan of action if profit is more than the 'most likely' profit

	Amount ($)
'Most likely' operating profit	400
'Optimistic' operating profit	800
Surplus	400

Action proposed if this extra profit is realised:

(a)   Buy extra cattle

(b)   Repay loan

Presentation of financial results

For some farms, especially large scale plantations, cooperatives and state farms, it is necessary to produce three financial statements each year so that the owners, members, or responsible government department will have a clear picture of the financial health of their enterprise. The three statements are as follows:

Table 4.8 Profit and loss statement

	Activity A (crop) ($)	Activity B (livestock) ($)	Activity C (other) ($)	Total ($)
Receipts				
Sales of farm products	1 000			1 000
Livestock sales		1 500		1 500
Less purchases		−600		−600
Changes in inventory	100	−40		60
Contract work (off-farm)			150	150
Total activity income	1 100	860	150	2 110
Less activity variable costs	500	400	20	920
Activity gross margin	600	460	130	1 190
Less operating overhead				800
Operating profit				390

(a) The profit statement (Table 4.8) shows the profit or loss made from the year's farming operations.

(b) The statement of sources and use of funds (Table 4.9) shows where the money came from and how it was used. This statement is helpful in drawing up the cash flow budget for the following year.

(c) The balance sheet, or equity, or net worth statement (Table 4.10) shows the value of the assets, estimated realistically according to market values at a given date, minus the debts. It is mainly concerned with the capital gains or losses of the farm business, and shows the net worth of the enterprise, or the owner's equity. These items can be arranged, as in Table 4.10, to show quickly the current financial position of the farm enterprise. In the example shown, the farm is sound enough from the capital aspect, but current liabilities at $500 exceed current assets at $400. If his creditors pressed him the farmer might be obliged to sell some of his cattle to be able to satisfy them.

When presenting such statements it is customary also to provide the corresponding figures for the previous year to facilitate comparison.

Table 4.9 Statement of sources and the use of funds

Sources	Amount ($)	
Cash sales of farm products	1 000	
Cash sales of livestock	800	
Deferred payments from previous years	200	
Additional loans	1 500	
Additional sundry creditors	100	
Sales of capital items	600	
Other cash receipts	100	
Total sources of cash (A)		4 300
Uses		
Cash variable costs	600	
Cash overhead costs	400	
Capital investment	500	
Interest	400	
Loan and creditor repayment	200	
Taxes	300	
Living expenses	800	
Increase in debtors	100	
Other cash payments	50	
Total uses of cash (B)		3 350
Net cash flow for year (A–B)		950
Plus cash balance at start of year		600
Cash balance at end of year		1 550

Table 4.10 Statement of assets and liabilities

	Amount ($)	
Assets		
Fixed assets:		
land and buildings	15 000	
Total fixed assets		15 000
Working assets:		
machinery	1 500	
furniture	300	
cattle	600	
poultry	100	
Total working assets		2 500
Current assets:		
grain in hand	200	
feed in hand	50	
commercial bank account	150	
Total current assets		400
Total assets (A)		17 900
Liabilities		
Long term:		
agricultural bank loan	5 000	
Total long term liabilities		5 000
Current:		
Cooperative store account	200	
Other creditors	300	
Total current liabilities		500
Total liabilities (B)		5 500
Equity or net worth (A–B)		12 300

Return on capital

The term 'resources' refers to all the factors or means of production which are at the disposal of the farmer. The most important are: land, buildings, and improvements such as accrued fertility and irrigation facilities; machinery; livestock; fertiliser; fuel; labour; management skills and credit. Depending on the conditions of land tenure, many of these resources can be converted to cash, by selling them. The cash sum which would be available from the sale, after paying off any debts owed on the farm, is the farmer's own capital. It is also known as his equity or net worth.

If we express the farm's annual profit, after paying interest and taxes, as a percentage of this capital, the resulting figure is a measure of the effectiveness of its management. It provides a guide to those responsible for the use of the capital whether that is an individual, a cooperative or a government department. It also allows the person concerned to compare the performance of this capital, invested as it is, with alternative possible investments.

The percentage return on capital (equity) is calculated as follows:

$$\frac{\text{Annual profit after interest and tax}}{\text{Capital}} \times 100$$

The farmer's capital (or equity, or net worth) is worked out by adding the market value of all the resources the farm enterprise owns, and subtracting from the figure the total of all the money it owes. This is illustrated in Table 4.11.

A farmer's capital is sometimes expressed as a percentage of the total resources under his control. The equity percentage of the farmer described above is calculated as follows:

$$\frac{\genfrac{}{}{0pt}{}{\text{Resources owned}}{\text{(assets)}} - \genfrac{}{}{0pt}{}{\text{Money owed}}{\text{(liabilities)}}}{\genfrac{}{}{0pt}{}{\text{Resources owned}}{\text{(assets)}}} \times 100$$

$$= \frac{19\ 500 - 6\ 500}{19\ 500} \times 100 = 66\%$$

Table 4.11 Calculation of farmer's capital

	Amount ($)	
Market value of resources owned (assets)		
Land and buildings (where owned by the farmer)	15 000	
Animals	2 000	
Machinery	1 000	
Unsold products stored on farm	500	
Money in bank account no. 1	1 000	
Total (A)		19 500
Value of money owed (liabilities)		
Money lender	1 000	
Development bank	3 000	
Cooperative	2 000	
Bank account no. 2	500	
Total (B)		6 500
Farmer's capital (or equity, or net worth) A–B		13 000

The main purpose of calculating the return on a farmer's capital is to show him how efficiently he is running the annual operations of his farm business. If the figure was only 1%, and other managers with similar land, climate and capital were obtaining 4%, the farmer should ask himself the following questions:

(a) Could I increase the rate of return on my capital by using better methods, borrowing extra money to improve production, or changing the mixture of activities on the farm?
(b) Should I transfer my capital from this locality to a farm in a different locality where the return on capital is likely to be higher?
(c) Should I transfer my capital out of farming altogether, and put it into some other form of investment, such as a transport business or a shop?
(d) Is the return on capital low because of a sharp increase in asset worth (or capital gain)? This could be advantageous under certain conditions of taxation and inflation.

(e) Should I use my increased asset value to borrow to make on-farm income-increasing investments?

The more rapid the annual increase in asset worth, the harder it is to maintain a constant rate of return on a farmer's capital. For example, it is even possible for the percentage return to decrease while the profit increases due to a sharp rise in the value of land or of livestock. The following figures illustrate this:

	Year 1	Year 2
Profit after paying tax and interest ($)	650	800
Value of farmer's capital ($)	13 000	18 000
Annual % return on capital	$\frac{650}{13\ 000} \times \frac{100}{1}$ = 5%	$\frac{800}{18\ 000} \times \frac{100}{1}$ = 4.4%
Increase in asset worth ($)	5 000	
Net gain over year ($) ($5 000 + $150)	5 150	

An increase in land value means that there is more collateral against which to borrow money for use in increasing farm income. It can also mean that higher land taxes have to be paid, and in some countries more inheritance taxes unless the title is passed on to children before the death of the owner. These consequences must be taken into account by the farmer.

The course most commonly chosen by farmers whose return on capital is low is first of all to try and raise income by better management. If the returns are still low, then alternative uses for the capital should be investigated.

Although the rate of return on a farmer's capital (equity) is one valuable measure of the use of capital on a farm, other measures also have some applications. All possibilities should be investigated.

Return on extra capital

This is one of the most important measures of capital use. In many cases, if additional capital is used to increase the existing farm resources, an increase in profits will result. When extra capital is put into drainage, irrigation or land clearing on an already existing farm, the farmer will want to know how well that extra capital was used. One useful way of judging this is to express the extra net profit that is obtained as a percentage of the extra capital that was invested. Thus:

Rate of return on extra capital =

$$\frac{\text{Extra net profit after paying extra interest and extra tax}}{\text{Extra capital invested}} \times 100$$

In many cases, this figure can be as high as 50%.

If, when, say, extra land clearing is being considered, estimates show that the rate of return on extra capital will be only 9–10%, the farmer should think very carefully about going ahead with it. There is usually some uncertainty associated with the weather, prices and other natural hazards. Also he often has to borrow the extra capital in order to carry out the improvement project, and the extra profit, after paying interest on the money borrowed and tax on the extra income earned, has to be high enough to pay back the instalments on the loan.

As a general rule, it is unwise to invest in a new project on an existing farm unless the rate of return on extra capital is at least 20%. If the return on the farmer's capital stands at 5% and the estimated return on extra capital of a project on the farm is 20%, then as long as the project performs as expected, the return on the farmer's capital will rise above 5%.

Calculating the return on extra capital is a simple way of testing whether or not a project should be adopted. This is very important when capital is scarce and has alternative uses.

Other names for extra capital are marginal capital and added capital.

Return on total capital

The market value of the total resources on a farm is often known as the total capital of the farm. It is calculated by adding up the market value of the land and improvements, and the value of the animals, machinery, grain and fodder reserves.

In calculating the annual rate of return earned by these resources, no account is taken of the debts owed. All that is taken into account is the earning rate of the total bundle of resources employed in the business.

In practice, the farmer or manager has to manipulate the total resources under his control, not just the proportion which is debt-free. If there is, for instance, a 30% debt on the property, it is not rational for a farmer to concentrate his efforts on only 70% of the area or on 70% of the animals on the property.

Therefore, the rate of return on capital is calculated by expressing the annual operating profit as a percentage of the total capital as follows:

Percentage return on total capital =

$$\frac{\text{Operating profit}}{\text{Total capital}} \times 100$$

Rate of return on total capital does not take account of interest, loan repayments, living costs, new capital and tax payments. All of these are unique or specific to the financial and family structure, and, also, to the standard of living of each farmer. It provides a guide to the earnings of the total resources as currently managed, unconfused by personal factors. It measures the following for each manager:

(a) His effectiveness as a combiner of annual inputs such as labour, irrigation, fertiliser, seed and machinery services to produce an annual income from the set of fixed resources he is currently employing in agriculture.
(b) The rate of earning of his capital, committed as it is to the farm, relative to the rate of earning of that capital if it were employed in some other income-producing field. such as transport or government bonds. The interest rate on bonds or the yield of safe investments provides a good indication of the minimum relative fruitfulness with which capital can be employed in the economy.

Return on historical capital

Historical capital usually means the value of the farm plus machinery and animals at the time of purchase or at incorporation as a cooperative or farming enterprise. It gives a misleading impression of the current earning capacity of the investment. For example, if a farm has an annual operating profit of $1 000, an historical value of $10 000 and a current value of $20 000, then rates of return are 10% and 5% respectively.

The rate of earning of the resources is measured more accurately by taking the return on total capital, i.e. 5%, because this gives a basis for comparison with the earning rate of today's value of the capital in other uses.

Capital gains

Increase in capital worth may occur simply from a rise in the market value of land. It may also be increased by well-chosen investments in clearing land, supplying water, acquiring good breeding stock, for example. It is calculated by deducting the cost of capital investments made from the total increase in value of the assets over a given period. There is, however, no direct cause and effect relationship between capital investment and capital gain. For example, an expenditure of $500 on farm buildings does not necessarily mean that the value of the farm will rise by $500. They may not suit the plans of prospective buyers and may thus be valued by them at much less.

Summary of Part A: Analysis

Five concepts have been dealt with in the first part of this chapter: cash flows; costs and receipts; gross margins; farm profits and profit budgets; and return on capital. Knowledge of these is an essential part of the mental equipment of anyone—farmer, manager, accountant, rural cooperative manager, banker or planner—who wants to understand the economic and financial basis of a farm business. An understanding of these basic analytic concepts is a necessary first step to being able to use them for decision-making and planning.

Concerning the financial side of their business, farmers are especially interested in how much money comes in and how much money goes out during, say, each month, quarter or year. Hence the important place given to the concept of cash flows. For semi-subsistence farmers, a net food flow budget is also helpful. Cash flows are the most relevant budgets for practising farmers, but costs and receipts are not all of the same nature. Any analysis intended to provide a basis for the improvement of farm performance has to take into account the difference between, for example, vari-

able costs and capital costs or between cash income and increase in inventories. The basic difference between these various kinds of cost and receipt have been explained here.

Gross margins are one of the commonest analytical and planning techniques in modern farm business planning. Other names given to this concept are activity profit, activity net revenue and activity direct profit. Although the gross margin is useful, easily calculated and readily understood, there are certain qualifications about its use which have to be borne in mind if it is not to prove misleading.

One of the most controversial concepts is profit. Farmers, economists, accountants, tax authorities and planners rarely agree on the meaning of profit. An explanation of the definition which we find most useful has been given and some applications of its use in budgeting and planning were discussed.

We saw that a farmer's own capital (or equity) is connected with the capital gain or loss aspect of the use of the resources under his control. The point was made that annual profits alone give too limited a view of the farm as a business.

Issues for discussion on Part A

1 Define management ability by listing the qualities of a good farm manager. Which of the qualities you have listed can be learnt only from practical experience? Which, if any, can be learnt from books, schools, courses, etc.? If some of the qualities you have listed cannot be learnt from either practical experience, books or formal courses, how can they be acquired?

2 List the sources from which the farmers you know can keep up to date with new developments which could improve the profitability of the farm businesses they manage or control.

3 What are the major management and decision problems of the subsistence and semi-subsistence farms that you know? How do the farmers on these farms handle the problem of variable yields?

4 On the farms with which you are familiar, and which employ workers, do you think that farm efficiency is reduced by the unsatisfactory attitude or performance of workers? If so, what lies behind this and what can the manager do to correct it?

5 Draw up a cash flow budget for the next year for (a) a small farm and (b) a large farm.

6 List last year's full financial figures for a medium-sized farm under the following headings:
(a) Costs: total overheads, operating overheads, capital costs, finance costs, variable costs.
(b) Receipts: cash sales, increase or decrease in fodder and stock inventories, dividends and rebates, capital sales, value of home grown food consumed.
Calculate the following: total gross margin, total operating profit, net surplus or deficit on the year's operations.

7 Draw up a profit budget for a farm for next year on the lines of Worksheets 6, 7, 8, 9 and 10 shown in relation to farm profits and profit budgets.

8 Give some examples of how the principle of diminishing returns can help a farmer or manager that you know to make better decisions. What are the main factors limiting the application of this principle on the farm?

9 'The stage of maximum physical production (output) is rarely the most profitable stage in any activity.' Show your understanding of this statement by illustrating how you would calculate the point of maximum profit for any given activity. Illustrate how you would work out the stage of maximum profitable production for an activity on a farm you know.

10 Show how you would use gross margins to help plan next year's operations on a semi-subsistence farm and on a small commercial farm.

11 Explain why the year's profit, in a farm management accounting sense, is not the sum of money which is in the farmers' bank at the end of the year.

12 Calculate the return on farmer's capital on a farm with which you are familiar. What conclusions do you draw from the results?

Part B: Operations

Decision-making

Decision-making in farming, as in all businesses, involves making a choice from possible alternative actions. It is one of the most important activities which a farmer or farm manager has to carry out. It is also an act of management that cannot be ignored or postponed. Failure to take decisive action, when a choice is possible, is itself a decision for which the consequences are just as real as those resulting from an overt decision/action by the decision-maker.

In recent years, a great deal of research has been directed to studying the processes of decision-making in industry, commerce and agriculture. The main outcome of these studies has been the development of procedures to help the decision-maker approach his problem in a systematic manner. The principal benefit to be gained from this more formal approach lies in the greater likelihood of making a good decision. This is because all pertinent information is consciously brought together and a consistent, logical and pragmatic choice-determining process is used to select the action or set of actions most likely to achieve the desired objective. Such a procedure does require, of course, very clear objectives.

In briefly outlining this overall decision-making procedure, it is first necessary to distinguish a 'good' decision from a 'right' decision. A good decision is a rational decision. It assigns weights to each of the relevant factors involved in the decision. The weights assigned reflect the decision-maker's real beliefs founded on his experience and the information he was able to obtain about the alternatives facing him. A good decision is also consistent with the decision-maker's preferences.

Since most decisions are made in the face of uncertainty, there is no guarantee that a 'good' decision will be the 'right' decision, i.e. whilst the decision-maker may act rationally, following formal decision-making procedures, he has no control over the outcome. For example, instead of selling his crop for $50 per tonne, a farmer may decide to store it with the prospect of getting $70 in one month's time. His information and experience leads him to assign a 90% chance (probability 0.9) on getting $70 per tonne in one month's time, but only a 10% chance (probability 0.1) of getting $40 per tonne. Due to some unusual factor in the market, the actual price received is $40. In this case, the good decision has a bad outcome, so it was a wrong decision.

Probabilities

A good understanding of probabilities is extremely valuable in decision-making. It enables a farmer to apply some measure to the risk he takes.

When a coin is thrown into the air the probability of it landing heads upwards is 1 out of 2, i.e. 50%, or 0.5 as it is commonly written in probability analysis. The likelihood of the coin falling tails upwards is also 1 out of 2 or 0.5. A more complex version of this simple example is the throwing of two six-sided dice. The probabilities of obtaining different totals by adding the numbers shown on each of the two dice after throwing are as follows:

Total	Chance out of 36	Chance out of 100	Approximate probability
2	1	2.7	0.03
3	2	5.4	0.05
4	3	8.3	0.08
5	4	11.1	0.11
6	5	13.5	0.14
7	6	16.4	0.17
8	5	13.5	0.14
9	4	11.1	0.11
10	3	8.3	0.08
11	2	5.4	0.05
12	1	2.7	0.03

The extreme totals are much less probable, while those totals which can be formed by several different throws are the most probable.

Assessing risks in terms of the probability of various outcomes is a great help in production planning. Thus a farmer who saw possibilities in growing vegetables on the flood plain of a river, would ascertain how many times within memory the river had flooded to cause the loss of a crop. If it appeared that flooding occurred, on the average, once in every five years, the risk factor (20% chance of crop failure due to flood) would become a basic element in his production plan. If the profit from cultivating this 4 years is sufficient to cover the consequences of a total loss of all his outlays one year and still leave an attractive margin, then production would be advantageous. The risk of flooding would have been recognised, appraised, and allowed for in the production plan.

Variability in rainfall can be considered in the same way. If in only three years out of five the rainfall in a particular area is sufficient and timely enough to support a good crop, the returns from these three years must be sufficient to cover the losses on the other two, and still leave a profit. Otherwise it would be unwise to start cultivation in this area without access to supplementary irrigation.

The problem is somewhat more complicated where there is a close interaction between a major input and a variable influence such as rainfall. If fertiliser is applied generously and rainfall is inadequate then the farmer sustains a cash loss on the fertiliser applied. On the other hand, if he does not apply the optimum amount of fertiliser for fear of lack of rainfall, then if there is adequate rain, he forgoes the possibility of a much larger yield, and a corresponding higher return on his inputs. The optimum position would generally be to apply that amount of fertiliser which would maximise returns at the level of rainfall which is most probable.

It is often said that few farmers do in fact maximise the profits obtainable by the application of additional inputs in accordance with probabilities. One difficulty is lack of knowledge, for example, of the frequency distribution of rainfall. Only a few areas have long term systematic records to provide reliable data on rainfall. In the absence of such records farmers follow tradition and their own experience which will obviously be coloured by recent events. Another difficulty is that many farmers have too little capital to take the risk of applying fertiliser when the possibility of inadequate rainfall could mean that it was applied at a loss in some years. These farmers do not have the financial staying power to carry the risk and wait for the very good results that might be obtained in other years. For example, it is necessary to apply extra fertiliser to IRRI rice to get the full benefit of its response. This necessity delayed the adoption of IRRI rice in some parts of India where dry seasons or inadequate irrigation facilities would result in negative returns to outlays on fertiliser.

Attitudes towards risk

Farm structure is an important factor here. Many farmers in Africa and Asia operate so small a unit that, even in good years, they have little margin beyond their essential needs. Often managers of large farms which are organised as cooperatives are reluctant to take risks because they are responsible to a large number of members. This is why state farms are sometimes used to try out new ventures. The manager is not involved financially and the government has large reserves.

The analysis of decision-making in relation to risk should be made in terms of total net income rather than in terms of a change in income. The decision-maker has two comparable figures to assess: the certain income he can get from his present activity; and the certainty equivalent, for him, of the new activity which has uncertain outcomes. The meaning of certainty equivalent should become clear in the following example.

The reader is asked to state the smallest sum of money he would have to receive definitely to stop him taking part in a gamble for $500 based on whether a coin fell heads or tails. The figure that he nominates is his certainty equivalent. A recent experiment conducted by the author with a group of 30 farm managers from tropical countries gave the results shown in Table 4.12.

The table shows that farmers (like other people) vary greatly in their attitude to risk. This uniqueness of each individual's attitude to risk is the basis of modern procedures which help formalise farmers' decision-making.

Moving from left to right in Table 4.12, we can see that all the group would rather take part in the gamble than receive less than $100. Three managers were so averse to taking risks or needed the money so badly, that they preferred to take $100 for certain, rather than risk $500 or nothing. Similarly, two of the group opted for $150 rather than gamble. For the largest number of farmers, their certainty equivalent was the outcome that

could be expected from a large number of throws, i.e. $250. We classify this group as 'risk indifferent' for this decision. If larger amounts were involved, their choice may alter.

The next three groups of people are 'risk takers'. A combination of their preferences to gain $500, and their beliefs that the coin will come down 'heads', leads them to want a certain payment which is more than the expected value of the risky choice before they would desist from taking the risky decision. The main alternative open to these managers can be presented as a decision tree shown in Fig. 4.7.

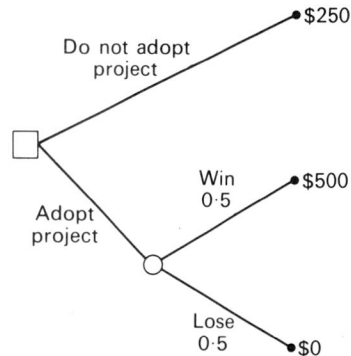

Fig. 4.7

The certain opportunity cost of an individual's decision to take a risky choice is the value of his certainty equivalent. An individual's certainty equivalent varies according to his state of wealth, the sums of money involved in the risky decisions, and his psychological make-up. It also varies over time.

Use of certainty equivalents

In the example used, there was no out-of-pocket loss. The decision-maker stood either to gain by the amount of his stated certainty equivalent, gain a larger amount ($500), or to be no worse off than he was before.

Table 4.12 Range of certainty equivalents of thirty farm managers

Certainty equivalent ($)	Less than 100	100	150	200	250	300	350	400	More than 400
Number of managers	0	3	2	4	12	5	2	2	0

Often the choice facing a manager is between maintaining his present income, or taking a new venture which could either increase or decrease his income. Let us assume that a farmer's present net income is $1 000. If he undertakes a new activity which he has been investigating, it should result either in a $500 increase in income (with a probability of 0.8) or a loss of $400 (probability 0.2). His decision tree for alternative action is shown in Fig. 4.8.

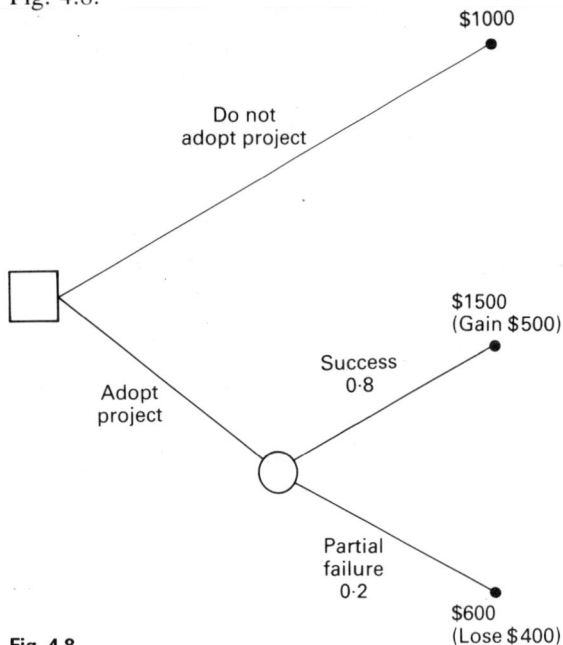

$1000

Do not
adopt project

$1500
(Gain $500)

Success
0·8

Adopt
project

Partial
failure
0·2

$600
(Lose $400)

Fig. 4.8

The decision tree has two main types of fork. The act fork, which is represented by a small square, shows where the decision-maker has to choose between two actions. The event fork, which is represented by a small circle, shows where one of two events can occur.

The most probable outcome from this set of alternatives over a number of seasons is shown below.

$$\$(500 \times 0.8) - (400 \times 0.2) = \$400 - 80$$
$$= \$320 \text{ addition to income.}$$

For most small farmers the main problem is to assess the probability of success in applying new

technology or adopting new crops. A clear view of the degree of risk involved could help in persuading many of them to adopt new methods and try innovations. If they can count on effective assistance from farm advisers or input suppliers, the risk may be less than they imagined.

Fig. 4.9 Decision trees: 'I have been thinking about those decision trees — how long does it take for them to bear fruit?'

Financial basis for decisions on crop and animal production

Crop production

One of the purposes of analysing crop activities, apart from obtaining the gross margin, is to distinguish between pre-harvest costs and harvesting and marketing costs. When a farm manager knows the value of these two sets of cost, he is in a position to make better decisions about future cropping activities.

As an example, assume that there are two crops, one of which (crop A) has a high harvesting and marketing cost (labour, storage, processing or transport), but low preharvest costs. The other (crop B) has relatively low harvesting and marketing costs, but high growing costs. With average yields, the total variable costs (pre-harvest, harvesting and marketing) are the same. Table 4.13 shows the costs of each crop per hectare. The proportion of those for crop A are typical for simple vegetable crops, while crop B is likely to be a grain crop such as maize.

If the manager took account only of the total variable costs in his planning, he would be likely to draw the wrong conclusions. Since both crops have a total variable cost of $30, he might conclude that there would be no difference in the amount of money which would be lost if the crop failed to grow to maturity. But in many cases, crops reach a stage close to harvesting, and then cannot be harvested because of unfavourable weather, damage caused by insects and diseases, or because there is no market. In such cases, the manager loses only $10 per hectare with crop A, but $20 with crop B.

Table 4.13 Variable costs per hectare of two crops

	Crop A ($)	Crop B ($)
Pre-harvest costs	10	20
Harvesting and marketing	20	10
Total variable costs	30	30

Table 4.14 brings out in more detail the importance of distinguishing between growing costs and

harvesting and marketing costs in crop-planning decisions. The first column of Table 4.14 shows four possible yields for crop A: the normal yield (Y_A kg); a yield of 50% more than the normal (1.5 Y_A kg); a yield of 50% less than normal (0.5 Y_A kg); and no yield (0.0 Y_A kg). Yield varies even though the growing costs are the same because of weather conditions such as hot winds at flowering time, heavy wind and rains near harvest time, drought and water shortage arising after the growing costs have been incurred. The probability of the particular yield occurring is shown in the second column of the table. Thus 0.25 means that 25 years out of 100 years there will be a yield of Y_A kg, i.e. there is a 25% chance that the yield will be Y_A kg. The next four columns show the harvest and marketing costs; the total variable costs (which are the sum of the growing costs and the harvest and marketing costs); the gross income; and the gross margin (the difference between the total gross income and the total variable costs).

Since the probability of each level of yield occurring is the same in this case, i.e. 0.25, the average expected gross margin is obtained by adding the four individual gross margins and dividing by four. If the probabilities were not equal, then it would be necessary to multiply each gross margin by its probability and then to sum the four resulting products. This procedure is illustrated in Table 4.15.

With crop A (low pre-harvest costs) the average expected gross margin is higher. Also, the losses in the years of crop failure are low.

Where the probability of crop failure is higher than 0.25, the influence of pre-harvest costs on the outcome is even greater than that shown in Table 4.14. In Table 4.15 the same gross margins according to yield have been used, but different probabilities (0.45, 0.10 and 0.35) of the various yields have been introduced. In a bad year the losses with crop B are greater than for crop A, and also the average expected gross margin is lower, even though one year out of ten, the gross margin for crop B is $115 and for crop A £110. Thus for a manager to make good decisions about the types of crops he will plant, he needs to know not only the total variable costs, but also the pre-harvest costs.

Table 4.14 Gross margins of two crops under a range of yield assumptions

Crop A Pre-harvest cost = $10   Average gross income = $100

Yield assumptions	Probability of yield occurring	Harvest and market cost ($)	Variable cost ($)	Gross income ($)	Gross margin ($)
Y_A kg (normal)	0.25	20	30	100	70
1.5 Y_A kg (50% more)	0.25	30	40	150	110
0.5 Y_A kg (50% less)	0.25	10	20	50	30
0.0 Y_A kg (failure)	0.25	0	10	0	−10

Average expected gross margin =

$$\frac{(70 + 110 + 30 - 10)}{4} = \$50$$

Crop B Pre-harvest cost = $20   Average gross income = $100

Yield assumptions	Probability of yield occurring	Harvest and market cost ($)	Variable cost ($)	Gross income ($)	Gross margin ($)
Y_B kg	0.25	10	30	100	70
1.5 Y_B kg	0.25	15	35	150	115
0.5 Y_B kg	0.25	5	25	50	25
0.0 Y_B kg	0.25	0	20	0	−20

Average expected gross margin =

$$\frac{(70 + 115 + 25 - 20)}{4} = \$47.5$$

Table 4.15 Expected gross margins of two crops with similar variable costs in a normal year, but with different pre-harvest costs

Crop A Pre-harvest cost = $10

Crop B Pre-harvest cost = $20

Yield	Gross margin (1) ($)	Probability (2)	Expected gross margin (1 × 2) ($)	Yield	Gross margin (1) ($)	Probability (2)	Expected gross margin (1 × 2) ($)
Y_A	70	0.45	+31.50	Y_B	70	0.45	+31.50
1.5 Y_A	110	0.10	+11.0	1.5 Y_B	115	0.10	+11.50
0.05 Y_A	30	0.10	+3.00	0.5 Y_B	25	0.10	+2.50
0.0 Y_A	−10	0.35	−3.50	0.0 Y_B	−20	0.35	−7.00
Expected gross margin			42.00	**Expected gross margin**			38.50

Deciding whether to harvest a crop

A small farmer growing crops mainly to feed his family may have no choice but to harvest whatever is growing but this is not true for all agricultural enterprises. Many rubber small-holders in Indonesia, for example, do not go to the trouble of tapping their trees when rubber prices are very low.

The main economic factors which determine whether or not a crop should be harvested are:

(a) harvesting and marketing costs;
(b) gross income:
(c) costs of, or income from, the crop residue if the crop is not harvested.

The fact that money has already been spent on growing costs is not relevant to the decision whether or not to harvest. This is true even when the total variable costs are more than the total gross income. Such a situation calls for minimising losses rather than maximising profits.

If there are no extra costs incurred when the crop is not harvested (e.g. having to chop it up and work it into the soil), or if no income can be earned from the unharvested crop by, say, feeding it to animals, then the crop should be harvested as long as the gross income from the sale of the crop exceeds the costs of harvesting and marketing.

When there is either a cost or an income associated with the unharvested crop, this rule has to be modified. For example, a farmer may face the following situation due to a fall in price of a perishable vegetable crop which he has grown:

	$ per ha	
Pre-harvest growing costs	40	(A)
Harvest and market costs	30	(B)
Expected income	25	(C)
Expected cost of disposing of crop residue if crop not harvested	10	(D)

If he does not harvest the crop, his costs are $50, i.e. (A) + (D). If he harvests the crop, his costs are $45, i.e. (A) + (B) − (C). So he is better off by $5 to harvest in this case, even though the harvest and marketing costs exceed the expected crop income. As the $40 growing cost is common to both calculations it can be ignored. This illustrates that growing costs are irrelevant at harvest time to the decision whether or not to harvest.

The rule which can be deduced from this example is that if the harvest and marketing costs minus the income from the sale of the crop is less than the cost of disposing of the unharvested crop, then the crop should be harvested, regardless of the amount of money spent on growing costs.

The next example deals with the case where there is income, rather than costs, associated with not harvesting the crop, e.g. where the unharvested crop can be used for fattening animals.

	$ per ha	
Harvest and market costs	30	(A)
Expected income from selling	35	(B)
Income if not harvested but fed to animals	15	(C)
Profit from harvesting	5	(B−A)
Profit from not harvesting	15	

Here, the rule is that, if the income from selling the crop minus the harvesting and marketing costs is less than the income from using the unharvested crop residue, then the crop should not be harvested.

By treating income as a minus cost (a cost of −$15 is really an income of $15), we can express the decision rules as formulae, where GI = gross income; H = harvest and marketing cost; D = disposal cost of (or income from) crop if not harvested. Thus if $GI - H + D$ is less than 0, then don't harvest. If it is more than 0, then harvest. Substituting from the second example above:

$$\$35 - \$30 + (-\$15) = -\$10.$$

So the decision should be not to harvest.

Crop rotations

Continuous cropping usually leads to a decline in soil nutrients and structure; a build-up of weeds and plant pathogens; and often increased erosion. In tropical countries, the 'bush fallow' or shifting cultivation is the simplest way of counteracting these harmful effects. One alternative is to use a rotation of different crops, often involving one or more seasons of a legume or a 'green manure' crop. Other alternatives, more complex but not necessarily the best, are to use chemical fertilisers and mechanical methods.

The technique of gross margins is used in the economic analysis and planning of crop rotations. However, gross margins of the separate crops (or phases) of the rotation should not be examined in isolation. The gross margin per hectare per year for the whole rotation is the only useful measure of the economic worth of a rotation. The following example illustrates this.

Assume on a farm of 30 hectares, that three years of pasture is needed to maintain the soil fertility after three years of cropping. The gross margin from the cattle grazing the pasture is $15 per hectare per year, and the gross margin from the crops is $30 per hectare per year (each phase being for 3 years). The farm has 15 hectares in pasture and 15 in crop at any one time to maintain the rotation. The total gross margin per year from the rotation is then:

Pasture and cattle	Crop	Total
(15 ha × $15)	(15 ha × $30)	
$225	$450	$675

Yearly average per hectare = $ $\dfrac{675}{30}$ = $22.50

The farmer sees that the gross margin of the crop phase is twice that of the pasture and cattle phase. He wonders whether he can expand the activity with the highest gross margin and grow five years of crops after three years of pasture. However, he estimates that average crop yields will then be less. Also more hired labour for weeding and extra fertiliser will be needed. Taking into account these factors he estimates that the average annual gross margin per ha per year from the crops would be $25 instead of $30.

With an eight-year rotation (three years pasture and five years crop) on the 30 hectares, there would be $\dfrac{3}{8} \times \dfrac{30}{1}$ or 11.25 hectares of pasture and 18.75 hectares of crop. At first sight, one would think that because more crop is being grown and its gross margin is still much higher than that of pasture the

new rotation should be more profitable than the original 3:3 rotation.

Analysis of the proposed rotation shows:

Pasture and cattle	Crop	Total
(11.25 ha × $15)	(18.75 ha × $25)	
$168.75	$468.75	$637.50

Yearly average per hectare = $ $\dfrac{637.50}{30}$ = $21.25

The GM (gross margin) per hectare per year for the original rotation was $22.5, so the farmer would in fact be worse off expanding the phase in the rotation with the higher gross margin. This is not always so, of course.

It was only by analysing the GM per hectare per year for the whole rotation that a true economic comparison of the two rotations could be obtained.

The reader should note that, in this example, land was taken as the limiting factor. Where other constraints, such as labour to handle seasonal peak workloads, are more important, these should take first place in the analysis.

Sometimes farmers are reluctant to start a rotation even though it may produce, in the medium term, higher gross margins than continuous single cropping. Their reason is that to change from continuous cropping to a pasture-crop system often means a temporary drop in income during the first few years when the pasture phase is being established. To the semi-subsistence farmer this would mean that his family risk being inadequately fed during this period. To overcome such difficulties, it may be necessary to obtain credit during that period.

Animal production

Despite the apparent diversity and complexity of livestock activities, it is not difficult to apply economic principles to animal production processes. This can supply useful guides for decisions. Livestock may be seen as a mechanism for converting raw materials into saleable products. Factors affecting the efficiency of the conversion mechanism are: feed, health, genetic strain, stage of growth, rate of weight gain, suitability for the environment, exercise, psychological and environmental stress.

Feed The quality is very important, but here we are concerned only with the concept of feed cost.

Health This can be maintained by using vaccines and veterinary services, and paying due attention to hygiene and husbandry. Generally, expenditure on this account should be regarded as essential. It is usually much less than the cost of diseases.

Genetic strain Certain strains of a species are superior to others in their ability to convert feed to animal product. Animal breeders have been particularly successful in developing efficient strains of pigs and poultry because of the short intervals between generations and the relatively large numbers of progeny that they produce at any one time. In most countries, use of this more efficient stock is essential for the financial success of a pig or poultry farm. Geneticists have not achieved the same success with beef cattle and sheep. Hence it is harder for individual producers to purchase significant numbers of cattle and sheep with predictably superior feed conversion efficiencies. However, the use of artificial insemination to increase the number of progeny of superior males has helped to improve feed conversion efficiency in the dairy industry.

Stage of growth This has a big influence on the economic outcome of a feeding operation, in many cases far more than genetic strain. Feed conversion ratios for cattle at different stages and weights are shown in Table 4.16. This ratio is

$$\frac{\text{kg feed consumed}}{\text{kg liveweight gain}}$$

The higher the ratio, the less efficient is the animal. Generally, younger animals add more weight for a given feed intake (i.e. they are more efficient), than older ones. An improved strain may have a fast growth rate but it will need to feed to support this. Poor feed availability can limit the usefulness of potentially more efficient stock. This is often the case under traditional production conditions in various parts of Africa.

Environment All animal species have their environmental limitations. It is difficult to raise

Table 4.16 Feed conversion ratios for cattle

Bodyweight (kg)	Mass of digestive nutrients, 85% grain (kg per kg liveweight gain)
200	3.4
250	3.7
300	4.0
350	4.4
400	4.7
450	5.0

many breeds of sheep in the wet tropics. Within the species, certain strains are better adapted to particular environments. Thus *Bos indicus* or humped breeds of cattle are generally better acclimatised to the dry tropics than *Bos taurus* or humpless breeds. In the discussion on economic analysis later it is assumed that the animals are suited to the environment.

Exercise If an animal expends energy grazing, then its feed requirements, above maintenance, are increased. In feed lots, the exercise requirement is approximately 15% above maintenance. When animals are grazing medium to good quality pastures it increases to 35%. On poor, sparse pastures, as in parts of Sahelian Africa, it rises to as much as 60% above maintenance.

Stress Many disease conditions increase energy requirements. So does the psychological stress resulting from excessive crowding of livestock, rough handling, or frequent disturbance by man, dogs or pests. Low temperatures and windy conditions also raise energy needs. Very high temperatures reduce appetite and feed intake.

Conversion costs and returns

The main costs where cattle are bought in, fattened and sold are:

(a) overheads;
(b) feed, including interest on outlays for feed;
(c) labour and running costs of any plant or machinery used;
(d) husbandry, disease control, vaccines, etc.;
(e) interest on purchase price of animals over period held;

(f) marketing charges, transport, commissions, fees, government or cooperative levies.

For a given feed cost, husbandry and marketing charges tend to rise in proportion with the number of animals put through the feed lot. Thus these can be regarded as variable costs, i.e. costs which vary as throughput rises or falls.

To calculate the profit margin from feeding cattle, the initial purchase price of the stock is deducted from the gross income from sale of the finished stock. This allows for loss through death. For purposes of economic analysis, it is convenient to subtract from this net gain the husbandry and marketing costs. We will call the figure so obtained 'the net value of animal product less husbandry and marketing charges' or 'net animal revenue'.

The annual gross margin is calculated by subtracting feed costs from the 'net animal revenue' figure. By using this modified expression of income or gain from the feeding operation, we are able to analyse broadly any feeding operation as a one-input one-output system. The overheads, since they remain constant, do not affect the point of maximum profitability, which is reached when marginal costs and marginal returns are equal.

Modifying the income picture by deducting husbandry and marketing costs means that there are only three components for analysis: overhead costs, feed costs and 'net animal revenue'. The situation is expressed graphically in Fig. 4.10.

The output is controlled by the level of feed input. As the level of feed increases, the marginal return decreases, as would be expected from the principle of diminishing returns. A stage is reached

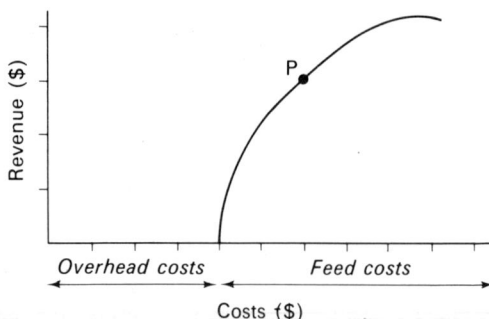

Fig. 4.10 Maximisation of net animal revenue

(P), where the cost of an additional unit of feed would be only slightly less than the value of the net animal product which resulted from it. This is the point of maximum profit, for a fixed level of overheads, i.e. where the marginal return is approximately equal to the marginal cost.

Probably no livestock feeder, in practice, is in a position to organise his feed inputs to such a delicate stage, so that

$$\frac{\text{marginal return}}{\text{marginal costs}} = 1.$$

He is more likely to stop at the point where the ratio is 2 or more.

All livestock operations can be analysed in terms of three components listed above: overheads, feed and 'net animal product less husbandry and marketing'. Once we leave the factory-type environment of the feed lot, the piggery and the poultry farm, where the feed costs are readily identified, there arises the problem of accurately defining the 'feed cost' figure for items such as pasture, silage, hay and irrigation water.

Such feed costs must include fees payable for grazing and water rights, the cost of supplementary feed and of growing and conserving pasture and/or fodder crops. On mixed farms, it is often difficult to separate the cost of feed used for pigs, poultry and cattle. Total feed costs may then be allocated between them in proportion to the relative quantities normally consumed by each type of livestock.

In the early years of pasture or crop production, a good deal of the fertiliser cost could be regarded more as capital input than a maintenance cost. One convention treats the first two years' fertiliser as capital, the balance as maintenance. Where the problem of allocation on a particular project or soil type is critical, much more refinement is needed.

On irrigation areas devoted to animal production, the cost of water, either bought direct from the irrigation authority or supplied from the farm's own pump, is part of the cost of producing feed for the animals. It must therefore be viewed as a feed cost.

With the exception of grossly under-stocked pasture, the amount of feed supplied will determine the level of output from a given animal-based system of feed conversion. By isolating the role of feed in output, the manager is in a position to use the principle of diminishing returns in determining how much he should spend on feed.

Steps in deciding whether to adopt a new activity

Before a commercial farmer, farm manager or farm decision-maker adopts a new activity, or expands an existing one, the following points need to be taken into account:

(a) market prospects for the new or extra products;
(b) physical and technical aspects of making the change;
(c) change in profit, assuming 'normal' seasons and prices;
(d) risk and variability associated with the change;
(e) amount of extra capital investment needed to bring about the change;
(f) return on extra capital invested;
(g) net cash flow, over time, expected to result from the change;
(h) expected change in assets and debts over time;
(i) human and social aspects.

On a semi-subsistence farm, the contribution to the family food supply and the degree of risk, are of the first importance. These points should be looked at systematically to permit valid comparisons between alternative changes. For a simple change in activities without extra capital investment only points (a) to (d) need be considered. Details of each point are explained below.

Market prospects
The decision-maker should determine when and how he would sell the product resulting from the change. He needs to find out from as many sources (people and publications) as practicable, the likely market and the range of possible prices for his product, especially at the time it will be ready for sale. With some special products, a large increase in production from just one farm could result in a reduction in price.

As far as possible, he should also find out what the likely increase in supply of the product from other producers would be. After giving due weight to these factors, he should be in a position to make a reasonable assumption about the prices that can be expected. Because it is so important, we shall come back to this point later.

Physical and technical aspects
The physical aspects to consider are the resources now available (labour, soil type, animals, machinery) to carry out the change, and whether extra resources will have to be obtained. Technical requirements for making a success of the plan may include specific types of fertiliser, animal husbandry techniques and new methods of harvesting and marketing. Avoiding an economic overall seasonal workload may be important for farmers with fixed labour availabilities.

It is also necessary that the farmer and/or his workers have the necessary skills and knowledge for the project. If they do not, they may have to acquire them. Many projects which look attractive on paper (i.e. before they are begun) turn out to be failures because the farmer and his workers lack the ability to carry them out.

To ensure that all relevant aspects of the change are taken into account, it is best to draw up a detailed plan of the land, machinery, fertiliser, water, labour and skills needed, expected yields and number and types of animals. Some allowance should be made for inefficiency in the early stages of the change, especially if the farmer is unfamiliar with the new activity.

If the physical and technical bases of the operation are not sound, its economics are also likely to be unsound. Time spent on budgeting and other financial calculations can then be wasted.

Change in profit
This is a key test of the merit of the proposed change. The calculation for this is known as a 'partial' budget. The word 'partial' means that attention is focused only on those costs and revenues which would alter as a result of any change made.

Worksheets 11 (p. 126) and 12 (p. 127) are used for calculating partial budgets.

Risk and variability
Because of the variable nature of the weather and agricultural markets, no farm plan is ever likely to

work out exactly as expected. Therefore, the farmer must work out what would happen if prices or yields were less favourable and more favourable than expected. The percentage chances (or probability) of these events happening should also be specified. Worksheet 13 (p. 127) shows the procedure.

Capital aspects

Even if the plan is physically possible and leads to an expected improvement in profit, a loan may be needed to put it into effect. The amount of extra capital needed should allow for any sales of plant, livestock or other assets no longer required if the plan is executed. The standard lay-out for this calculation is shown on Worksheet 14 (p. 128) and is known as a capital budget.

Percentage return on extra capital

This is another important measure of the merit of a proposed change. It is calculated by expressing the expected increase in profit as a percentage of the extra capital put into the change.

As it can often take three or four years before the new activity is stabilised and working properly, the extra profit figure used in the calculation should be that obtained when the extra income becomes fairly stable. For example, if the profit before the change is $1 000, and the profit after the change is as shown in the graph in Fig. 4.11, we would choose $1 500 as the basis for calculating the extra profit figure of $500.

If the extra capital invested was $2 500 then the rate of return on extra capital would be

$$\frac{500}{2\ 500} \times \frac{100}{1} = 20\%$$

Usually, it is not wise for a farmer to invest in a new farming development unless the rate of return on marginal capital, after interest, is at least 16–18%, for two main reasons:

(a) the risks involved;
(b) the need to pay back loans from the extra profit.

The method of calculating the expected rate of return on extra capital described above can be

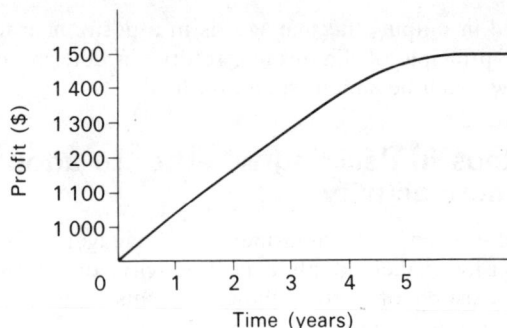

Fig. 4.11 Expected profit after change

carried out quickly although it is not strictly accurate. It is a useful screening device for selecting developments. If the percentage return is high, then the development warrants further study. If it is low, it can usually be rejected, and an alternative development studied.

Pre-loan net cash flows

Even though two developments may show a similar rate of return on an extra capital investment of say $2 500, this does not mean that they are equally attractive to a farmer. For example, the total farm annual net cash flows before borrowing (cash received minus cash spent in a year excluding loans needed) may differ between two possible developments (see Fig. 4.12).

Development A has large cash deficits in the early years, but high positive cash flows from about the third year on. Development B has only a small deficit in the early years but also a low positive cash flow from the third year to year five.

The cash flows shown above are those before borrowing, i.e. they indicate the amount of money which has to be borrowed in the early years if the farm is to remain solvent. In the case of Development A, this may be too large for the bank to consider. Although the medium term prospects are good, the farmer may find it hard to obtain finance. Even if he obtains a loan, should markets or seasons turn adverse in the first or second year, the farmer may find that he underestimated his need for loans. He may then face bankruptcy or at least severe financial difficulties. With Development B, the risk is low, but so are the profits in years three

124

(a)

Development A

Net cash flow before borrowing ($)

Time (years)

(b)

Development B

Net cash flow before borrowing ($)

Time (years)

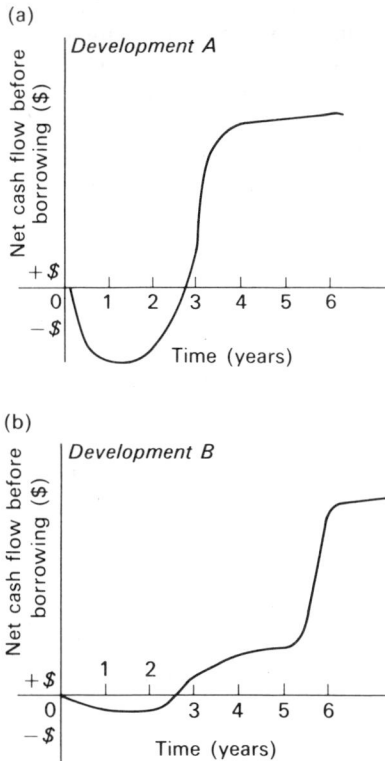

Fig. 4.12 Expected annual total farm net cash flows before borrowing, resulting from the adoption of two different developments

to five. Net cash flow from year five onwards is similar to that for Development A. The format for calculating cash flows is shown in Worksheet 15 (p. 128).

The choice of which development to accept will depend on the farmer's attitude to risk, his access to credit, the value he attaches to an early rather than a late pay-off, and the relative size of the positive and negative cash flows of the two developments.

So before a rational choice can be made between two developments the farmer should know not only the return on marginal capital, but also the pattern of pre-loan net cash flows.

Expected change in assets and debts

A new activity frequently uses borrowed funds. The increase in debts means higher interest charges and principal repayments. At the same time the investment should raise the value of a farm. However, spending, say, $1 000 on improving a farm is no guarantee that its market value will increase by $1 000. Sometimes it can increase by more, sometimes by less.

When a new development is being undertaken, it is usually worthwhile to calculate the expected change in value of assets and debts over the first 4–5 years of the development's life. There are two main reasons for this:

(a) to avoid the possibility that the level of debts will rise too high in relation to the assets. If debts become too high, there is a danger of bankruptcy;
(b) to assess the likely change in net worth (or equity) as a result of the project.

Depending on the conditions of ownership, increase in net asset worth and market value can be a valuable feature of an improvement or intensification programme. The movement in assets and liabilities can be shown on a form such as Worksheet 16 (p. 129).

Human and social aspects

Even though a planned change may look attractive on both economic and technical grounds, the expected result may never occur, because of human and social obstacles.

Lack of know-how and skill has already been indicated as one reason for plans not paying off. The customs and beliefs of the persons involved, their attitude to work, their sense of what is fair, their desire to obtain more of the benefits, their levels of expectation, may also lead them to frustrate the programme. So the manager has to assess whether these factors are likely to cause trouble, what steps he can take to avoid it, and at what cost. Such human and social factors can be particularly important for the success of programmes which introduce changes within the more traditional environments.

There will still be intangible factors, difficult to quantify, in arriving at a decision whether or not to go ahead with a change. They include the farmer/manager's own preferences, values, and ambitions. A final decision is possible only after the intangibles have been taken into account.

An illustration on Worksheets

The following budget Worksheets are used to illustrate the expected financial effects of growing five hectares of maize instead of the five hectares of sorghum currently grown, on a medium-sized farm. It is assumed that the farmer already has some debts, which he is gradually paying off.

There are six Worksheets. The first two (sheets 11 and 12) set out a partial budget, i.e. they look only at the costs and income which would change if the farmer were to grow maize instead of sorghum.

The left hand side of Worksheet 11 shows the annual profit (before deducting overhead costs) from the present activity, detailing the income and costs of growing sorghum. The right hand side of the Worksheet shows the figures for maize including interest on any new capital needed for the maize activity, such as a planter. The figures for maize are those expected when production has become stabilised.

When a new activity is planned that does not replace an existing one, no entry is made on the left hand side of the Worksheet.

Worksheet 12 shows the difference in 'profit' between the proposed new situation and the present. Account is taken of whether costs or income in other parts of the farm would alter if the change was made. Also, since extra profits may be taxed, allowance is made for this. The final figure shows the difference in profit after paying interest on the extra capital needed to bring about the change, and taxes on the extra net income.

'L' shows the net financial benefit which we would expect if the change was made. If capital has to be invested in order to carry out the new activity, we can assess its earning role by expressing 'L' as a percentage of the net amount of capital invested. If the rate of return after interest and tax is less that 20% then the project is not very sound.

The maize will bring a higher expected income than the sorghum, but its costs are higher. Even so, the expected increase in profit from the maize, after paying tax and interest on the extra capital needed, is $333.

Worksheet 13 shows how the extra profit from the switch to maize might vary. It also demonstrates the effect of a crop failure on the *total*

Worksheet 11: Partial budget of proposed change

	($)	($)		($)	($)
Present activity: 5 hectares sorghum			**Proposed activity:** 5 hectares maize		
Annual income from crops and/or animals	750		Annual income from crops and/or animals	1 250	
Total (A)		750	Total (D)		1 250
Annual running costs (*not* capital costs):			Annual running costs (*not* capital costs):		
Direct running costs (e.g. seed, fertiliser, wages, husbandry, medicines, repairs)	360		Direct running costs (seeds, wages, feed, etc.)	500	
Depreciation only on items directly involved in the present activity	40		Depreciation only on items directly involved in this activity	50	
Total (B)		400	Interest on any capital invested to make the change*	30	
Annual 'profit' from present situation or activity (A–B)	350 C		Total (E)		580
			Expected annual 'profit' from new activity if the change is made (D–E)	670 F	

* This can be calculated only after completing Worksheet 14.

Worksheet 12: Appraisal of expected difference in annual operating profit if change is made

	($)	($)		($)	($)
Expected difference in profit if changes is made (F–C)	670		Extra tax on net difference in annual 'profit' (K)	37	
	350				
		320 G	Increase in annual 'profit' from change after paying interest and tax (J–K)	370	
				37	
Has anything been overlooked? Would costs or returns on any other parts of the farm alter if change to new activity is made? If so, what would be the *NET* amount involved? (**H**)	+50				333 L
Net difference in annual 'profit' if change is made (**G +/− H**)		370 G			

Worksheet 13: Expected variation in increase of 'profit' if the change is made

		($)	Chance (%)	
Outcome A:	'Most likely' profit increase	333	70	
Outcome B:	'Pessimistic' profit increase	−300	10	
Outcome C:	'Optimistic' profit increase	500	20	

Effect on *total* farm finances if outcomes B and C occurred:

Effect	**Outcome B**	**Outcome C**
Serious	In first year	
Not important		
Good		Yes

Plan of action if outcome B: Do not replace machinery
Plan of action if outcome A: Reduce debts: replace machinery

farm finances, and the effect of an especially high yield.

There is a strong chance that the switch to maize will be profitable but there is also the possibility of the farmer making a loss. His decision to go ahead with the programme will depend on the state of his total finances, and on his attitude to risk.

Worksheet 14 is a capital budget sheet which shows the net amount of extra capital needed to make the change. It also shows the expected

Worksheet 14: Capital aspects of proposed change

	($)	($)
New capital expenditure involved in change		
Animals	0	
Machinery — secondhand maize planter	200	
Structures — maize storage	100	
Other	0	
Total (A)		300
Capital items which would be sold if the change is made		
Animals	0	
Machines	0	
Other	0	
Total (B)		0
	300	
	0	
Net capital cost of making change (A–B)		300 C

	($)
Annual interest on capital borrowed to make change	
Total capital $300 × interest rate 10% (D)	30
Data to calculate rate of return on extra capital	
Increase in 'profit' from change after paying interest and tax on extra net income (Item L from Worksheet 12)	333 E
Net capital cost of change (C)	300
Rate of return on extra capital needed (E as per cent of C above)	
$\dfrac{333}{300} \times \dfrac{100}{1}$ %	
	111 F

Worksheet 15: Expected total farm net cash flow before borrowing if change is made

	Years	1 ($)	2 ($)	3 ($)	4 ($)	5 ($)	6 ($)
Cash receipts (excluding loans)							
Sales of all farm products		3 500	3 500	3 500			
Other receipts (not loans)		200	200	200			
Total (A)		3 700	3 700	3 700			
Cash payments							
Variable costs		1 200	1 300	1 350			
Overhead costs		600	700	750			
Loan repayments		500	500	400			
Capital investment		500					
Interest		200	100	50			
Living costs		600	800	850			
Taxes		300	300	300			
Total (B)		3 900	3 600	3 750			
Net cash flow before borrowing (A–B)		−200	+100	−50			
Annual borrowing needed to meet payment deficiency		200		50			

128

percentage rate of earnings of the extra invested capital.

The only investments needed are for a maize planter and special storage for the grain. No capital items will be sold. The expected increase in profit, expressed as a percentage of the extra capital invested, is 111%, which is a very attractive use of capital or cash resources.

Worksheet 15 shows the expected net cash flow for the whole farm if the change is made. It is necessary to show the effect of the extra borrowing and income on the *total* farm finances because the farmer has other borrowings and there has been a loss of revenue from the sorghum. These items cannot be ignored when the farmer is making the decision whether or not to make the change. In those cases where no extra borrowings or capital investment are needed to make the change, there is no need to fill in the capital, cash flow and equity sheets.

This view of the expected cash position of the total farm finances shows that the farmer would only need to borrow a small amount of extra money in the first year. He is still able to keep up the repayments on his long term loan of $5 000. In the later years he is able to reduce his debts.

In Worksheet 16 we show the movement in the farmer's capital or equity (i.e. assets less debts) which is expected to occur over the next three years if the change is made. The data analysed in this

Worksheet 16: Expected movement in value of assets and debts

	Years	1 ($)	2 ($)	3 ($)	4 ($)	5 ($)
Assets						
Land and improvements		15 000	15 500	16 000		
Machinery		1 500	1 300	1 400		
Livestock		3 000	3 000	3 000		
Bank						
Total (A)		19 500	19 800	20 400		
Debts						
Short term loans		1 000	1 200	1 000 .		
Long term loans		5 000	4 500	4 300		
Sundry creditors		500	500	500		
Total (B)		6 500	6 200	5 800		
Equity or net worth (C)						
(A–B)		13 000	13 600	14 600		
Equity $= \dfrac{C}{A} \times 100\%$		66.6	69.6	71.5		
Annual debt service cost						
Interest		200	100	50		
Loan repayment		500	500	400		
Total		700	600	450		

worksheet show that a gradual increase in equity due to a slight increase in land value plus a reduction in debt can be expected.

Deciding on the price of a new product

The first step in deciding on a change is to assess the likely market for the new product. If the price assumed in the partial budget is greater than the actual price received when the crop is sold, and the farmer has to borrow money to grow the new product, then he could run into financial difficulties.

Let us assume that a small farmer is contemplating a change to a new product. He does not have access to many reliable sources of marketing information so he asks his extension officer what price he could expect for the new product. The steps which the extension officer, or the farmer and the extension officer between them, should take in arriving at the expected price are described below. Worksheet 17 is intended to help to make this procedure more systematic. An explanation of the steps set out in the worksheet follows.

(a) and (b) **Define the harvest period and the variety of the product** The price will vary according to the seasons and variety of the product. After defining the growing seasons the farmer can propose those varieties which are suitable.

(c) **Choose the market** The decision about which market the farmer should use to sell his product need not be final at this early stage, unless the farmer has accepted a contract to supply a certain amount of the product to a processor or merchant. As harvest approaches, the prices possible from alternative outlets should be investigated more carefully.

(d) **Investigate whether there is a fixed price** If there is, the extension officer should determine whether it is related to a fixed amount and/or grade or quality. This could be the case with a government marketing board, for example.

(e) **Study past prices** The purpose of this is to help the farmer estimate future prices. The farmer and/or the extension officer should look at the supply and demand factors which influenced prices at the expected selling time over the last three or four years. The extension officer will probably need to refer to the market statistics section of the appropriate government Ministry. For example, if the price one year ago was low, and he believed this was due mainly to a large supply, he might put in the table: District yields were very high; the hectarage planted was also higher than normal, both here and in other parts of the country with similar selling periods.

(f) **Estimate future price** Having completed (e) the extension officer should have an idea of the relative importance of the factors which influence prices for the product. On the basis of this information, he has then to estimate the price for an average quality product when it is time to sell it. The estimate will be based on his expectations of the supply, and the anticipated demand for the product.

Several sources are available from which the extension officer can collect the information he needs. First, there is his own and the farmer's experience. Even if the farmer has not grown the product before, he must consciously or unconsciously have some information, which gave him the idea that it would be profitable. However, this information could be unreliable, so it is wise to check it with the experience of others. These might include other farmers growing the product in the area, merchants and cooperatives, the extension service, the government marketing service, relevant publications, statistics and the radio.

The estimate should be for the 'most likely' price for an average quality product. This is the easiest estimate for the extension worker because he will often not know the prices which different grades or qualities bring.

(g) **Adjust price for quality** Where the price depends very much on a certain grade or quality and there is a special market for the best quality product, the farmer should calculate the likely spread in the quality of his product, e.g. 30% first quality; 60% second quality; 10% third quality. If the average price applies to second quality, it is likely that the farmer will receive more than that because he has 30% first quality.

The incorporation of quality in price estimation is especially important when the farmer is aiming at a high quality product, because this often needs a special production technique which can involve higher costs. He must therefore know what percentage he can sell at the high price. He must also know whether or not he can sell the lower qualities and if so what price he can expect.

Since the line of production is new to the farmer, the extension adviser should not over-estimate the likely quality. Lack of experience can result in a lower overall quality being produced than that obtained by farmers who have been growing the product for some time.

(h) Estimate the range of possible prices No matter how well the 'most likely' price has been estimated at this given time, the overall supply at harvest will always depend on conditions during the production period: weather, insects, diseases, etc. So in addition to using the 'average' or 'most likely' price, it is also necessary to estimate the chances of receiving prices lower and higher than this. Even

if the government has announced fixed buying prices, the farmer must assess, on the basis of past experience, how far such prices will be maintained in his area.

The farmer must then consider what courses of action are open to him if he appears to make very little profit or if future prices drop below the 'most likely' ones which he estimated. Should he not be able to sell all his crop at the price expected he should plan how to use the crop to produce the greatest profit.

When future prices and the chances of their occurring have been estimated, the farmer should consider for how long these price estimates will be valid. He should not plan too far ahead on the basis of figures which may well change in the near future.

Worksheet 17: Procedure for estimating market price of a farmer's product

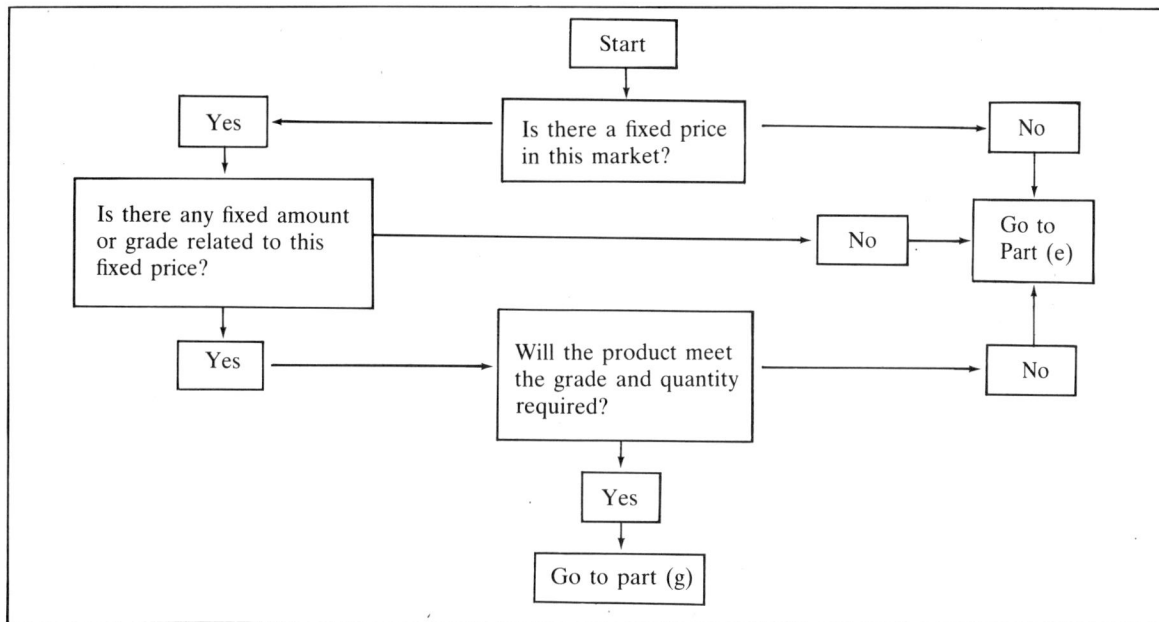

(a) Define the harvest or sale period:
From .... to ....
(b) List the varieties and choose the most suitable.
(c) Consider the market possibilities and choose the best place and method.
(d) Having chosen likely markets, do the flow chart above.

(e) Investigate past prices. Try to recall what the prices for an average quality product were during the past 3 years:

	1 year ago	2 years ago	3 years ago
Price			

Explain if possible, in terms of supply and demand, the reasons for the prices being what they were during the past 3 years.

	Price 1 year ago	Price 2 years ago	Price 3 years ago
Supply was the main reason (specify details)			
Demand was the main reason (specify details)			
Both supply and demand were 'abnormal' (specify details)			

(f) Estimate future price:

Estimate, from as many informed sources as practicable, where supply will be greater, smaller or about the same as either last year or some 'normal' (base) year.

Estimate likewise whether the demand is likely to increase, decrease or remain stable, relative to a base year.

Decide what the net effect of the supply and demand (above) will have on the future price when the product is going to be sold.

Estimate future price, at time of sale for average quality product: ....

(g) Adjust price for quality:

Does this expected price depend on the quality or grade?

If yes: what do you think will be the quality of the product:

	High	Normal	Low
Percent			

Taking the quality of the total crop into consideration, do you think the average price obtained for the whole crop will differ from the price in (e)?

To what extent?

Difference (in % or money): ....

(h) Estimate the range of possible prices:

Indicate if the government is likely to intervene with maximum price .... or minimum price .... Other interventions: ....

Estimate the effect on prices available to the farmer.

(i) Decide the most likely future price for the farmer's product and the likely variation of this price, taking points (f) and (g) into account. In addition evaluate the possibility of the following prices occurring:

	Percentage change
Most likely future price	
Pessimistic future price	
Optimistic future price	

Estimate the period for which the most likely price estimate will remain valid: e.g. 6 months, 1 year, 2 years.

Taking account of variability

So far, the examples used in our discussions of budgeting have used single values for costs, yields and prices, e.g. annual costs $500, annual income of $1 000 yield 1 000 kg per hectare. In practice, there is often a range of possible outcomes. Any farmer or farm manager who does not take account of the likely variability will find himself inadequately prepared to take the appropriate action if the actual outcome is different from the one he expected when he was drawing up his plans.

We will discuss some of the techniques available to help the farm manager make provision for variability.

Variability of total outcome

The first technique looks at the total picture and incorporates various probabilities. A budget using 'most likely' single values is prepared and the expected annual profits or the annual net cash flows, are calculated. Then the possible variations around the 'most likely' figure are estimated, together with their percentage chance of happening. The farmer then has to specify what action he has planned in the event of an outcome, other than the 'most likely' one, occurring.

The example given in Table 4.17 shows one format for considering the total variability given.

Table 4.17

	Net financial outcome ($)	Chance (%)
Most likely	1 000	60
Pessimistic	600	35
Optimistic	1 300	15

If pessimistic outcome:
How seriously will this affect the total finances of the farm?
(Very seriously/seriously/not seriously)
What action(s) can be taken if the pessimistic outcome occurred?

If optimistic outcome:
What effect will this have on the total finances of the farm?
(Great benefit/moderate benefit/little benefit)
What action(s) can be taken if the optimistic outcome occurs?

Flexible budgets
Flexible budgets can be used when a range of outcomes is possible, or where the costs of inputs or the prices and yields of outputs are likely to vary.

Yield, price per kg and variable cost per hectare are key parameters in a cropping activity. The steps involved in constructing a flexible budget are to:

(a) identify the key parameters in the activity or project:
(b) construct a profit equation by expressing the relationship of the parameters in simple mathematical form:
(c) solve the equation using different parameter values and expressing the results either in figures or in graphical form.

The following examples illustrate flexible budgeting. For maize production the profit equation can be written as follows:

Profit per hectare = $Y \times P - V$
(where Y = yield, P = price, V = variable costs)

If fertiliser is an important parameter which is likely to vary in the amount applied, and in cost, then it can be identified separately. Thus:

Profit per hectare = $Y \times P - (F + Vo)$

Fig. 4.13 Comparison of budget with actual result: 'It's a good thing I budgeted 70% pessimistic this year.'

133

Here, Y and P have the same meanings as in the previous example, F means fertiliser costs and Vo means variable costs other than fertiliser. If the yield of maize is 1 500 kg, the price 5 cents per kg, fertiliser costs $30 and other variable costs (including marketing) $25 per hectare, the profit equation would be:

$$\text{Profit per hectare} = 1\,500 \times 0.05 - (30 + 25)$$
$$= 75 - 55$$
$$= \$20$$

Different values of the key parameters can be substituted in the profit equation, thereby giving a quick and simple means of budgeting in situations where inputs and outcomes vary.

Here is an example involving animals. Cattle for fattening can be bought for $C per head, fattened on pasture at R animals per hectare and sold for $P per head. Medicines and husbandry costs $M per head, and selling costs amount to 0.05 of the sale price. Thus for every animal sold for price P, only 0.95 P is received by the farmer. The profit equation is as follows:

$$\text{Profit per hectare} = R\,(0.95\,P - C - M)$$

Here again, the profit under different parameter values can be easily calculated by substituting in the profit equation.

Fig. 4.14 is a typical application of the use of graphs to show a range of outcomes where the parameters vary. The x-axis shows the purchase price, the y-axis the selling price, and the sloping lines show the profit or gross margin per head. These allow for pasture and medicine costs at a constant $8 per head. Fig. 4.14 then shows that if, say, the purchase cost of the cattle was $64, and the selling price was $110, the gross margin would be $38 per head. The profit per hectare for the stocking rate of 0.8 steer per hectare can either be calculated (0.8 × $38) or alternatively shown on the sloping lines which at present show the profit per head.

Separate graphs can be constructed for different stocking rates, or different variable costs. Many farmers construct graphs such as the one in our example for activities in which they engage

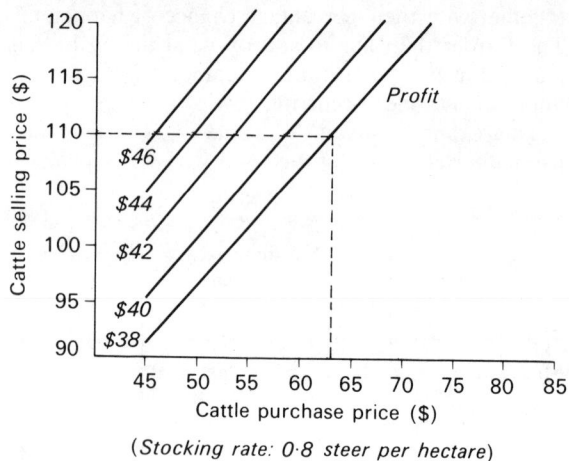

(*Stocking rate: 0·8 steer per hectare*)

Fig. 4.14 Graphic presentation of a flexible budget

regularly. They often put them on the wall of their workroom for quick reference.

Break-even budgets
Another technique which is useful in handling variability when planning is to use 'break-even' budgets. This involves calculating what the minimum value the key parameters (e.g. price and/or yield) would have to fall to before the 'profit' from the proposed new activity became zero, i.e. before the activity just broke even. If the break-even minimum value(s) of the key parameter(s) is very low and has a low chance of occurring, the farmer can feel reasonably confident about going ahead with the new activity.

Sensitivity analysis
In many activities or projects, the net profit depends on the values of just two or three key parameters. Sensitivity analysis, which is normally based on a flexible budget approach shows:

(a) those parameters (yield, prices or costs), which have the greatest effect on net profit;
(b) the extent to which the size of the net profit is sensitive to a change in the value of one or more of these parameters.

For example, in a given maize production activity, the size of the net profit or gross margin (GM) may depend mainly on the yield (Y) and the cost of fertiliser (F) used, because the net price, after deducting harvesting and marketing costs (Pn) is known with considerable certainty, and the pre-harvest variable costs, other than fertiliser (Vpo) are also unlikely to vary greatly.

Then relationships can be expressed in the profit equation:

$$\text{GM per hectare} = (Y \times Pn) - Vpo - F$$

If the yield is fairly closely related to the amount (and hence the cost) of fertiliser used, the farmer or manager can substitute likely values of Y and F in the equation and so test the sensitivity of the gross margin to changes in these likely values.

The range of gross margins that result from the sensitivity test will give him a basis for deciding on the amount of fertiliser he will need to use in order to give him the 'most likely' highest gross margin.

The data from the sensitivity test further stimulate him to focus his attention on the need to use the proper crop production techniques for obtaining the expected result. Thus he is likely to be more conscious of the need to take timely and appropriate action if, say, weeds threaten his crop. Also, he will be on the lookout for early signs of insect pests or disease which could cause the yield to fall.

Sensitivity analysis can also be applied to the total net profits of projects, and here it serves three functions:

(a) indicating the range of possible financial outcomes;
(b) emphasising to the manager the need to use the proper crop production techniques and the need to be flexible and timely in his response to both adverse and favourable developments;
(c) stimulating him to think about, and to plan, courses of action in the event of the outcome other than the 'most likely' outcome.

Measures for reducing the harmful effects of adverse outcomes

The techniques discussed in the previous section are used mainly to indicate the likely effect of variability and to stimulate the farmer or manager to make contingency plans. First, we will discuss some of the measures available to help farmers reduce income variance (i.e. to keep net profits at

a stable level) in the face of price and climatic variability. Then we will consider measures to prevent the farm business running into financial difficulty or perhaps bankruptcy.

Means of reducing income variance include the following.

Yield insurance Hail, flood, fire and sometimes drought insurance can be obtained for crops in a number of countries. Livestock are more difficult to insure. The premium is in proportion with the risk borne by the insurance company.

Growing crops for which there is a guaranteed price In many countries, governments set the price or guarantee a minimum price for some products. The farmer has the choice of growing these products and thus reducing his income variance. In some years, however, his income would be higher if he grew products for which there was no fixed price.

Diversification Frequently this is wise when yields and prices can vary greatly. On the other hand, specialisation has obvious advantages, since resources (including accumulated managerial skills) can be devoted to producing the product which will give the highest return. Where two activities are competitive, the inclusion of the less profitable activity in the farm plan is usually not warranted except for biological reasons, such as in crop rotations.

The net effect of price and climatic variability on changes in gross margin of the various activities for a particular farm or region can be tabulated. The changes are related to each other by a 'correlation coefficient'. This coefficient shows how the gross margin of one activity changes as the gross margin of another changes and can range from +1 to −1. Where the correlation coefficient is between 0 and +1, the gross margins of the activities are said to have a positive correlation coefficient. This is a situation where one gross margin increases as the other increases. Where the coefficient is between 0 and −1, an increase in the gross margin of one activity is associated with a decrease in the other.

Diversification allows flexibility in the use of resources and lowers income variability in all cases except those where enterprise returns are perfectly correlated. This is where a reduction in the gross margin of one activity is matched by a similar reduction in the gross margin of the other as in rain-fed rice and maize.

To reduce the harmful effect of risk it is desirable to diversify into activities which have negative correlation coefficients of gross margin, provided that the profitabilities are not greatly different. In practice, it is found that the gross margins of most activities are positively correlated, the coefficient ranging from +0.4 to +0.8.

In areas of great production uncertainty, there is little benefit in terms of reduced income variance to be obtained from diversification. As production certainty increases there is an increase in the benefits from diversification into activities whose gross margins show least correlations, e.g. poultry and beef or into those which have complementary or supplementary relations with each other.

Contracting to processors or merchants Such contracts guarantee a fixed price for a specified amount of product. This arrangement is common with tobacco, sugar cane, poultry products, fruit and vegetables for processing, etc.

Hedging on a futures market Where such markets are in operation a farmer can sell his product for a known price now, rather than wait for an uncertain price three to four months hence.

Avoiding financial difficulties

The most practical steps in avoiding serious financial trouble are as follows.

Keep borrowings to a level where they can be serviced The ability to service debt depends on the level of the annual cash surplus which results from the year's operations, before deducting interest and principal payments. It is calculated as follows:

Gross cash income	....
Less Cash operating costs	....
Living expenses	....
Net plant replacement costs	....
New capital investment	....
Taxes and other cash outgoings	....
Total cash outgoing before debt servicing	....
Annual cash surplus (available for interest and loan repayment)	....

In calculating the annual cash surplus, depreciation is omitted.

The higher the annual cash surplus, the higher the debt that can be serviced and the lower the critical equity percentage needed for the viability of the farm business.

$$\text{Equity} = \frac{\text{Assets} - \text{liabilities}}{\text{Assets}} \times \frac{100}{1}$$

Whenever undertaking a programme which involves borrowing, the farmer or manager needs to consider how much money he would have left to service his debts (i.e. pay off interest and loans), if the programme did not work out as expected. He should also consider what would happen if the amount of money in that event was not enough to service the debts. Would his banker lend him some money for next year? If so, could he meet the extra interest and repayment burden at the end of next year? With what probability? These questions need to be answered before a farmer decides on how much money he is going to borrow.

Have a contingency allowance When drawing up plans for the next year, or for three or four years ahead, the farmer should build into his budget a contingency allowance to cover items of unexpected cost or reduced income. For example, with cattle activities in areas when drought sometimes occurs, a sum of say $5 or $6 per head should be built into the costs to allow for the possibility of having to buy feed or grazing. If, in the event, there is no need to use it in the current year, it can be put into a readily cashable, interest-earning investment against the day that it will be needed.

Similarly, on crop farms, if there is a chance of a total crop failure, say once every five years, an allowance of one-fifth of the total pre-harvest variable crop costs can be added to each year's costs, and the money put into some interest-earning investment which can be readily converted to cash. If this precaution is taken there will be, in general, funds available to meet the pre-harvest costs in the year following a crop failure.

Have a flexible plan When one activity fails during the early or middle part of the year, it is often still possible to follow it quickly with another. This will compensate the loss on the first activity.

The farmer must prepare himself, both in terms of knowing the technical requirements of the next activity, and making arrangements to obtain quick access to the inputs needed, otherwise he may not be in a position to make a successful change of plan. Flexibility is one of the keys to successful farm management, and is often the explanation for one farmer being financially successful whilst his neighbour is a business failure.

Use fire, theft and liability insurance if available Heavy financial losses can result if a farmer's assets are stolen or destroyed by fire. The farmer may have to meet major claims for damage caused by himself, his employees or stock, or compensation for injuries incurred by people working for him. Wherever such risks are significant he is advised to insure against them if reliable facilities are available.

For the semi-subsistence farmer, the major ways of avoiding financial difficulties are:

(a) diversification of activities where it will ensure a more reliable food supply;
(b) storage where produce can be protected against deterioration, pests and predators;
(c) keeping savings in a readily convertible form.

Discounting, productive values and inflation

'Time is money' has two meanings for the farm manager. First, there is a cost, in terms of income forgone, if he fails to complete certain operations on time, e.g. sowing, harvesting and disease control. Second, he usually values $1 received today more highly than $1 received in, say, six years' time. Here, we will deal with the second meaning. The correct answer to the problem of whether to buy a new tractor which will last ten years, or a cheaper second-hand one which will last five years and is then traded in for a similar one, involves putting a value on money spent or received in future years. So does the choice between planting part of the farm with fruit or timber trees, and sowing it with improved pastures for livestock. The decision on the best policy is made easier by using the technique of discounting, which allows valid comparisons to be made between alternative investments which have differing flow patterns of costs and returns in future years. Here we are concerned with discounting for the 'time' effect of money. This is quite distinct from discounting for inflation.

As a farm management tool, discounting is of greatest value when the investment period exceeds three to four years. For planning over shorter periods it is less useful. To compare alternative medium to long-term farm development plans, we need to understand both compounding and discounting; they are both based on a similar concept.

Compounding

The technique of compounding is best explained by an example. Suppose we invest $200 now at a compound interest rate of 5%. What will the value of the $200 be in five years' time?

At the end of the first year, we still have the $200. There is also $10 interest which the $200 has earned. This $10 interest is added to the $200 to make a sum invested of $210. At the end of the second year we receive 5% interest on $210. Every year the interest earned can be reinvested. The investment will be worth $255.24 in five years' time, provided the interest is kept and re-invested at 5%.

The formula for calculating the end value of a compound investment is:

$$A = PV (1 + R)^n$$

where A is the future amount to which the investment will grow; PV is the present value of the sum invested; R is the interest rate expressed as a decimal; and n is the number of years for which the investment is made.

Discounting

Discounting is the opposite process to compounding. Here, we calculate the present value of a sum of money to be spend (or received) in the future.

The formula for calculating present values of future cash flows is:

$$PV = \frac{A}{(1 + R)^n}$$

Where PV is the present value of the future amount; A is the future amount; R is the interest

137

rate expressed as a decimal; and n is the number of years it will take to receive the money, A.

Thus, the present value of $255.24 to be received in five years' time, assuming an interest rate of 5%, is:

$$PV = \frac{255.24}{1.2763} = \$200 \text{ (approx.)}$$

The discount tables given in Appendix 1, have been calculated on this basis. They show the present value of a dollar discounted at different interest rates for different periods of time. Similarly, the compound interest tables show the future value of money invested today at compound interest for various periods.

For example, in Appendix 1, if we look at the column headed 5% interest rate, and go down to row 10, we see the figure 0.6139. This means that $1 due to be received in 10 years, with an interest rate of 5%, has a value today of $0.6139. Similarly, $1 000 would be worth today $613.9. If $613.9 were now invested for 10 years at 5% compound interest it would grow to $1 000 in 10 years' time.

From Appendix 2 we can calculate the growth of an investment at compound interest. Thus $1 invested at 5% grows to $1.6289 in 10 years' time.

It is possible to choose an investment which does not provide enough money for living expenses in the early years. To avoid this it is a good practice to consider only the annual net cash flows (cash income less all cash costs) in excess of a minimum personal income. A long term investment that requires an unreasonable reduction in the operator's personal income is generally not satisfactory. There is, however, no limit on how much a plan may increase it.

Appendix 3 provides figures for an annuity whose present value is one. This helps a borrower work out how much principal and interest he needs to find each year to amortise his loan.

Thus, when borrowing $10 000 at 15% interest for nine years the factor is 0.2096 (say 0.21). The annual payment with compound (not flat) interest is:

$$\$10\ 000 \times 0.21 = \$2\ 100$$

This is a useful table for both borrowers and financiers.

Interest rate for use in project appraisal

When comparing investments using the discounting technique, we have to decide what rate of interest (or discount rate) will be used. It will depend on two factors: the opportunity cost of the capital available to the manager, i.e. the rate it could earn in other acceptable investments on or off the farm; and the manager's personal attitude to different investment opportunities, e.g. whether he is prepared to accept the interest paid by a savings bank as a reasonable investment, or whether he is willing to take more risk and invest in potentially more profitable investments.

Farm investments should return as much as would be obtained if the funds were spent on alternative investments. Where a farm is already well developed and the availability of funds is not a limiting factor, the relevant discount rate is the current market interest rate. A manager of a part-developed farm with only limited funds is in a completely different situation. His on-farm investment may earn a much higher return on capital (say 15%, after interest and tax) so the discount rate he would apply to off-farm investments for the purpose of evaluation would be 15%.

In the following example two projects, A and B, each have a life of 5 years and require an investment of $1 500. Net cash flows, after deducting a minimum personal requirement of $500 per year, are as follows:

Total undiscounted value ($)		Year				
		1	2	3	4	5
Project A	2 400	600	600	600	600	—
Project B	3 000	—	—	—	—	3 000

The answer to the question 'Which is better?' depends on the discount rate. This in turn depends on the rate of interest that the $1 500 could earn in alternative investment.

We will appraise the two projects using two discount rates, namely 5% and 15%. The present values of the projects are shown in Table 4.18.

Table 4.18 Net present values of projects A and B at two discount rates

	Total present value ($)	Year 1 ($)	2 ($)	3 ($)	4 ($)	5 ($)
Project A						
Net cash flow undiscounted	2 400	600	600	600	600	
Present value discounted at 5%	2 125	571	544	517	403	
Present value discounted at 15%	1 744	521	453	394	376	
Project B						
Net cash flow undiscounted	3 000					3 000
Present value discounted at 5%	2 349					2 349
Present value discounted at 15%	1 491					1 491

In Table 4.18 we illustrate two fundamental points about project appraisal:

(a) The project with the highest present value is the most profitable so usually should be the one chosen.
(b) The ranking of projects can change when the discount rate is increased, i.e. project B is best at low opportunity interest rates, project A is best when there are attractive (15%) alternative uses for investment funds.

Productive value

The estimated market value or the productive value of any resource (for example a farm, a business or a share) can be calculated by using the discounting formula. It is possible to calculate the present value of an asset which produces a flow of income over time. Thus if the operating profit of a farm being examined is $6 per hectare and 5% is the ruling rate for investments of comparable safety, we can say that the current productive value of the farm is:

$$PV = \frac{\$6}{0.05} = \$120$$

In some areas, agricultural land values are so high that even good managers have difficulty in maintaining a rate of return of more than 4% from farm operations. In these areas, personal, social or capital growth considerations may lead the owner or potential buyer to accept a lower rate of return than he could earn on the money market. Productive values do not take account of capital gain or loss.

Caution should be exercised when capitalising operating profit. The following should be taken into account.

(a) Small changes in the operating profit have large effects on capitalised or productive value.
(b) The interest rate used has a great effect on the total capital value calculated, e.g.
operating profit $6, interest rate 5%, productive value $120;
operating profit $6, interest rate 3%, productive value $200;
operating profit $4, interest rate 5%, productive value $80.
(c) The capitalised productive value refers to the value of the farm in operating condition, i.e. land, stock, plant and improvements. Thus, to get the value of the land and fixed improvements, the value of the stock and plant have to be deducted from the capitalised value.
(d) Most authorities on land valuation have ruled against productive valuation in favour of market value, though the former is useful in estimating a theoretical value of the land based on its income-earning capacity.

We saw earlier that there is not necessarily any relationship between the market price and productive value of land. In fact they are rarely the same.

Inflation

This is an expansion of the supply of money in relation to goods, and in consequence a decline in its value. Thus, a loaf of bread may have cost 12 cents five years ago; today, the price of a similar loaf is 22 cents. More generally, it may take 22 cents of today's money to buy the same amount of goods and services as did 12 cents five years ago.

The most common measure of the degree of inflation is a consumer price index. Periodically, the price of an agreed package of basic goods and services required by consumers is recorded. Changes in this composite price from its price in a given base year are expressed as changes in an index number. If the index number changes from 100 to 105 over a year, the rate of inflation has been 5% for that year.

This does not mean, of course, that the prices of all the products the farmer sells, and of those he must buy, will have inflated at that rate. Each is subject to differing pressures. In tropical countries the price of products exported to world markets, and of imported supplies such as fertiliser, will be subject to very different influences from, for example, the cost of local labour.

In making a budget it is generally best to use current or 'real' costs and prices. The budget will then be in common terms throughout. Estimating the rate at which the prices of different items are likely to inflate would in any event, be very difficult.

The present values of the net flows over four or five years can be calculated by discounting at the relevant interest rate; the project with the highest net present value, should be the one selected. Even though the actual financial outcome of the project, in inflated currency, will be different from the budgeted result using today's prices, the basis of selecting the project is sound.

Assumptions in projecting future costs, prices and yields

The only way to predict costs in a budget, unless we have special knowledge about future changes,

is to assume that they will continue to rise at the same rate as they have in the past. The assessment of prices to be expected for products sold is discussed later in this chapter. Prices could be raised in the latter part of the budget period if a new yield — or quality — seems likely to be available then.

Principles of equimarginal returns and substitution

So far, we have only considered the input-output relationship for a single activity. Maximum profits are earned when the marginal or extra cost (MC) equals the marginal return (MR). The same rule applies to all enterprises where there are unlimited funds available. With limited funds, it is not always possible to apply inputs to each activity.

Equimarginal returns

We will now consider, with an example, how to maximise profits when funds are limited and there are alternative uses for them. Assume the farmer/manager grows three crops: rice, maize and sorghum, and that prices (cents per kg) are as follows: rice 2.5, maize 2.0, sorghum 1.0 and fertiliser 3.0. Yields and financial returns for different applications of fertiliser are shown in Table 4.19. The figures marked show the last stage where marginal returns exceed marginal costs. More data would be required to show the exact amount of fertiliser needed to equate marginal returns with marginal costs. Such information is often difficult to obtain in tropical countries, but the example is included to help illustrate a basic principle of resource allocation.

With unlimited funds, the most profitable amount of fertiliser to apply to rice is about 600 kg; on maize about 300 kg; on sorghum about 700 kg. With these levels of application the additional returns are $3.50 for rice, $3.60 for maize and $3.20 for sorghum. These returns just exceed the additional cost of the fertiliser.

Suppose we have only $27 available for fertilising three one-hectare crops. The money is spent to best effect by first applying fertiliser to the crop where the marginal return per unit of fertiliser is highest, and then to the crop which has the next highest

Table 4.19 Additional yield and return from a range of fertiliser applications to rice, maize and sorghum

Fertiliser Application per ha (kg)	Cost per ha at 3 cents per kg ($)	Added cost per ha ($)	Rice			Maize			Sorghum		
			Yield per ha (kg)	Return per ha ($)	Value of extra product per ha ($)	Yield per ha (kg)	Return per ha ($)	Value of extra product per ha ($)	Yield per ha (kg)	Return per ha ($)	Value of extra product per ha ($)
0	0		900	22.50	10.00	1 000	20.00	6.60	2 000	20.00	10.40
100	3.00	3	1 300	32.50	8.50	1 330	26.60	5.00	3 040	30.40	9.00
200	6.00	3	1 640	41.00	7.00	1 580	31.60	3.60	3 940	39.40	7.70
300	9.00	3	1 920	48.00	5.80	1 760	35.20	2.60	4 710	47.10	6.50
400	12.00	3	2 150	53.75	4.50	1 890	37.80	1.70	5 360	53.60	5.40
500	15.00	3	2 330	58.25	3.50	1 975	39.50	0.90	5 900	59.00	4.30
600	18.00	3	2 470	61.75	2.50	2 020	40.40	0	6 330	633.00	3.20
700	21.00	3	2 570	64.25	1.70	2 020	40.40	−0.70	6 650	665.00	2.20
800	24.00	3	2 638	65.95		1 985	39.70		6 870	687.00	
Total for application of $24					43.35			19.70			48.70

marginal return, and so on. The value of extra product is shown in Table 4.19. The first $3 would be spent on 100 kg of fertiliser for sorghum, giving a marginal return of $10.40. The next $3 would be spent on 100 kg of fertiliser for rice, giving a marginal return of $10.00. Determination of the best way of allocating the $27 worth of fertiliser is illustrated in Table 4.20. The $3 units of fertiliser are allocated in such a way as to pick up successively the highest marginal products shown in Table 4.19.

The $27 is best spent by allocating four $3 units of fertiliser to rice, one to maize and four to sorghum. The total income obtained from spending the $24 in this way is $71 ($30.80 + $6.60 + $33.60) compared with $67.80 ($25.50 + $15.20 + $27.10) if the fertiliser were spread equally among the three crops.

If funds were unlimited, expenditure on each enterprise would continue, until the added (marginal) returns equalled added (marginal) costs. When funds are limited they are allocated between activities so that the highest levels of marginal returns get priority, until the level of the marginal returns for each activity is approximately equal.

Table 4.20 Optimum allocation of fertiliser to rice, maize and sorghum

Cumulative fertiliser cost ($)	Marginal return from $3 of fertiliser applied to:		
	rice ($)	maize ($)	sorghum ($)
3			10.40
6	10.00		
9			9.00
12	8.05		
15			7.70
18	7.00		
21		6.60	
24			6.50
27	5.75		
Total marginal return	30.80	6.60	33.60

This principle of allocation is known as the equi-marginal returns principle.

Opportunity cost

The opportunity cost of a farm management decision is the amount of money which is given up by choosing one alternative rather than another.

The principle of equimarginal returns is the basis of the opportunity cost concept. For example, in Table 4.19 the first 100 kg of fertiliser applied to maize yields $6.60, and to sorghum $10.40. We say that the opportunity cost of fertilising maize with the first 100 kg of fertiliser is $10.40, i.e. we forgo $10.40 in order to obtain $6.60. In this case, the

opportunity cost is positive and hence should be avoided. On the other hand, the opportunity cost of applying fertiliser to sorghum rather than maize is negative. We forgo $6.60 to gain $10.40, and this is obviously good business.

The main point of the opportunity cost concept is that alternative investments must be taken into

Fig. 4.15 'Premium, 20% of estimated crop value; pay-out on crop failure, 50% of crop value.'

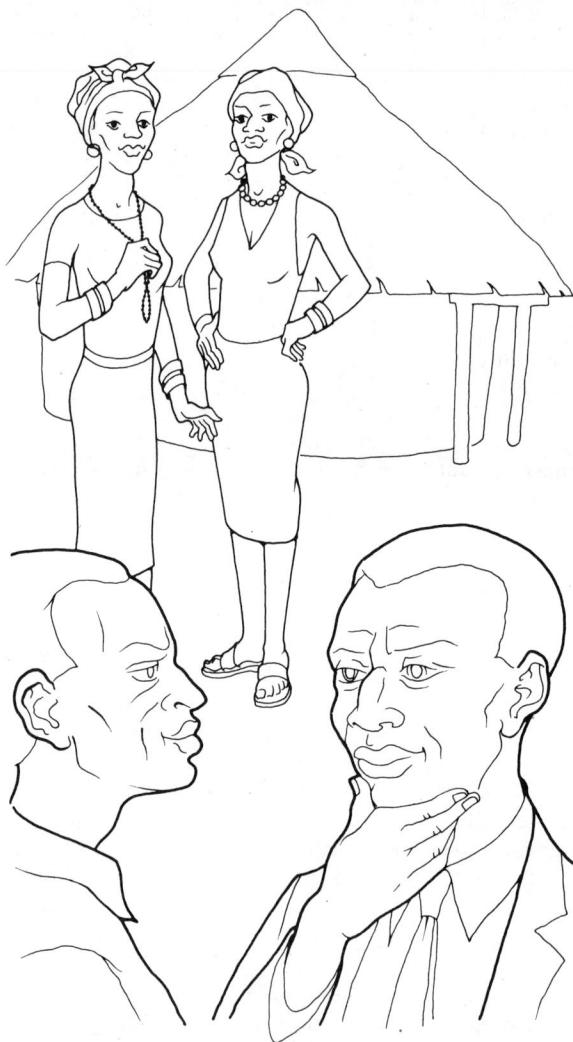

Fig. 4.16 Opportunity costs: 'Who says labour costs can be set at zero for social purposes? What do you think is the opportunity cost of a hard day's work in the sun, for me with two new wives?'

142

account if maximum returns on resources invested are to be obtained. By using the concept of opportunity cost the farmer/manager has a warning system, to use whenever he is contemplating any form of expenditure. His reaction will be to say to himself. 'Although the added return from this expenditure is $5 per $1 added, am I giving up the chance to earn $10 extra return by putting the money into some other activity?'

Substitution

It is usually possible to produce two different products, or a combination of two products, from one resource, e.g. milk and/or beef from a given amount of feed; maize and/or rice from a hectare of land; crop and/or livestock from a unit of labour or capital. Moreover, the same farm product can usually be produced in a number of different ways, e.g. liveweight gain from various combinations of grain and hay; a given yield of irrigated crop from different mixes of water and fertiliser.

The principle of substitution helps in selecting the most profitable combination of two or more resources or products. We will examine the application of the principle where the aim is to maximise profit where alternative products can be produced with similar resources, e.g. either grain or beef can be produced on a given area of land. Note that for simplicity we have assumed linear relationships as activities are expanded or contracted. As indicated earlier, there may be diminishing returns as activities expand.

Maximising profits where alternative products can be produced from similar resources

Here we will assume that we have 100 hectares of arable land. Each hectare can produce grain giving a gross margin of $30, or carry one head of cattle, with a gross margin of $26. The production possibilities, when we consider land alone, are shown in Fig. 4.17.

We can have 100 cattle with no grain, 100 hectares grain with no cattle or any combination of the two indicated by line BC.

If gross margins were the sole criteria of profitability, and capital and labour were in plentiful

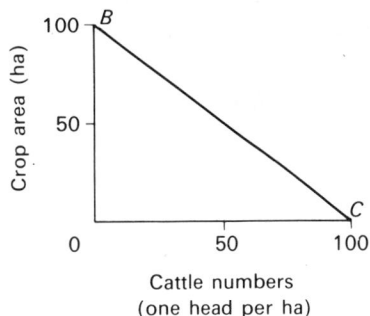

Fig. 4.17 Production possibilities from 100 hectares of arable land

supply, the most profitable plan would be to grow 100 hectares of grain, giving a total gross margin of $30.00.

This is not a very realistic suggestion in many areas, because it is usually not possible to crop continuously and maintain yields. Also capital and labour are often limited. So let us assume that there needs to be a four-year pasture (grass and legume) phase to restore fertility removed by four years of cropping. Thus in a stable rotation, only 50 hectares can be cropped in any one year.

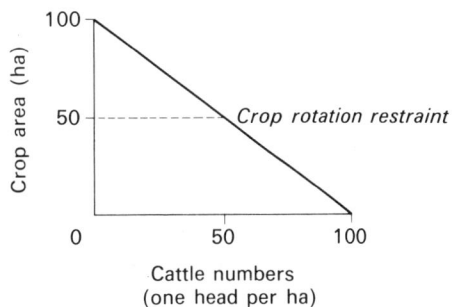

Fig. 4.18 Crop rotation constraint

In Fig. 4.18 we show that for reasons of soil fertility, we cannot grow more than 50 hectares of grain, but that up to 100 cattle can be run.

However, there may not be enough capital and labour for 100 cattle or 50 hectares of crop. The total capital and labour availability and the

143

requirements for a one hectare unit of crop and a one head unit of cattle are as follows:

	Capital available	Crop (1 ha unit)	Cattle (1 head unit)
Working capital ($)	4 000	40	50
Labour at critical period (hours)	40	0.6	0.4

There is enough capital to grow 100 hectares of crop,

$$\frac{4\,000}{40}$$ or 80 hectares of cattle, $$\frac{4\,000}{50}$$

at 1 head per hectare. The existing labour supply permits the manager to grow either 66 hectares of crop, $\frac{40}{0.6}$ or to run 100 hectares of cattle (100 head), or a combination within these limits. The soil fertility, capital and critical labour period restraints are shown in Fig. 4.19). The shaded zone in the figure is called the feasible area of production, i.e. production is possible, without exceeding any restraints imposed by available capital, labour or fertility. It is more profitable to produce at the boundary ABCD than at, say, point X, because the level of production at X is lower than at any point on the boundary. Thus there is enough capital, land and labour to grow a maximum of 50 ha of grain. Some cattle can also be run, along to point B, when we meet a restraint on the supply of labour. Thus, at point B, we have a plan involving 50 hectares of grain, and 30 cattle, which use 30 hectares, a total of 80 hectares, leaving 20 hectares unused.

The shaded section ABCD shows that it is feasible but perhaps not profitable to produce at point C. This will involve giving up grain and replacing it with cattle. Is such action justified? The substitution ratio of critical labour of cattle for crop is the ratio at which labour is freed for every hectare of crop given up as shown below:

$$\frac{\text{Crop labour replaced}}{\text{Cattle labour added}} = \frac{0.6}{0.4} = 1.5$$

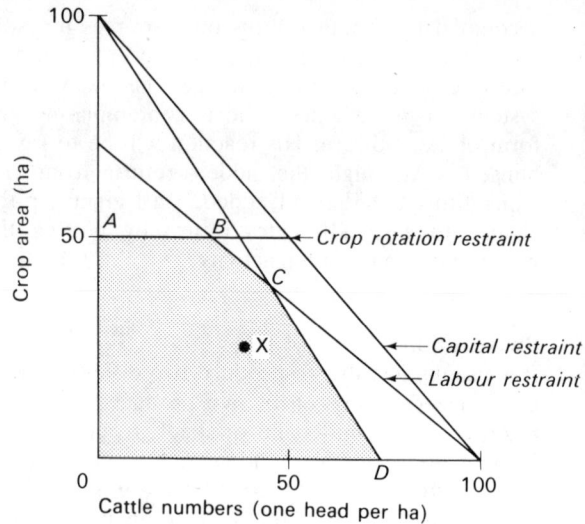

Fig. 4.19 Feasible production area

Thus every hectare of crop forgone frees enough labour to run 1.5 hectare of cattle. The effect on gross margin (GM) is as follows:

Loss of 1 hectare crop × GM = 1.0 × $30 = $30
Gain of 1.5 cattle × GM = 1.5 × $26 = $39
Net gain per hectare = $9

By reducing crop hectarage to 35 and increasing cattle to 52 hectares, the gross margin increases by 15 × $9 or approximately $135. In this situation, 87 hectares are used, 13 unused.

The next restraint met is working capital. For every hectare of crop given up after point C, working capital substitutes at

$$\frac{0.40}{0.50} = 0.8$$

Thus one hectare freed from crop allows only 0.8 hectares of cattle. This is clearly not profitable, because the gross margin from crop is higher than the gross margin from cattle.

Thus, given the restraints specified, the most profitable plan is:

	Gross margin ($)
35 hectares crop × $30	1 050
52 hectares cattle (52 head) × $26	1 352
Total	2 402

144

This plan uses all available labour and capital, but not all the land. In practice, the surplus land could be used by spreading the cattle over all the non-arable land; possibly this could lead to higher gross margins per head of cattle through better nutrition. Alternatively, the farmer/manager could try to hire more labour at the critical time even at a high cost, so that the 50 hectares grain programme was maintained.

The graphical presentation of a farm planning problem which has been illustrated cannot be used when there are more than three activities. Even with three activities, a three-dimensional figure is needed. Many farm planning jobs involve more than 20 activities and as many restraints. Provided the data are available, optimum allocations can be worked out with the aid of algebra. The technique of linear programming has proved of considerable value in helping to plan multi-activity farms and businesses. It is based on the principle of substitution and uses substitution ratios as described here.

Substitution to minimise costs
In the example in the previous section we showed how to produce maximum profits where alternative products can be produced from the same resources, subject to certain restraints. The principle of substitution is also used to find out the least-cost combination of resources needed to produce a given result. For example, a feed mixture is required to produce say 50 kg liveweight gain in 50 days in a group of cattle weighing 200 kg. It should contain specified amounts of energy foods, amino acids, fibre, minerals and vitamins. If the price and content of the various sources of nutrients are known, e.g. hay, grain, protein meal, mineral supplements, then linear programming can be used to select the least-cost combination of the different nutrient sources.

Although the example quoted refers to a feed mix problem, the principle can be used whenever a situation calls for minimising the cost of the input mixes needed to produce a specified outcome.

Computers in farm planning
In our discussions on the application of the principle of substitution, it was indicated that linear programming could be used to solve problems such as:

(a) ascertaining the best combination of activities, given certain restraints such as limited areas of suitable soil, shortages of labour and capital, restricted supply of feed at certain times of the year and the need to maintain soil fertility by use of legume rotations;
(b) working out least-cost combinations of components for a feed ration.

Computers can complete the complex calculations involved in a matter of minutes. They are also used in farm management accounting, and in simulating or making models and experimenting by varying the important parameters.

In this way computers can be of use in working out the 'most advantageous' production programmes for model smallholder farms in specific ecological zones.

Use of farm accounts and records
Over the past decades there have been three important advances in the application of management accounting principles to farm management.

(a) The accounts are timely and show the current market situation.
(b) Inputs are related to outputs.
(c) The accounts are designed to assist with forward planning, and are not merely a record of historical performance.

Accounts for farm management
Farm management accounting has a number of distinctive features. Approximate market value, and not the historical cost, is the basis of valuation of most resources analysed; inputs are related to outputs. The production year, rather than the fiscal year, established by tax authorities, is the basic accounting period. Thus the initial month of the accounting year will vary with the main activities pursued on the farm and the locality. It may start in March, April or July. Full information is available to the manager within weeks of the end of the production year. Physical records play a very important part in the preparation of the accounts,

e.g. tractor and labour usage: feed consumption by various kinds of livestock; sex and age composition of flocks and herds; crop yields. Deferred payments for sales are related to the year of production, not the year of receipt. Regular up-to-date reports of actual progress against budgeted projections are a feature of farm accounting.

Farm management accounting aims to provide farmer and manager with realistic information on the current status of both the farm business as a whole, and of individual activities. The data derived from the accounts are somewhat limited, but can also be used for forward planning.

Farm records

There are numerous books and pamphlets available to help farmers decide on the sort of records they should keep if they are to prepare accurate accounts under their local conditions. We will therefore not discuss them in detail here.

It should be remembered that accounts are a record of what has occurred or is occurring; budgets tell us what might be in the future. Accounts, however, are sometimes useful when borrowing. They are particularly necessary where farmers are subject to income tax to avoid over-payment. In some countries they may be helpful in obtaining subsidies.

Multi-column sheets are one of the most useful aids in keeping farm financial records. Each column can be given a heading which fits the specific situation on the farm. One farm may need only 8 or 9 columns, another as many as 27. Table 4.21 is a very simple form of multi-column sheet for payments with the first four columns used to identify and evidence the transaction. A more elaborate sheet may show variable costs for each activity rather than lumping them together as in this example.

Some of the other jobs for which multi-column sheets can be used are to:

(a) record receipts from the different farm activities;
(b) show annual machinery depreciation;
(c) record details of costs and income from each activity, e.g. seed, fertiliser, spray, labour, water, machinery, harvesting, processing, transport and selling costs of maize;
(d) record machinery used on different farm activities;
(e) show how total wages were allocated between different workers.

In maintaining such records it is important to keep in mind the purposes for which they will be used. Otherwise farmers may find themselves with a lot of detail, but no broad allocations that are strategic for decision-making.

Calculators, mini-computors and accounting machines

These machines have been designed to add, subtract, multiply, etc. a series of figures and type the results onto sheets according to a pre-arranged format. They are especially useful for comparing

Table 4.21 Multi-column payments sheet

Date	Details of transaction	Cheque No.	Cheque total ($)	Cash ($)	Overhead costs ($)	Variable costs ($)	Capital costs ($)	Personal drawings ($)
1973								
2/7	Land taxes			300	300			
10/7	100 bags fertiliser — for maize	624	200			200		
20/7	Purchase of new plough	625	300				300	
30/7	Payment of school fees			130				130
30/7	Wages			100		100		
	Total payments		500	530	300	300	300	130

actual against budgeted figures, for recording cost allocations to different activities, and for showing the overall financial state of a business.

A simple electric model could be very useful for a large farmer. The services of such machines can sometimes be obtained on a contract or fee basis from the offices of farm accounting specialists. These specialists can often advise on record-keeping systems and comparative performance at the same time. To the smaller farmer portable calculators using long life batteries can be very helpful. At present many farmers do not take as much interest in economic analysis as they should, because of the need to make calculations by hand.

Summary of Part B: Operations

The purpose of the second part of this chapter was to help the farmer make better decisions and plans, and manage his operations more effectively.

We discussed general decision-making; the financial basis of decision-making on crop and animal farms; the steps involved in deciding whether to adopt a new activity; the measures available for coping with variability when planning and managing a farm; the planning and appraisal of medium to long term projects using discounting procedures; the application of the principles of equimarginal returns and substitution; and finally, some features of farm management accounting and record keeping.

The discussion of the principles and applications of modern decision theory showed how to analyse and present a decision problem in a systematic way. It stressed that decision-makers were acting rationally if they made choices which were consistent with their beliefs and their attitude to risk. The notion of a person's certainty equivalent was shown to be central to the application of decision theory to any real world problem. It explains why many semi-subsistence farmers are reluctant to grow new crops.

Two major decisions on crop farms were dealt with in the next section: which crops should be grown; and whether or not to harvest a crop. In both decisions the importance of distinguishing between pre-harvest or growing costs, and harvesting and marketing costs was made. The fundamental economic and technical basis of all livestock activities was presented; a method of financial analysis was outlined; and the importance of the feed cost in animal production systems was stressed.

Since one of the more important decisions a farmer or manager has to make is whether or not to adopt a new activity, to expand an existing activity, or to invest in a new or expanded project, we have outlined the step-by-step procedure he should follow in arriving at his decision. In addition, a check list has been provided to help the farmer and/or his adviser settle on the prices he should estimate for his products.

Since variability of yields, prices and costs is a feature of most agricultural production systems, the farmer, when planning, has to make provision for this. Several techniques to cope with variability were illustrated, the chief of which is known as flexible budgeting. Once the plan is put into operation, variation from the original plan will still occur. Some steps which the farmer can take to cope with the unfavourable and favourable aspects of such variation were presented.

With medium and long term investments, the farmer often has to wait several years before he starts to get a return on the capital he has put in. Since capital is often scarce, and has alternative uses on the farm, the farmer needs some way of evaluating these medium and long term investments so that he can compare them with alternatives which have a quicker pay-off. We described the technique of discounting, which allows such comparisons to be made. It also permits a farmer or manager to decide how much he should pay to acquire an income-earning farm resource.

Inflation is a further problem in medium and long term planning. Ways of dealing with it in planning were discussed.

The application of two important economic principles—equimarginal returns and substitution—was introduced. The first principle shows how best to allocate limited resources such as water or capital among several competing activities or projects. The second, substitution, helps in deciding what activities should be carried out on a farm when a number are possible, but where there are certain restraints such as soil type, labour, and capital. The concept of substitution can also help in producing a product at the lowest cost when there are a number of different ways of doing it. The application of the principle of substitution through the computer-based technique of linear programming was outlined. Finally, the distinction between accounting for tax purposes and accounting for farm management was made, and some suggestions for a simple farm record system were given.

Issues for discussion

1 Select a financial problem which is relevant to you, and which involves making a decision between alternatives whose outcome is uncertain. State your certainty equivalent for the risky outcomes. For example, you may have sure income in your present job, but you are offered the chance of joining a friend in a farming venture. If it succeeds, you will make more money than you do at present. If it does not, you will be worse off.

2 How do you think the ideas described under 'Decision-making' could be applied on both a commercial and a semi-subsistence farm which you know? What are the main difficulties in applying these ideas?

3 List the total variable costs of five crops with which you are familiar. Divide their costs into two categories: (a) growing or pre-harvest costs; (b) harvesting and marketing costs. How do you think that a farmer would use this information to decide which crops he would grow? Give an example of where it would pay to harvest a crop even though the gross income from the sale of the crop is less than the harvesting and marketing cost of the crop.

4 If you were trying to help a commercial and a semi-subsistence farmer decide whether to replace one crop with another, what steps would you take to help them arrive at their decisions?

5 If you were a farmer and wanted to develop your farm by, say, clearing land, improving pastures, putting in an irrigation system or buying machinery, how would you decide the following:
(a) whether you should go ahead with the project?
(b) whether you should borrow money to carry out the project?
(c) what terms (i.e. the interest rate, the period of repayment and repayment 'holidays') you would

need to get on the loan in order to carry out the project successfully?
(d) what precautions you would take to prevent yourself getting into serious financial trouble in the event of the project not working out as well as expected?

6 Draw up a flexible budget equation for a crop or animal activity by identifying the main parameters. Also present it in graphical form, showing the effect of changing one or more of the key parameters.

7 Taking two farms (a small one and a medium-sized one), list the practical measures or steps which are available to the farmer/manager to help reduce the harmful effects on his finances of price, climate, or yield variability.

8 Draw up a five-year development budget for a farm that you know, using net cash flows.

9 Test the sensitivity of the annual net cash flows to changes in the key parameters.

10 Do you think that the technique of discounting has any application in appraising medium to long term projects on any farm with which you are familiar? If not, why not?

11 What practical measures can the farmers you know take to offset the harmful effects of inflation? Does inflation have any advantages for some (or all) of these farmers?

12 The principle of equimarginal returns can be an important guide to decision-making when a farmer has to choose between alternative uses for his funds. In view of the shortage of data on most farms, can you see any useful application for the principle on the farms that you know?

13 Has the principle of substitution any real-life application on any farms that you know?

14 Over the next five years can you see any useful contributions being made by computers to the farm management and planning problems of any farms you know?

15 There is no point in the farmer keeping physical and financial records unless he is going to use them for planning management or decision-making. Make a list of the minimum number and type of records which a small farmer and a medium-sized farmer should keep. (Remember: the farmer must be able to use the data to help him make farm management decisions.)

Further reading

Barnard, C. (1979) *Farm planning and control*, Cambridge University Press, Cambridge.

Belov, F. (1956) *The history of a Soviet collective farm*, Routledge and Kegan Paul, London.

Boehle, M. and Eidman, V. R. (1984) *Farm management*, John Wiley and Sons, New York.

Castle, E. N. (1973) *Farm business management: The decision-making process*, 2nd ed., Collier Macmillan, New York.

Clayton, E. S. (1964) *Agrarian development in peasant economies*, Pergamon Press, Oxford.

Cleave, J. H. (1974) *African farmers: Labour use in the development of smallholder agriculture*, Praeger, New York.

Collinson, M. (1972) *Farm management in peasant agriculture: A handbook for rural development planning in Africa*, Praeger, New York.

Dillon, J. (1980) *Farm management research for small farmer development*, FAO, Rome.

Friedrich, K. H. (1971) *Manual for farm management investigations in developing countries*, FAO, Rome.

Harper, M. (1973) *Kenya smallholders: their attitudes and problems*, FAO, Rome.

Lloyd, D. H. (1968) *A systematic approach to business analysis without accounts data*, University of Reading, Reading.

Makeham, J. P. (1985) *The farming game*, Gill Publications, Armidale, NSW Australia.

Makeham, J. P. and Malcolm, L. R. (1986) *The economics of tropical farm management*, Cambridge University Press, Cambridge.

Phillips, T. A. (1961) *Farm management in West Africa*, Longman, London.

Ruthenberg, H. (1980) *Farming systems in the Tropics*, 3rd ed., Oxford University Press, Oxford.

Upton, M. (1987) *African farm management*, Cambridge University Press, Cambridge.

Upton, M. and Anthonio, Q. B. O. (1970) *Farming as a business*, Oxford University Press, Oxford.

World Bank (1980–86) Various publications on farm management and extension, World Bank, Washington DC.

5 Development economics

This chapter sets out to explain how countries become richer and able to offer their people more services and better prospects of a good life. It then looks at the part agriculture plays in this process. In countries with no important mineral resources, agriculture has generally to carry the main burden. It has to provide funds to run the government; it must provide a basis for industrial and commercial development; the foods needs of rapidly growing populations must be met; produce must also be exported to earn foreign exchange.

Development is not just a matter of producing more from agriculture and investing the proceeds wisely. The people in agriculture must feel that they all have a chance to share in the benefits. Otherwise, in their discontent, they may tear down the institutions most conducive to long term progress. This means that, at least, they should have a chance to work and learn, and not be held back by reactionary social structures. Progressive arrangements for the use of land and access to finance are essential. These issues are also discussed in this chapter.

The last parts of the chapter are concerned with how tropical countries can earn the foreign exchange needed to pay for essential imports, and with ways in which their governments can hasten the pace of development. These focus on sound policies and financial management and a shrewd use of international aid. The preparation of specific investment projects and their coordination with ongoing programmes is also treated.

Economic growth

Economic growth or development is the improvement of people's level of living. This is measured not only in terms of money, but also of quality. It may be useful to regard 'growth' as relating to the more material elements, whereas 'development' has also a social and cultural content. Major indicators of this level are:

(a) income per person;
(b) life expectancy at birth;
(c) infant mortality rate;
(d) food supplies in terms of calories available per person in relation to calorific requirements;
(e) proportion of children aged 5–15 years attending school;
(f) percentages of males and females in the total population above some appropriate age that are literate;
(g) proportion of the economically active population that are unemployed;
(h) proportions of the economically active population that are in the principal industrial and occupational categories;
(i) personal consumption as a percentage of national income.

The physical content of the level of living is measured by the quantity of goods and services consumed by each person over a given period. Each of the above indicators measures one part of this level and generally the indicators all shift as economic growth occurs. Many indicators are highly correlated with the level of income per person and this can be used, therefore, as a general indicator. However, it is by no means a complete indicator, as Western societies plagued by problems of traffic congestion, pollution and declining personal services are now fully aware.

The estimates of income per person in Table 5.1 show an immense gap between the average income in the industrial market economies, and that in Africa. It may seem a gap which no rate of development foreseeable in the immediate future could expect to bridge. However, if allowance is made for the higher costs of services and other disadvantages in North America, Western Europe and Japan, the gap is not so wide as it might seem.

In many developing countries the average income per person is nearly constant. Total income is growing, but the population is growing at the same rate. In other countries incomes have risen in money terms but so have prices and costs. The result is that real income shows little gain. If this process, known as inflation, goes on at a much faster rate in one country than another, products that have to be sold on world markets cease to be

(a)

Fig. 5.1 The quality of living

Table 5.1 Average income per person and percentage of population in agriculture, 1980. (*Source*: **World Bank**, *World Bank Development Report 1986*)

	Average income per person ($)	Percentage of labour force engaged in agriculture
Low-income countries		
Africa	260	79
China	290	70
India	240	70
Middle-income oil importers		
East Asia and Pacific	1 310	54
Latin America and Caribbean	1 760	34
High-income oil exporters	13 290	36
Industrial market economies	10 530	7

competitive and the country's currency usually has to be devalued. Nevertheless change and growth are taking place. With the spread of technology and changes in consumption habits, living standards in the important subsistence sector are moving upwards in most tropical countries. New dynamic forces in the commercial sectors are radically altering the way of life and the aspirations of the people.

A distinction is sometimes drawn between growth, self-sustained growth, and accelerated growth. Self-sustained growth usually means that certain motivators are built into the economy in such a way that it grows automatically. Accelerated growth means that the rate of growth is itself increasing, e.g: from 3% annually to 4%, 5%, etc. Countries beginning development rather late have often achieved high growth rates. These 'late-comers' can benefit from the accumulated knowledge, experience and innovations of countries that started earlier. They have a better chance of avoiding some of the pitfalls.

Development relationships

From Table 5.1 it may be seen that the average income per person tends to correspond inversely with the percentage of people engaged in agriculture. In Africa, the average income is $260 and 79% of the people are engaged in agriculture. The corresponding income and percentage for Latin America and the Caribbean is $1 760 and 34%. Agriculture, together with livestock raising, fishing and hunting, is often called the primary sector of an economy. The secondary sector is made up of manufacturing, power production, mining, building and construction. The tertiary sector is all other economic activities including trade, transport and other services. The money value of the output of

151

Table 5.2 Relationships between development indicators and income levels. (*Source:* Adapted from **Chenery, H. R.** (1971) 'Growth and change' in *Finance and development*, 3)

	Average annual income per person				
	$50	$200	$600	$1 000	$2 000
Percentage of total domestic output					
Primary sector: agriculture	58	36	22	16	10
Secondary sector: industries	7	20	29	33	39
Tertiary sector: services	30	38	40	40	39
Tertiary sector: utilities	5	7	9	10	12
Percentages of labour force					
Primary labour	75	59	35	24	8
Industrial labour	4	17	28	33	40
Utilities and services labour	21	27	36	42	52
Urban population (as % of total population)	7	34	52	58	65
Birth rate per thousand	47	37	28	22	17
Death rate per thousand	20	11	9	9	11
School enrolment ratio	18	53	74	82	91
Adult literacy rate	15	55	80	89	93
Savings as % of national income	9	15	19	22	25
Investment as % of national output	12	18	22	24	25
Tax revenue as % of national income	10	17	25	30	28

a worker is usually much higher in the secondary and tertiary sectors, but he usually has to pay more for housing, food and clothing than the farmer.

Table 5.2 is instructive because it relates various indicators of the level of living to average income per person. It is based on data assembled from 100 countries. While dollar values have changed since 1970, it shows how close is the relationship between income and the percentage of children who go to school and adults who are able to read and write. Birth and death rates are inversely related to income. As might be expected, savings and investment both increase as income rises.

Two factors are recognised as playing a vital role in the process of economic growth: one is capital and the other management.

The role of capital

A man can produce much more if he has capital than if he works only with his hands or with very simple tools. How much more he can produce depends on the relative usefulness of capital for the kind of production in which he is engaged. Thus the investment of capital in a bullock and plough to replace hand tillage will add much more to output than a subsequent investment in a rather elaborate building to house the bullock. The relationship between capital and what it produces is known as the incremental capital output ratio or capital coefficient. This means the amount of capital associated with an increase in output. A ratio of 2:5 would mean that an additional annual output of $1 000 flows from the use of $2 500 of new capital.

Within an economy, capital increases through savings and loans from other countries. So the rate of savings (plus loans) largely determines the amount of capital available. The way this is invested determines the increase in output that follows. Thus if the rate of savings is 5% and the incremental capital output ratio is 2:5, then the rate of growth would be as follows:

$$\frac{5 \times 100}{2.5} = 2\%.$$

In practice the rate of savings in an under-developed economy is about 5%, and the rate of growth about 2%. Since the population tends to increase at this rate also, there is little movement upwards in real income per person. In more developed economies the savings rate may be 15% or more, even 25%. This is one of the reasons why economic growth is often fastest in countries that are already quite well off.

The role of management

At one time it was thought that the accumulation of capital by savings and supplementing these by borrowing, lay at the heart of economic development. Later the vital role of management was recognised. Lack of skilled management is one of greatest problems in tropical countries. Two types of managerial ability are essential for organising production along modern lines. The first is in management of economic policy and public administration. The second type is management of production and marketing enterprises. To quote Alfred Marshall, 'Management of this kind directs production so that a given effort may be most effective in supplying wants [under the complex conditions of modern life and brings together] the capital and labour required for the work, engineers its general plan and superintends its minor details.'

While it is now generally accepted that the State must play an important role in development, how to carry out this role is not well understood. Even when an administrative system has trained civil servants, it may be poorly equipped to take a positive role. In India, Pakistan and elsewhere, for instance, a class of administrators was left, at the time of independence, who had been trained to act in accordance with an elaborate set of rules. Too

frequently they attempted to apply the rules and regulations meant for routine administration to the management of economic enterprises in a period of rapid change. Observing the rules seemed more important than getting results. There was more attention to status and seniority than to efficiency and initiative. This is still true of many tropical countries.

A further influence on the management of public enterprises has been confusion between the accrual of profit and its use. Disapproval of the use of profit for conspicuous consumption often blinds officials from seeing that profit is also a source of savings badly needed for economic development. This has already been recognised in some Eastern European countries where formerly profit was a bad word. Now incentives for profit-making are being provided.

It must be understood that economic development involves constant change. When administrators accept this, it should be easier for them to exercise economic controls in a positive way. The government administration in Japan, for example, is used to growth. This has been favoured because the administration had a clear understanding of its role in relation to business enterprise.

Too much control has also had its impact on the management of private enterprises in many developing countries. The result has been that they are conditioned to protective policies and political pressures, and do not concentrate on efficiency.

So far we have only explained the nature of economic growth. It is measured in terms of physical goods and services. However, this can be very misleading as regards the quality of life. For a favourable rate of growth, access to capital is essential, with management playing a vital role in putting capital to good use.

Theories of economic growth

The concept of widening markets, first emphasised by Adam Smith, author of *The Wealth of Nations* published in 1776, is crucial to nearly all explanations of economic growth. Where the markets open to producers are small and local, as had been the case in many parts of Europe until shortly before Adam Smith's time, there is little scope either for specialisation or for the accumulation of capital. The result was that many human and natural resources were not employed to capacity. They awaited a greater demand for their output, which could only come from expanded markets. Expansion of markets through increased demand is an indispensable stimulation to growth.

Growth stages

Choosing the predominant type of activity in a society as a criterion, Adam Smith distinguished the following stages of growth: hunting, pastoral, agricultural, commercial, and manufacturing. Karl Marx focused attention on the distribution of wealth as a class basis. Other approaches have been based on the type of money exchange, the area of transactions, and the organisation of production. In the 1930s, Colin Clark classified growth by the nature of employment: as a country develops, the proportion of its working population engaged in the primary sector declines, and that in the tertiary sector increases; the proportion engaged in the secondary sector first rises, then begins to fall.

Economic factors have far-reaching effects upon social, cultural and political life and vice versa. This interaction is a feature of Rostow's stages of growth analysis. He distinguished five stages: the traditional society; the preconditions for take-off; the take-off; the drive to maturity; and the age of high mass consumption. One can easily criticise Rostow's analysis as regards its general application, but it brings out some important points. Establishing a favourable political and social background is a primary factor for development. People must appreciate, desire and be prepared for growth before it can take place. Secondly, it shifts the focus from simply the rate of investment to a deeper one which takes into account people's attitudes. Attitudes have an important influence on the conditions of production and demand. Critics of growth stage theories assert that they only describe the historical growth process, and do not say what caused it; that they explain how transition to an industrial stage was associated with nationalist movements and the emergence of nation states, but do not analyse the factors causing this transition. Marx does not actually discuss how social classes are formed.

Growth stage analyses are best seen as an intermediate step between a descriptive catalogue of contributions and a full-scale mathematical development model. They provide some suggestions as to what causes what, in the process of development. Mathematical models endeavour to measure the degree of cause and effect in the growth process. Inevitably this involves much simplification of what actually happens. This can lead to correspondingly unrealistic conclusions.

Challenge and response

The analysis associated with Toynbee and Gerschenkron focuses on tensions generated by the contrast between present conditions in the developing countries and potentials shown by the advanced countries. The more the advanced countries demonstrate growth in technology, the greater seems the potential to do the same in a backward country by borrowing their technology. Leaders in the less advanced countries then come under continuing pressure to catch up. The challenge must be great, otherwise the response may be blocked by the many obstacles to be overcome. Gerschenkron, like Rostow, considers the political unification of a country to be a necessary prerequisite for the challenge–response mechanism to operate.

The big push

More recent theories of economic growth concentrate on investment. They are concerned with the size of the investment programme and how it is allocated. The theory of the big push is associated with the name of Rosenstein-Rodan, and Leibenstein's 'critical minimum effort'. Its main point is that there is a minimum level of resources that must be devoted to a development programme if it is to have any chance of success. This is because many of the critical investments needed cannot be made in small steps. Investments should also be integrated so that each one helps to make the others more profitable. From this come the external economies that are so important in accelerating the pace of development.

Balanced growth

Some of the arguments used in the big push thesis are central to the doctrine of balanced growth. This maintains that investment has to be made in various directions simultaneously to take into account complementary demands. People engaged in new activities become each others' customers. More important is the role of external economies. The balanced growth argument is the justification for comprehensive planning. Independent decisions by individual investors would not be able to take account of the external economies arising from a planned diversified programme.

Balance can of course be looked at in two ways, horizontal and vertical. If consumers want certain types of goods they will also want others that are complementary and production should develop accordingly: this is horizontal balance. Vertical balance is when all the successive processes needed for a group of final products are developed at the same time. This does not mean that investment should be channelled towards each and every activity at the same time. Nor does it imply that all sectors should grow at the same rate; some may decline. What is important is that the various linkages which make for success in particular lines of development are there at the right time.

Thus economists' explanations of growth have centred on the widening of markets. They have been tempted into separating growth by stages. Though illuminating, these do not show how the process is set in motion and kept going. National identity has a role in quickening the pace of growth, both through stimulating a spirit of emulation of other countries and in opening the opportunity to plan on a larger national scale.

Congruence of Marxism and the development planners

Limitations seen in current prices as signals for longer term investment, especially in developing countries, led in the 1950s and '60s to a consensus in favour of development planning. In the words of Scitovsky (*Journal of Political Economy*, April 1954): 'the proper coordination of investment decisions requires a signalling device to transmit information about present plans and future considerations as they are determined by present plans; the pricing system fails to provide this. Hence the belief that there is need either for centralized investment planning or for some additional communication system

to supplement the pricing system as a signalling device.' In 1957 Gunnar Myrdal wrote that it was 'universally urged' that low income countries 'should have an overall, integrated national plan. Because of the various deficiencies in a backward country it is also accepted by everyone that the government will have to take over many functions which in most advanced countries in the Western world were left to private business.' (*Economic theory and under-developed regions*, Methuen, London, 1957).

There was a contrary view with P. T. Bauer its most vigorous spokesman. His attacks on such hallowed notions as the vicious circle of poverty, nostrums such as central planning and international aid, and his defences of the decentralised decision-making process of the market were perhaps too strongly expressed to command much support. It was thought that Bauer's views came from his experience of the cash crop economies of West Africa and Malaysia. They were less relevant to stagnant food crop economies in semi-arid areas or where vicious circles did arise out of adverse circumstances as in Bangladesh. There were also clear cases where successful smallholder cash crop industries would not have got started without outside support and intervention, as under the Kenya Tea Development Authority.

By the late 1970s, however, Bauer was back in fashion along with the Chicago school of Friedman. Experience of centralised planning in practice had led to disillusionment. It was based on inadequate information and its management was inefficient. The distorting effects of import and export controls and over-valued exchange rates became evident. Interest shifted back to the efficient allocation of resources and to comparative advantage.

Role of agriculture in economic development

Because of the predominance of agriculture in most tropical economies, the farm sector has a key role in economic development, especially in the initial stages. This contribution has often been underestimated. Planners and economists in developing countries saw that the more advanced economies were nearly all industrialised. They drew the conclusion that the major effort should be directed towards industrialisation, often to the neglect of agriculture. The results have usually been unfortunate. Essential though industrialisation is in economic development, it must be accompanied by progress in agriculture if the economy is not to run into serious difficulties, as in the USSR and Argentina, for example. It is dangerous to argue from historical analogy. There may be important differences in population factors and competition on world markets.

The intensive application of technology to agriculture, reaching into the developing countries as the 'Green Revolution', led to another shift in thought. Use of the new high yielding varieties, together with increased applications of fertiliser and an adequate water regime, resulted in rapid development where conditions were favourable. Attention has since focused on areas where water supplies are uncertain and on the special problems of Africa with a population increase of around 3% per year.

The interlocking relationship between agriculture, population and the growth of employment in other economic sectors have been the subject of major studies. FAO prepared its Indicative World Plan in the 1960s and, in 1981, 'Agriculture at the year 2000'. In 1986 the International Food Policy Research Institute issued a parallel set of projections to the year 2000. Its production and consumption estimates for the developing countries are somewhat higher than those of FAO; also, detailed account is taken of China.

Meeting food requirements

The most obvious and important contribution of agriculture is to meet the additional demand for food resulting from population growth and higher incomes, and to remedy nutritional deficiencies. Because of the 'population explosion' following better health services, developing countries face a far more difficult task now than those countries which went through this stage earlier. Family planning to regulate population growth is being promoted in many countries. However, it will be a long time before it has significant effect.

The population problem becomes more acute as towns and cities grow. Country people will feed themselves except in time of natural disaster or economic distress. The key problem is to feed the towns. The demand for food depends not only on population, but also on income. With higher incomes people consume more food and also more expensive types and better qualities of food which need greater agricultural resources for their production. This implies a shift in the pattern of production towards sugar, fats, livestock products, fruit and vegetables, which are consumed in much larger quantities as incomes rise.

In Table 5.3 we summarise population growth, food production and food use up to the year 2000 for the different developing regions, based on trends 1960–80. The population growth foreseen for Asia at 1.5% per year is well below the expected rate of increase in food production of 1.9%. A surplus of 50 million tonnes is foreseen, including 7 million tonnes in China. In contrast, against a population growth rate of 3.3% in Africa the increase in food production with an average of only 2.1%, leaves a major shortfall. The table also demonstrates the impact of feed use for animal production. This is needed to meet the demands of higher income consumers. While food production in North Africa, the Middle East and Latin America is expected to cover direct consumption up to 2000, there will be a deficit when the use of feed to support livestock is also taken into account. How to meet the projected demand for livestock products, and the rate at which production of these foods could be accelerated in practice, are key issues in these regions. While use of food for livestock is expected to grow also in Africa in relation to direct human use, it is not foreseen as very significant.

In most tropical countries the domestic market is expected to be the main driving force for modernisation, greater productivity of land and labour, and higher farm incomes. Rapidly growing urban centres should pull ever-widening areas of the countryside into the market economy. In the developing countries in 1962, 82 members of the rural population had only 18 non-rural members to support as well as themselves. This will shift to 70 and 30 respectively, then to 60 and 40. Farmers will have to double their output for domestic markets to maintain existing urban consumption patterns.

Table 5.3 Projected growth rates of population, production and domestic use of major food crops, by region, 1980–2000. (*Source*: **International Food Policy Research Institute** (1986) *Food in the third world: past trends and projections to 2000*)

Region	Population	Production	Domestic use			Share of feed in domestic use (%)	
			Total	Food	Feed	1980	2000
Asia	1.5	2.9	2.3	1.9	4.4	12	17
North Africa/Middle East	2.7	2.9	3.8	2.5	6.1	26	39
Sub-Saharan Africa	3.3	2.1	3.6	3.5	5.5	6	9
Latin America	2.1	3.0	3.2	2.3	4.0	40	47

Farmers situated close to cities, served by good transport, or favoured by access to irrigation, will reap the main benefit. Those less well placed may be affected very little.

It is in those areas that feel the pull of monetary demand that new techniques must take over from traditional farming. However, this will only happen if credit, input supply, marketing, transport, processing and agricultural extension systems, as well as prices, keep pace with monetary demand.

Agricultural development should also take account of specific nutritional requirements. Diets in tropical countries tend to be dominated by the basic food crops — rice, maize, millet, sorghum or cassava — which grow best under the prevailing conditions. This often means that the lower income groups, and especially women and children, do not get enough protein. Corrective measures include promoting the production and marketing of other foods which are high in protein, the enrichment of basic foods during processing, and the provision of meals to children at school and other special arrangements for vulnerable groups. Breeding new varieties of the staple food with a higher protein availability will help in the long term.

What happens if agricultural production fails to keep pace with this growth of demand? The first result will be a rise in food prices. As food represents 60% or more of total consumer expenditure in low income countries, the inflationary effect of a rise in food prices can be very serious. People can subsist for long periods with inadequate housing, or insufficient clothing or other manufac- tured goods; but they cannot survive without enough food, let alone continue to work efficiently. Nothing causes unrest more quickly. If food prices rise and production fails to respond, then recourse must be made to imports. Stocks of surplus foods in other countries may be drawn on by special concession. Otherwise, imports must be paid for in foreign exchange. This has then to be diverted from imports of essential capital goods, so slowing down economic development generally.

Providing industrial raw materials
Agricultural raw materials are important for devel- opment because of their export possibilities and the help they can give to industrialisation. Textile manufacturing, leather tanning, rubber curing, timber processing, oilseed crushing, sugar manufac- ture and refining, for example, can be very labour intensive. Large numbers of people may be absorbed and trained to move on later to more skilled types of industrial work. Such industries can often be operated economically on a fairly small scale and require relatively little capital. They can be located in rural areas where the raw material is available, so helping to build up local centres and slow down the drift of population to the big cities. According to FAO estimates, with an agricultural growth rate of 3.4% would go one of 7% in agro- allied industries.

Earning foreign exchange
Demand for imports into the tropical countries, even though concentrated on essentials, is likely to

rise at least as fast as GDP. For many of them, agricultural products account for most of their exports (see Table 5.4). Many countries obtain over 70% of their export earnings from farm products, and some over 90%.

Full exploitation of the productive capacity of the tropical countries for agricultural exports would put amounts onto world markets far in excess of what could be absorbed without a disastrous effect on prices. Increased offerings of cocoa, coffee and tea, for example, would be likely to bring a declining total amount of foreign exchange to each country. Export prospects are better for beef and veal, processed fish and crustacea, fishmeal, processed hard wood, leather, silk and some fruit and vegetables. However, overall agricultural exports from the developing to the developed countries are not expected to grow much more than by 1% per annum. Industrial exports may offer much better prospects for countries with adaptable low cost labour, as demonstrated in Taiwan, Korea and Mauritius. The scope for expanding export earnings from agricultural products is discussed later in this chapter.

Agriculture can also improve the balance of payments by saving on imports. Many developing countries import large quantities of agricultural products. With improved methods of production, processing and marketing a large part of these supplies could be produced economically at home. Half of the agricultural products imported into developing countries during the 1960s were cereals. Almost another fifth were fats, oils and sugar. These last items, and some cereals, can be produced in many tropical countries at economic prices. Comparative advantage must be the criterion. Some proposals for import substitution in national plans involve such high production costs as to damage the interests of the country. Higher food costs affect consumers directly and lead to demands for higher wages. Higher costs of inputs such as fertilisers, or agricultural raw materials, prejudice the marketability of the final output.

Table 5.4 Share of agricultural products in total export earnings: country averages 1975–77. (*Source*: **World Bank**, *Commodity trade and price trends 1979*)

All agricultural products	Individual products (%)
Over 90 %	
Lesotho	Wool 90, wheat 10
Burundi	Coffee 94
Uganda	Coffee 84
Gambia	Groundnuts 56, groundnut oil 34
Over 70%	
Malawi	Tobacco 47, tea 20, sugar 11
Ghana	Cocoa 66, timber 11
Mauritius	Sugar 78
Union of Myanma (Burma)	Rice 46, timber 20
Ivory Coast	Coffee 33, cocoa 19, timber 17
Honduras	Bananas 25, coffee 22, timber 11
Sudan	Cotton 51, groundnuts 18
Sri Lanka	Tea 51, rubber 17
Dominican Republic	Sugar 43, coffee 13
Ethiopia	Coffee 56, hides/skins 10

Source of capital

The classical theory is that since agriculture accounts for the major part of both the labour force and the economic output of most developing countries, taxation and capital formation must both come largely from agriculture. There must, however, be a balance. Economic development does not require a one-way flow of capital out of agriculture. Rather, it calls for a flow of capital into agriculture in the form of fertiliser, water, new seeds, skills, equipment and services in order to obtain a still larger return flow of capital.

If too much capital is taken away from agriculture in taxes, both the incentive and the means to expand production may disappear. This, in turn, would retard industrial development by limiting the growth of the rural market for manufactured goods. Fortunately, many of the developing countries have already passed the stage where agriculture is the only major source of revenue or of investment resources. However, it is in the least-developed countries that it is likely to remain the main source. Since it is hardly practicable to tax subsistence farmers, the main burden usually falls on those who grow crops for export. This may discourage the most productive sector.

By no means all the transfer of resources from agriculture to other sectors takes place through the medium of taxation. Farmers also help to finance trading and manufacturing enterprises by direct investment or through commercial banks, and also through interest payment to creditors in those sectors. FAO has estimated that about 18% of income from agriculture goes into savings in Asia and 22% in Latin America. Expected rates of investment in agriculture were between 9 and 10%. Thus in these countries there would be a substantial margin of savings left over for investment in other sectors.

Source of manpower

While agriculture will continue to be the main source of employment in most tropical countries, a greatly increased productivity is needed for economic growth. Labour can then be released for other occupations. As Adam Smith put it succinctly 200 years ago:

If the labour of one family can provide food for two, the labour of half the society becomes sufficient to provide food for the whole. The other half, therefore, or at least the greater part of them, can be employed in providing other things, or satisfying other wants and fancies of mankind.

This labour must be transferred to other occupations if there is to be a growing market for agricultural products. In a country with 80% of its population in agriculture, each farm family has, as its domestic market, only one quarter of a non-farm family.

Arthur Lewis's famous two-sector model of development was based on unlimited supplies of rural labour. An increasingly profitable industrial sector would provide low wage employment in the towns. In turn, the agricultural sector would feed a growing workforce on the basis of rising productivity. However, this presumed a population growth around 1.5%. Actual population growth has been much faster; it has exceeded the absorptive capacity of developing industrial sectors, reducing the operational relevance of his elegant theory. (See G. M. Meier and D. Seers (eds.) 1984, *Pioneers in development*, Oxford University Press, New York.) A problem now in many tropical countries is the widening pool of urban unemployed. It is exacerbated by traditional education inherited from metropolitan countries. Often it does not provide the balance of skills needed.

Market for industry

In the early stages of economic growth, agriculture with its large share of the population provides the main market for the products of new industries. The faster growing and more prosperous the agriculture of a country, the more quickly it shifts from a subsistence to a monetised basis, and the more favourable are the conditions for industrialisation. This is a part of the two-way development process between agriculture and the rest of the economy.

In the first place, the growth of an urban market is the main stimulus to agricultural development. The availability of manufactured consumer goods then provides a strong incentive for farmers to increase production for the market. Manufacture of farm tools and implements, fertilisers, pesticides and other materials useful for production requisites serves both as an incentive to agriculture and also contributes directly to its productivity. Growth in one sector should stimulate growth in the other. However, in 27 countries the average increase in GWP per caput 1980–85 was less than 1%; for many more it was below 3%. This limits the ability of agriculture to provide markets for industrial sectors. Assuming an income elasticity of demand for non-agricultural goods of 1.0 to 1.5, the rate of growth of such demand including the population effect would be between 3.1 and 3.8% per annum. This makes it all the more important to increase rural incomes through supplementary activities such as public works and village industries.

In addition to a consumption demand for industrial goods and services, agriculture will need more fertilisers, pesticides, tools and equipment. This would also stimulate domestic industry, but part would spill over into imports. This would put additional pressure on the balance of payments. The overall inference is that a shortage of foreign exchange, rather than a savings investment gap, will limit the feasible rate of economic growth. This does not mean that capital is the only limiting factor. Size of the market, raw materials and energy availability, technical and managerial skills are also extremely important.

Other key conditions for achieving economic growth in the tropical world are: continuance of a high level of demand in the already developed countries; pursuit of trade and aid policies designed to supply increasing foreign exchange; and help in developing technical and managerial skills.

Sustainability

This means 'keeping an effort going', 'ability to last out'. It is a vital criterion of development programmes for countries with limited resources. They must be within the capacity of a government and people to maintain. Otherwise, not only will outside aid for over-ambitious programmes be wasted; it will also divert scarce qualified manpower from productive activities that would bring more lasting benefit.

Sustainability has also a much broader perspective. A sustainable development strategy would be one that manages natural and human resources, as well as financial and physical assets, for increasing long term health and well being. It rejects policies and practices that support current living standards by depleting the productive base, including natural resources, and that leave future generations with poorer prospects and greater risks than our own.

Let us look first at the sustainability of institutions and services and then at the environment.

Institutions and services

Declining commodity values following the 1981 recession, accumulated debts and reduced foreign aid left many governments unable to support ongoing programmes and institutions. Scope for increasing domestic taxation was slight. External funds were obtainable on condition that they accepted an International Monetary Fund/World Bank recipe for adjusting the structure of their economy. While often regarded as an unwarranted interference, the action proposed was generally what the countries should have been doing anyway in their own longer run interest. Often their leaders had become trapped under political commitments and urban pressures. They were afraid to take remedial action because it could mean their own downfall.

Characteristic elements of a structural adjustment programme have been:

(a) a realistic exchange rate;
(b) fiscal and price incentives for both exports and the production of domestic food supplies;
(c) timely allocation of foreign exchange for transport and processing equipment, fuel and spare parts, agricultural inputs and incentive consumer goods for rural population;
(d) promotion of competitive marketing of agricultural inputs and products, reducing the role of high-cost or loss-making parastatals;
(e) strengthening of rural market networks to bring consumer good and input supply and output purchasing enterprises nearer to farmers;
(f) realistic rates of interest for agricultural credit so favouring the mobilisation of domestic savings;
(g) saving on management by consolidating overlapping institutions and hiving off to local beneficiaries road maintenance, treatment of animal diseases and other services within their technical capacity.

Overall, these measures favour enterprise in exporting and food production; they shift the balance away from urban residents and the bureaucracy.

Environment

Pressures on the environment stem from diverse roots: poverty, ignorance, greed, custom, climatic insufficiency — and development itself. Agricultural growth calls for irrigation and drainage, clearing forests, and using fertilisers and pesticides, all of which can cause environmental damage. Poverty is the worst form of 'pollution', yet raising the level of living means modifying the natural environment, often perilously in the tropical countries. Inherently they are more susceptible to environmental degradation or ecological imbalance than temperate zones. Burgeoning populations strain the supporting capacity of the land. So overgrazing leads to deterioration of the feed base; lack of water, or misuse of it, to desertification; and satisfying the need for fuelwood (as much as a tonne per family each year) to deforestation, thence to erosion, siltation and floods. Construction of roads, irrigation systems and processing plants can exacerbate these problems or create new hazards.

The critical issue is how to avoid or mitigate damage to the environment without slowing the pace of progress. The costs resulting from adverse environmental change can be enormous. Measures to forestall environmental degradation include:

(a) establishing forest belts and protected grasslands to control desertification;
(b) cutting and replanting controls for woodlands and the use of alternative sources of energy for cooking, for example rural electrification and biomass energy, and improvement of cooking stoves;
(c) treating irrigation canals to control mollusc hosts to schistosomiasis;
(d) livestock controls to prevent overgrazing and competition with wildlife migration;
(e) pricing of agricultural chemicals and power equipment to discourage excessive, profligate and inappropriate use;
(f) training of personnel to enhance their sensitivity to environmental concerns.

Applying such measures should be pragmatic, adapted to local conditions, not the implementation of rigid standards formulated elsewhere. The capital outlays involved may be small. Under-employed rural labour can be engaged with food aid. The great effort required is of central and local government to maintain such measures against continuing pressures to relax them.

Socio-economic factors affecting development

Development moves labour out of agriculture, but how are the mass of people who are dependent on it, to live in the meantime? The percentage of the total population engaged in agriculture is falling. Even so, the absolute number of people so engaged will continue to rise as populations increase. Yet in Asia, where the largest numbers are involved, most agricultural holdings are already too small for economic working and labour is under-employed for much of the year. There is little new land left to bring under cultivation. To make the problem worse there are not enough jobs away from farms to employ all who would leave farming and take up other work.

The employment problem

This problem may prove more intractable than that of food supply. With unemployment comes human misery, social unrest and political instability. The greatest threat to technological advance is the social disorganisation which could result from an increasing number of people with no means of obtaining an adequate living. A high rate of investment is needed to absorb an increasing number of non-agricultural people into productive employment.

Mechanisation can be discouraged in areas where there is surplus labour. Import restrictions and taxes on tractors and other labour-saving devices can induce farmers to use more labour by reducing its relative cost. Often, however, with the help of power and machinery, land may be cleared more thoroughly, ploughed more deeply and cropped more intensively with more labour used as a result. In Africa the expansion of rice growing often depends on the availability of tractors to carry out cultivations that must be completed during a limited season.

It is retrogressive to adopt employment policies that slow down the rate of economic growth. This only makes the problem worse in the long term. In India, the importation of the equipment used in the solvent extraction processing of oil seed was restricted at one time in order to protect the process as a village industry. The result was less incentive to grow oilseeds; wastage of oil and protein; and an inability to take advantage of expanding demand.

Employment in agriculture can be increased by changes in type of production such as the adoption of more labour-intensive crop and livestock raising. Examples are a shift from extensive grazing to intensive production of young stock, fat animals and dairy products; a shift out of grain into the production of fruit and vegetables, oilseeds and other cash crops; and setting up integrated plant/animal systems such as cattle under coconuts, crops/pigs/fish, etc. Notable for labour-intensity in East Africa have been the production of cashew nuts, fresh fruit and vegetables, and flowers. Not only does their production and harvesting call for detailed attention, but the various marketing operations — packing, quality control and processing — are also labour intensive. Such changes in the labour-absorptive capacity of agriculture can be brought about by provision of irrigation water; measures to put the land into the hands of family farmers and groups managers who will be more interested in using the labour available; shifts in exchange rates and in export and other duties on farm output; selective credit policies; and provision of the necessary extension and marketing assistance.

Labour which is unemployed seasonally or totally can be used to improve the rural infrastructure; to build roads and bridges, irrigation canals, drainage ditches, water reservoirs, farm buildings, access roads, schools and other communal buildings; and to plant fruit and forest trees. Surplus food, available free through the World Food Programme and other food aid channels, can be used in part payment of wages. Cash outlays on organisation and supplementary payments will be needed. But more important is the generation of social pressures to encourage work: 'slogans for the leaders and whips for the laggard'. There is a double pay-off in a popular sense of participation in development and the addition to productive capacity. In the meantime income should be distributed more evenly and widely. This will lead to greater consumer demand. However, care is needed to avoid flooding the available markets with extra output, which will lower prices. Consumer education and internal marketing should be strengthened at the same time, to promote demand for labour-intensive livestock, fruit and vegetable products as far as incomes permit.

Allegiances and resentments

Social factors may be major obstacles to change and development but they also favour it. First let us look at the barriers.

Many people have strong and deep feelings as to which people and groups deserve their allegiance, and which people they mistrust and oppose. The struggle to survive has induced two deeply ingrained attitudes: village loyalties, and even stronger bonds of kinship.

Village loyalties take the form of exchanges of mutual help among members of a village, or within clan groups living in several villages. Family ties are even stronger. Usually they extend to many more family members than husband, wife and children. With this often goes the view that official positions and special training are instruments for use against others, to the private advantage of their possessors. The attitude that family and village groups should be helped and outsiders preyed upon, can lead people to feel they are acting quite properly in cheating strangers, and making dishonest business commitments. In this way the loyalties of economically backward societies can become a formidable barrier to easy information and market exchanges with people they do not know well. Services can only be organised on a reciprocal basis between people willing to deal as fairly with others as with their friends and relatives. It has been claimed that the reason for bureaucratic corruption being so rare in Japan is that the prevailing culture extended the relationship of the family group to include the Emperor and the whole people.

Confidence in the stability of a government and its ability to protect individuals and their property is another great influence for development. Assurance that law and order will be maintained may be more important than observance of democratic election procedures. However, a politically powerful elite might maintain institutions that perpetuate backwardness. Thus a government must not only be strong and stable, it must also be oriented towards progress. The problem with many of the 'one party systems' through which stability is maintained, is their dependence on a single personality. He may be progressive at one stage in his career and reactionary at another. It may require some near catastrophe of famine or revolution before a particular governing class will turn to a new set of goals.

Social discontent can be a potent factor for development. Conspicuous examples of some people acquiring new possessions and ways of living spur on others to want the same things and to break

Fig. 5.2 Public office and family ties

felt they could do better than alien rulers in educating their people, bringing them into commercial society and securing a better level of living for all. Once in power these leaders are under pressure to keep their promises. They have to build up a feeling for the country, for the government and for the party behind the government, in order to counteract the traditional influences for separation: tribal, regional, class and kinship interests. Many of the leaders of newly-independent countries stand apart from the class or tribal system of the old social structure, but they may later have to appease such interests to keep in power, and this favourable factor diminishes.

Livestock raising and marketing in tropical countries is greatly influenced by socio-economic traditions. For many people in savanna and mountain Africa, ownership of cattle is a prestige symbol. It represents a command over resources upon which the livelihood of a whole social group has been founded. The social sanctions which limit the slaughter of livestock to special occasions, or prohibit it altogether (as in some groups in India) also reflect a need to preserve capital vital to the existence of the group. With better disease control and more security, traditions which were developed to maintain a herd can lead to serious over-grazing. Old-established attitudes may also keep livestock owners apart from sedentary crop producers when a direct link between livestock raising and the production of fodder crops could result in higher quality animals coming to market in a much shorter time.

Linking the village with progressive society

One of the biggest problems in rural development is securing an effective link between the progressive elements in society and the village tied to backward concepts by fear of new ideas and suspicion of outsiders' motives. There is no gain in sending into such a village an extension officer who is unable to identify local needs, and who recommends standard measures for improvement without first finding out if the associated conditions support them. Specific new techniques must be fitted into a closely linked series of associated practices.

A number of steps must be taken at the same time and a number of services must be working

such bonds as hold them back. Contact with Western universities and commercial enterprises often provokes dissatisfaction with low affluence and poor technical efficiency. From discontent can come revolution and a new authority committed to changing the old systems and quickening the pace of advance.

Recent achievement of independence has been a major force both for and sometimes against progress. The leaders of the independence movements

163

efficiently together if the expected benefits of change are to accrue. Recognition of this has led to the concept of the minimum complementary set of services. In combination they make it profitable to use improved technologies by linking rural villages and the outside world in a network of service exchanges. Commonly they include:

(a) input supply channels which provide improved seeds, fertilisers, insecticides, implements, tools and other production requisites;
(b) marketing channels that use methods which protect the interests of both buyers and sellers;
(c) extension services backed by applied research that enables them to provide advice to farmers which is effective under their particular condition;
(d) credit systems that enable farmers to obtain funds when needed to meet production outlays and essential consumption requirements;
(e) where relevant, irrigation agencies with staff able to allocate water supplies channelled from major dams and rivers to individual farms.

A human problem in providing these local support services is the reluctance of many government officers to work in rural areas. The man who has become educated and technically qualified feels that he has left his village behind. This is not merely a matter of material comfort, but also one of mental satisfaction and personal prestige. Officers serving in outlying areas could be offered special allowances and improved prospects of promotion. The long term solution lies in improving both living conditions in rural areas and communications with the cities.

Maximum use must also be made of local leaders and organisations already based in the villages. Farmers' participation that can transmit to authority advice on how these services are performing and, if necessary, take on some of them as a competing channel, can put new vitality into existing systems.

Strategies for rural development

The concentration of economic power and social and political influence in the hands of a traditional landlord or chief can be a major cause of rural backwardness. The chief may be well satisfied with the income and prestige accruing to him under existing conditions. He is then likely to resist, by all possible means, the spread of ideas and the implementation of programmes designed to bring about changes. The influence of religious leaders is often mobilised in this direction. They may see the spread of technical education, independent thought and greater economic mobility as reducing their control over rural people.

While it is not proposed that any country should follow one particular route, three main courses of rural development have been identified.

Modernisation strategies Technologies and entrepreneurial methods developed elsewhere are adapted to local conditions without specific reforms in social structure. Social changes are to be expected, however, as opportunities to take up new occupations and to move through the economy cause a shift in the balance of income and social power in favour of those who are most active and enterprising. Overall economic progress in countries pursuing such a strategy can be relatively fast. This is partly because they are attractive to foreign investment and so do not suffer from shortages of capital. Notable examples have been Malaysia, Kenya, Ivory Coast, Brazil and Colombia.

Reformist strategies These are based on legislative action to eliminate large scale landlord control by allocating holdings above a specific size to former tenants and to landless agricultural workers. Supporting services, credit, extension, marketing and input supply are provided up to the capacity of the country concerned. There is no specific policy for changing social relationships, but this results from the new status of the former tenants and the impact of the government sponsored supporting services. The former landlord continues to farm part of his land directly; often he does this more intensively and becomes a leader in demonstrating new technology.

Illustrations of the application of this strategy are India, Egypt, Venezuela and Taiwan.

Strategies of deep structural change Here profound changes in the entire rural social structure are regarded as essential for the acceleration of economic growth and for equal participation by the whole rural population. Development is planned not only to increase output but also to benefit groups that in the past were left behind. Through cooperatives and political organisations, agricultural workers are given a strong voice in the control of land, and credit and marketing. They can only be effective in such a role if they have the necessary education and skills. So widespread training in farm management, accounting, cooperative and business administration is essential. Agricultural technicians can then be recruited from the whole range of rural people and so reinforce the desired shift in social weights.

The expropriation policies often associated with such a strategy may restrict access to international capital. The capital needed for implementation will then have to be generated internally at the cost of a temporary lowering of living standards. Decisions based on dogma rather than experience and restricted scope for individual initiative may also slow the pace of growth. In counterbalance, however, is the much more intensive capitalisation of labour, feasible with devoted leadership and unhesitating compulsion. Examples of the use of this approach are China, Vietnam and Cuba.

The intention of this section was to examine the interplay of social and economic factors in development. In most of the tropical countries agriculture must provide employment for an increasing rural population. This can be done by fostering more intensive lines of production. Traditional attitudes which restrict the scope for development must be modified. Dissatisfaction with existing conditions can be a potent force for development. It impells young people to seek new ways of earning a living with better opportunities and to participate in decision-making on matters that affect their welfare. There are several strategies available for mobilising latent human resources into progressive activity.

Social considerations have a vital part in the development process. But it is difficult to assess their weight. Do the complaints of individuals and groups count more, for example, than the steady accretion of economic advantage to a silent majority? Certainly development will proceed fastest where the bulk of the rural population feel that they share in the benefits.

Land tenure systems

Land tenure systems are legal or customary relationships between government, society groups and individuals, concerning rights and duties in the use of land. They have developed over time to meet the practical needs of crop and livestock production in the way preferred by the dominant elements in a particular society. They may also be changed by government through implementing a land reform programme.

Land tenure systems are important to economic development because they influence the application of labour, capital and entrepreneurship. For example, without some security of tenure, land users will apply only those inputs that bring immediate benefits; they will have no interest in preserving soil fertility or building up equipment to make the land increasingly productive which would add to the capital resources of the country. This holds good not only for inputs such as fertilisers which result in a residual accretion of fertility after the immediate crop has been taken; it applies also to the use of labour. Improvement of water supplies, terracing and drainage, maintenance of farm buildings, and a variety of similar tasks are often undertaken in what might otherwise be leisure time, if there is security of tenure. A land tenure system should provide incentives to stimulate production and productivity. For them to be effective there should be flexibility in decision-making and scope for innovation.

The variety of different forms of land tenure is almost endless. The major types are: customary tenure including nomadic grazing rights; cash- or crop-sharing tenancies; owner operators; cooperative or group farming; and state farms.

Customary tenure
In this form the right to graze or cultivate agricultural land lies with groups or tribes. Individuals are allocated pieces of land by the chief of the group according to its customs. The land belongs to the tribe and cannot be alienated to individual members, but all members are entitled to work on portions of it.

This system is widespread in Africa, South-east Asia and the South Pacific. It has the basic defect that individuals cannot count on receiving the same piece of land each year. However, ways can be found round this, if the advantages are clear. Thus farmers planting cocoa trees in Ghana, for example, are allowed to retain their investment and pass the trees on to their children.

Systems of customary tenure can be modified by government action. Customary rights may be assumed in their entirety by a government which may then lease land to individual farmers, as is done in Nigeria. In Kenya, Malawi and Niger, individual properties have been created and land titles registered.

Special arrangements can be made to meet the production and processing requirements of particular crops. A legal basis has been provided in the Benin Republic, for example, for grouping sufficient oil palm units round a processing plant to keep it supplied with raw material. Holders of rights to the land making up the palm oil unit receive a rent and can also work on it for additional payment.

Nomadic and transhumant pastoral systems are based on continual or seasonal movements of livestock in search of grazing and water. They are common around the edges of the Sahara and in other dry areas offering limited grazing opportunities. The harsh conditions there determine the type of animals that can be raised, and the kinds of movements that must be undertaken.

Dependence on natural grazing has various limitations. The forage available can vary greatly from one place to another and between seasons. Watering points are often few and far between. In an effort to use all the forage available, and as a precaution against losses when there is a drought, herders tend to overstock. This causes a progressive deterioration of the grass cover, especially near watering places. The movements of nomadic herdsmen may also upset settled farmers bordering their territory.

The central issue is to balance stocking rates with the carrying capacity of the land and at the same time assure the nomad family a decent living. This usually involves establishment of an optimum size of range unit per family, supported by stocking controls, provision of improved watering and disease control facilities, supplementary sources of feed, and better marketing organisation. In Kenya,

one community of traditional cattle herders, the Masai, are enclosing their land with fences. In general, these pastoral economies are in crisis and pastoral populations are decreasing.

Fig. 5.3 'How can we keep these nomads off our growing crop?'

Cash tenancies or crop-sharing

Many tenancies stem from feudal relationships. A conqueror assigns land to his leaders in return for their allegiance. They give it to their own supporters who become the local landlords. The next step is to rent the land to people who will cultivate it, and return a share of the crop to the landlord.

Share cropping is sometimes criticised as reducing the tenant's incentive to apply production inputs, particularly fertiliser, at the optimum rate. Half the benefit of his outlay in fertiliser, for example, will go to the landlord. Similarly, the landlord will have less incentive to make improvements because he will receive only half the benefit. Thus too few resources will be applied both in production of crops and improvement of the land. Against this it is argued that an intelligent landlord and tenant will find a joint incentive in obtaining the maximum benefit from their land. The apparent low level of living of many crop-sharing tenants usually reflects low opportunity costs of labour rather than specific ill treatment by landlords. Competition for access to land forces up the terms that tenants accept. This is borne out by the more favourable conditions prevalent near Asian cities which offer good markets for farm products as well as non-farm employment to drain away excess farm population.

The most favourable feature of crop-sharing is the division of risks. Since it requires more supervision than other tenancies, crop sharing is likely to be adopted where this factor is outweighed by the advantages of sharing the risk. The system developed for the Gezira in Sudan has attracted much attention. A public board controls the planting, picking, and marketing of cotton and provides seed, pest control and other services on credit. Tenants are required to plant cotton on a certain percentage of their land; on the remainder they can plant other crops for their own use or disposal. Half of the cotton sales proceeds go to the tenant; the balance is kept as payment for land, irrigation water, services and taxes.

The tenant paying a fixed money rent bears all the risk of a crop failure, unless he can persuade the landowner to forgo part of the rent that year. However, he has greater incentive to apply additional inputs, labour and attention, in so far as all proceeds in excess of a fixed rent accrue to him. Competition for land can put him in a weak bargaining position with the owner regarding the amount of rent to be paid and renewal of the tenancy. Most developed countries have taken measures to protect tenants against exploitation on this account. These include legal protection against eviction without due cause; provision for payment of compensation for improvements made during the tenancy; and the fixing of rents at specific levels related to the value of major crops. The great advantage of an effectively supervised tenancy system is on the side of capital requirements. There is no need for a farmer to possess capital to buy land. Whatever capital he has can be applied directly to crop and livestock production.

Owner-operators

Under this system the land is owned by individuals who farm it directly with family and employed labour. This form of tenure offers good prospects of maximising labour inputs. The quality of management and the application of capital vary with the situation of the individual operator. Many are short of working capital because they have so much tied up in their land. The efficiency of this system can be reduced, moreover, by diseconomies in the use of machinery, as in the Indian Punjab. It can also be prejudiced by continuing sub-division of farms through inheritance until they are too small to permit rational use of available technology, or of the family labour available. This has occurred in Egypt, for example, and in many parts of South-east Asia.

Cooperative farming

The Soviet model is the best known example of this type of tenure. The *kolkhoz* or collective farm comprises the land and people of a whole village, or of several villages combined. It is directed by a committee with an elected chairman. Members are employed for a stipulated number of days, and share in the net earnings. In addition, they each have their own house and an individual plot not exceeding 0.5 hectares or 0.2 hectares of land under irrigation.

The collective farms of the USSR have not demonstrated high productivity in comparison with other systems under similar conditions. In the late 1980s they began leasing out operations to smaller units. Lack of individual incentive and difficulties in management may be continuing drawbacks to cooperative farming.

The cooperative model is most effective where it opens the way to significant economies of scale. This has been demonstrated in Bulgaria and Hungary where large collectives employ specialised managers .and apply advanced technology. In China, with mass hand labour involved, the cooperative system was abandoned after 30 years of perseverance. Parcels of land have been contracted out to family units by production group on condition that they supply fixed quantities of produce. Output in excess of the levy can be consumed or sold as they wish. Allocation is for 15 years to encourage investment in improvements. Equitable allocation of the various qualities of land available resulted in families receiving a number of small scattered pieces. Even so, agricultural output went up by 30% and peasant family incomes doubled.

State farms

State farms are generally set up to carry on a particular activity, e.g. seed multiplication, animal breeding, according to specific requirements. Under the Russian system the *sovkos* or state farm is intended to serve as a production model for the cooperative. It is also used to achieve specific increases in output required under development plans. Working capital is provided and a manager is appointed by the government. His instructions are binding, though keeping the goodwill of his staff helps greatly. In the USSR, state farms are autonomous bodies, with considerable latitude in organising their own operations. The workers have much the same status as an industrial labourer. Together with the manager they receive bonuses in addition to their normal wages if results exceed given targets.

A state farm can, of course, be run just like a plantation operated by a large commercial enterprise which employs a resident manager. Its efficiency depends on adequate capital, the quality of management employed and autonomy in operational decisions.

Land reform

This is a fundamental change in institutionalised relationships among people with respect to land. It can take a wide range of forms depending on the situation to be remedied. Where land holding is subject to tribal custom, the goal is to develop a system which encourages private or group investment. Individualisation of tenure is one solution. Assignment of titles to various kinds of groups is also being tried. Lines of reform for nomadic grazing have already been indicated.

There are substantial parts of Asia, Latin America and Africa where landholding is still feudal. Secure tenure for the man who actually cultivates the land is the main reform needed. In some cases there is legal protection of tenants against excessive rents, arbitrary evictions and failure to compensate for improvements. In practice this may not suffice because of the landlords' social and political influence at the local level. Usually the effective step is conversion of former tenants into full proprietors with government provision of necessary equipment and supporting services. Land in excess of a specified upper limit is distributed to former tenants and landless agricultural workers. In Egypt, this limit is about 20 hectares per person and 40 hectares per family. The problem in Egypt, in India, and elsewhere, is that to give all heads of families working in agriculture their own plot would bring the average farm size below that which permits efficient use of available technology. Indeed, most reform legislation prevents further division of the units assigned to individuals, and controls their sale or use as collateral for loans. The multiplication of individual units also magnifies the task of extension, credit, and input supply services. To make possible the use of advantageous cultivation and pest control methods, compulsory grouping for cotton rotation has been introduced in Egypt (see Fig. 5.4).

Land reform also includes consolidation: bringing together scattered individual holdings. This is difficult and slow. Where it is carried out on a voluntary basis a consensus is needed. It affects the livelihood and attachments of many small proprietors. Their holdings may still be very small even after consolidation.

Fig. 5.4 Grouping of holdings for cotton production
(a) Each shaded area denotes a grouping of villagers' plots

(b) The individual plots in the shaded area labelled X in (a)

Implementation of land reforms

It would be preferable to prepare for land reform programmes carefully, and train the necessary staff in advance. Most major land reform legislation, however, tends to be carried through rather abruptly with the coming to power of a new government committed to such a policy. It is therefore all the more important that those concerned with land reform programmes are aware of what is involved.

Financial and human resources are needed for the following:

(a) survey of existing ownership pattern;
(b) payment of compensation to former owners;
(c) redistribution of landownership;

(d) administration of the reform and provision of supporting services;
(e) construction of physical equipment in reform areas;
(f) provision of working capital for new farm units;
(g) initial losses in output and subsidies to new farmers.

Payment for land taken over from private owners is generally made in the form of a long term government bond. Funds to pay these off on maturity can be obtained through annual payments by the new owners.

A special agency to manage the land reforms needs to be established and its staff trained. In addition to surveying, reallocating and equipping the land, the agency will most probably have to set up special extension, input supply, credit, and marketing services to help the new farmers. The cost is likely to be heavy initially but direct expenditure on reform management should decline rapidly after a few years. Although the credit, supply, marketing and similar services will be a continuing requirement, they can in part at least, be made to pay for themselves.

In practice costs tend to be higher than necessary because the physical facilities provided are more elaborate than farmers need; the work is carried out in a hurry with public funds; and because of the tendency for bureaucracies to proliferate.

How far land reform results in a decline in production during the years immediately following reform, depends on the nature of the reform and how it is carried out. Transference of title to tenants and crop-sharers already on the land and accustomed to taking management decisions, involves minimal disturbance. Assignment of such responsibility to workers alone, or to groups who are accustomed only to carrying out instructions, is likely to create a serious hiatus unless major decisions are taken for them and the necessary support provided. Generally government services replace the former owners in this role: they need time to become effective.

Land reform should create farms large enough to provide their operators with satisfactory income under the prevailing conditions. This will step up the rate of capital formation in the economy as a whole. However, the major benefit is usually political. Pressure for land reform originates in social discontent. If such pressures are not eased, then the cost to the country in tension and strife may be great indeed. Most land reforms achieve a substantial redistribution of income-producing resources. Where, previously, high incomes were confined to a small elite and the consumption of the mass of the population was low, redistribution can give a great fillip to demand. The long term benefits of a broader rural income base and the replacement of dependent tenants by self-reliant farmers are a stimulus to industrial and commercial growth, and a social and political climate offering better prospects for peaceful development.

Agricultural banking and credit

Credit means access to capital for which payment will be made at a later due. Through credit, people are enabled to use capital at the time they need it. Interest is the price paid to mobilise the credit and to direct it into profitable channels. To illustrate this one may consider the relationship between a young man starting to farm and an older man with accumulated capital. The first wants money to buy equipment and supplies. With these he expects to increase output enough to be able to repay the loan and interest, as well as cover his living expenses. The second is looking for a source of income. He is willing to lend his money provided that he is sure of being repaid and receiving some reward in addition.

There are three types of credit that a farmer may need:

(a) short term credit (one production season) to pay for fertiliser, labour and sometimes to cover living costs while waiting for crops to mature and be sold;
(b) medium term credit (up to 3 or 5 years) to pay for irrigation pumps, equipment, work animals and breeding stock;
(c) long term credit (up to 10 to 15 years) to buy land, establish tree crops, construct buildings, terraces and major irrigation works.

Associated with agriculture are the credit needs of enterprises engaging in the marketing and storage of farm products and the supplying of inputs. They need seasonal credit to cover the period between acquiring products and being paid for them, and longer term credit to pay for transport, stores, office and other facilities.

The risks and costs of lending to agriculture can often be high:

(a) farm output can vary greatly under the impact of climate, plant diseases, etc.;
(b) the prices obtained by farmers for their produce can also vary;
(c) farm units are often small and dispersed, involving high administrative overhead and transaction costs.

To cover the cost of the funds, management expenses and the risk involved, interest rates on loans to small scale agriculture must necessarily be relatively high. They are high also where there is continuing inflation because the lender knows that he will be repaid money that will buy less than when he lent it.

Sources of credit for agriculture

In most countries there is now a range of sources to which the farmer can go for credit. These include relatives and friends, informal savings clubs, private moneylenders, traders who make advances to attract business, commercial banks and specialised agricultural and cooperative banks.

Family, relatives and friends These are usually the most immediate sources of credit but they may not be able to lend the amounts needed at the right time.

Savings clubs In many countries there are traditions of group saving to meet recognised credit needs. Generally they were primarily social. However, savings clubs in Zimbabwe, for example, have enabled members to take advantage of price discounts on fertiliser.

Private moneylenders and banks These begin as individual enterprises looking for profitable ways of using liquid capital in hand. Because of their contacts and reliability, they may be approached by people with capital to handle their surplus funds, and in this way private commercial banks have grown up. They have played a vital role in West Africa in financing the local purchasing of agricultural produce for export. On personal reputation and thumbprint signature, one Nigerian groundnut trader could obtain a $12 000 advance from Barclays Bank at the beginning of the buying season, with renewals as produce was delivered into recognised storage.

Generally, however, commercial banks are less interested in lending to small scale agriculture because of the small amounts involved in relation to the management cost. For this reason, and because the banks were often in foreign ownership, there have been moves to nationalise them, as in India, Sudan and Tanzania. By pooling the resources of competing private banks, the nationalised banking system in India has opened a large number of branches in rural areas. The goal is to have one for every 5 000 to 10 000 people. In Latin American countries such as Colombia and Venezuela, and in the Philippines, a wider spread of private banks in local ownership is being encouraged.

Input suppliers and marketing agencies The costs and risks of lending to small farmers are greatly reduced when they agree to sell their produce through the lender and he can deduct the loan repayment from the sales proceeds. This is the strength of the merchant moneylender. Generally he knows both the farmer and the products well. He can judge repayment capacity and assess cash flow prospects of borrowers better than banks. Funds for weddings and other social expenses can also be obtained from him. Such moneylenders are often criticised for their interest charges, but it is not easy to evolve cooperative or public organisations that can provide the same service at any less cost.

Linking of credit and marketing is easiest under vertically coordinated production/marketing channels associated with centralised processing, e.g. for sugar, cotton, oil seeds, milk, tea, tobacco. It is less secure for food crops, livestock or fish, where trader/farmer relations may be less stable. There is no major problem in combining credit supply with marketing if farmers can choose between alternative offers and are fully informed on credit costs and product prices. They can then compare the lower price likely to be paid by the trader advancing credit against a commitment to supply produce with the price to be expected elsewhere and the cost (and ease) of borrowing from an institution.

The advantage to the farmer of a credit and marketing contract is security of outlet and easy access to the inputs he needs. The marketing enterprise is sure of receiving the kind of supplies required both to satisfy its customers and operate processing facilities to capacity.

Where there is competition between distributors of inputs such as fertilisers, a farmer may be able to obtain them on short term credit from a local agent who is himself financed by the distributor. Credit for several years may be obtained from suppliers of farm machinery and equipment where repossession is feasible in the event of default.

Farmers' cooperatives These can provide the same services, if they have access to funds. On the whole they act as lending and collection channels for credit supplied by a centrally sponsored cooperative or agricultural cooperative bank. In China, Korea and to a lesser extent in India they are a major source of farm credit for input purchases.

Agricultural banks Specialised agricultural banks have been established in many tropical countries using government capital. Problems of access to the bank and elaborate lending procedures limit the usefulness of these banks to the smaller farmers. Without its own branch structure, an agricultural bank must either work through local cooperatives, particularly for short term credit, or else carry its service to villages in collaboraton with local authority. Some way of involving the local community seems essential if a centralised system is to operate effectively at the local level. While the purpose of establishing specialised agricultural banks is to ensure that farmers' needs receive full attention, the rural bank that offers financial services to any creditworthy borrower seems to have greater prospects of viability. There is complementarity in the needs of farm and non-farm rural borrowers: the burden of overhead costs is spread.

Governments of tropical countries, assisted by external aid, have made great efforts to expand institutional credit services to agriculture. Nevertheless, in the mid-1980s less than 50% of the farmers in Asia were served by them and in Africa only 10 to 20%.

Mobilisation of capital

Under predominantly subsistence conditions, the only important source of capital is non-monetary investment in land improvement or additions to cattle herds. With development, individuals begin to accumulate savings in cash and governments to collect revenue. Funds may also be obtained from more advanced economies.

The main sources from which capital can be mobilised to finance agriculture are as follows:

(a) private savings of farmers from their own operations;
(b) savings of private lenders and investors;
(c) savings of individuals and groups in banks and credit institutions;
(d) government domestic revenues;

(e) transfer of private foreign capital to direct investments in agricultural production, processing, marketing and provision of requisites;
(f) bilateral and multilateral loans and grants to governments.

To channel private funds into agriculture there must be a banking network reaching into the rural areas, and oriented to the financing opportunities available there. Farming must also be profitable; this requires that prices for agricultural products are attractive. In practice, higher returns on capital with less risk and cost have often been available from construction and commerce; private domestic funds have tended to flow in this direction. Foreign private investment in tropical countries also depends on favourable conditions, the political climates, and freedom to move capital and earnings.

A government can direct funds into agriculture in the following ways:

(a) By organising compulsory savings. Taxes can be levied on various economic activities. Compulsory savings from agriculture itself can be realised through the prices set by marketing boards or fertiliser supply agencies; through rates charged for the use of irrigation water; or by special development levies.
(b) By requiring that commercial banks lend a minimum proportion, e.g. 10%, of their funds to agriculture.
(c) By expanding the amount of credit available through its central bank. Loans made to agriculture by retail banks can be rediscounted soon after they are made, so permitting the retail bank to make further loans. Such expansionary credit policies accelerate the pace of development, but inflation may follow. The damaging effects of too much inflation must always be kept in mind. Unless citizens have confidence in the domestic value of a currency, they cannot be expected to save large amounts nor to make their savings available for use by others.

The primary role of a central bank is to watch over the financial state of a country's economy as a whole. It tries to keep the overall volume of bank credit at the highest level compatible with economic stability. The Indian Reserve Bank, which is the central bank of that country, has channelled large sums to agricultural financing institutions; it has also guaranteed loans by other banks. This has been done without much inflation because of the flexibility of the economy including ample supplies of under-employed labour.

Substantial capital for agriculture has been supplied to many countries via bilateral and multilateral grants, loans and gifts of grains, fertilisers and other products for local sale and as a basis for revolving credit funds. Agricultural loans by the World Bank 1975–85 amounted to $33 000 million by 1984. Conditions of obtaining such loans are that the country has met its obligations regarding previous loans; can designate an organisation competent to channel the loan into effective use; and can provide the necessary supporting services.

The scope for mobilising capital from within domestic agriculture has seemed so limited in many tropical countries that the government was regarded as the main source of new finance. It is politically tempting for a government to offer credit at very low rates of interest to favoured sets of borrowers. This does not, however, foster the development of a self-sustaining system. An ample supply of foreign capital and easy access to refinance facilities of the central bank at concessionary rates has discouraged banks from mobilising voluntary financial savings. Loans to farmers at interest rates far below the cost of providing the funds, taking into account inflation, encourages misuse of such credit. The national banking system is deprived of the deposits which people might make if local banking facilities were available and interest rates on savings attractive.

To farmers, it is more important that they can obtain a loan on time, with little formality, and for a convenient period, than that the interest rate be low. Under the Comilla (Bangladesh) Rural Development Project a levy of 5% was put on all institutional credit to help meet administrative and supervisory costs. This brought up the effective interest rate from 9% to 15%, and still it was accepted by the farmers.

Rather than provide credit which is so cheap that the supply tends to dry up, governments must look for ways of building up self-supporting savings and credit systems.

Credit management

Experience has shown that institutional credit to small-scale farmers cannot be provided in isolation. It must be integrated with a whole set of services. Essential for an effective production credit system are:

(a) a marketing system which provides a regular supply of inputs to farmers, and a specific outlet for their produce with fair prospects of assessing the price they will obtain;
(b) an extension service which can show farmers how to use credit to the best advantage under their conditions;
(c) a system of land tenure which assures stable occupancy and enables a farmer to benefit from improvements he makes on the land;
(d) a legal (i.e. clearly established and recognised) basis for using credit that is fair to both lender and borrower — it should be possible to borrow quickly and simply;
(e) recognition by the farmers themselves of the importance of business character as a basis for credit, i.e. the prompt payment of interest and instalments, provision of notice of any delays, and ability to handle borrowed funds wisely.

Where farmers are not familiar with the additional inputs that can be obtained with credit, and the changes in methods needed to take full advantage of them, a qualified adviser should visit them and discuss their plans in detail. This is much better than lending on the basis of a standard formula without direct knowledge of the farm concerned. The problem, however, in providing this degree of supervision lies in the number of specialised staff required and the cost.

Insurance of farmers against loss of crops or livestock through drought, floods or disease would also reduce credit repayment risks. It is easiest when restricted to the cash outlay on the crop and to specific natural hazards such as hail, flood, hurricanes. Where large numbers of small farmers are involved the costs are generally too high.

An effective credit system quickens the pace of development. It mobilises capital and enables it to move to where it can be employed most usefully. A key problem in tropical agriculture is how to arrange this so as to serve the needs of the smaller

Fig. 5.5 A detailed application, or credit for the asking?

farmers. Farm production planning, allocation of loans, input supply, marketing, and steps to attract savings, must all be integrated. So far as the farmer is concerned, the procedure must be simple.

Development planning

Planning is the putting together of development proposals that are interrelated. Because each helps the other, the development process should go faster with planning. There is less wastage of human and material effort than when all initiatives are left to individuals acting independently. For this to hold good, the development proposals must be attuned to the productive resources, management capacity and social structure of the country. Flexibility is also important; otherwise longer term projects may stagnate under short term financial constraints.

Putting plans into effect is more difficult with agriculture than in other fields. Production is usually in the hands of many small independent farmers. Their traditions are slow to change and crop yields can vary greatly with the weather. The era of a plan that was a blueprint for development came to an end with the oil price shock of the 1970s. Nevertheless, tools for coordinating the various factors that go into agricultural development remain essential equipment for the economists concerned.

Steps in planning

Seven steps may be distinguished in effective planning. These are:

1 Estimation of available resources.
2 Appraisal of current trends.
3 Projection of expected demand.
4 Projection of expected production.
5 Setting targets.
6 Establishment of projects and measures to achieve these targets.
7 Evaluation and follow-up of the measures adopted.

The first five of these are preparatory. The sixth and seventh are the action steps and call for special attention. Let us look first at the preparatory steps.

Resource estimation This means acquiring a detailed knowledge of the farms of a country, the methods used, and the land, labour and livestock available. Factors which determine a farmer's response to price incentives such as nature of tenure, access to markets, degree of commercial interest, are also important. The planner must know the rural people and what determines their use of agricultural resources, including family and religious attitudes. If many farmers are illiterate and tradition-bound, the number of people capable of introducing changes and teaching new skills is important.

Current trends The next step is to determine present agricultural trends and what changes are needed. Are crop yields rising? Is fertiliser being used more widely every year? Trends resulting from normal economic activity provide a base from which to work. If food production is already increasing at a slightly higher rate than population, there may be no need to change present agricultural programmes. Often, however, measures must be taken to keep food production in pace. Cotton is a vital foreign exchange earner for Sudan. Examination of current trends in yield and output will show that yields have changed little. The trend in output corresponds to the area under irrigated cultivation. So the planner knows that substantial increases in cotton supplies depend on expanding the land area served by irrigation.

Expected demand Forecasting future demand needs is a further step in planning. This depends on the rate of growth of the population; of the movement from rural to urban areas; and the rise in personal income. These factors will bring changes in habits and tastes. Demand forecasts make use of food consumption surveys which obtain direct information from samples of the population which are representative of the different income strata. From such surveys, and experience in other countries with similar conditions, income and price elasticities for various foods are estimated.

The planner will also try to ensure that low income consumers can get a nutritionally adequate diet at prices they can afford. They should be able to choose between alternative satisfactory food combinations according to their cost. Where resources permit, school meals and price subsidies for special groups can be provided to ensure that children and other vulnerable population groups are adequately fed.

Expected production In estimating future agricultural production, planners use what they call input/output yardsticks. Thus, an additional hectare of land under irrigation might be expected to give an additional 1.5 tonnes of cotton in Sudan, for example. In another situation the application of one extra tonne of fertiliser could be assumed to yield x tonnes of maize and so on. Naturally, such yardsticks have to be determined separately for different crops and soil and climatic conditions. They will also differ between the traditional and commercial sectors in many tropical countries.

Target setting This means establishing, for example, the number of irrigation wells to be installed; the quantity of improved seeds to be distributed; the area of land to be reclaimed within the period of the plan. Together with these targets go estimates of the materials and other inputs required and the probable expenditure. These will be subsidiary targets within overall targets for total agricultural output and farmer's income.

Setting target is largely a matter of bringing into balance current and projected levels of consumption and production; exports and imports. This is illustrated in Table 5.5 which relates to a model country with a population of 10 million in 1986. This is expected to increase by 15% over the seven years 1986–93. The target is to feed this population and also meet a 20% increase in consumption. Projection of current trends to 1993 shows exports to be much the same, but levels of demand which, in relation to domestic production and imports, leave a substantial gap for a number of products. In the case of milk products this amounts to 88 000 tonnes even after allowing for a doubling of imports. To avoid a reduction in individual consumption, domestic production must expand to cover the expected deficit. This would call for an annual rate of increase in production of 5.5%, as shown in the final column of the table, as against the expected rate of 2.6%. For oilseed and coffee,

Table 5.5 Calculation of agricultural production targets in a six-year development plan, 1987–92

Commodity	Annual average over base period, 1984–86 (tonnes × 10³)				Projections for 1992 (tonnes × 10³)						Annual rate of increase in production (%)	
					Demand			Supply				
	Consumption	Exports	Imports	Production	Domestic	Exports	Total	Imports	Production	Supply gap or excess	Projected	Target
Millet	800			800	960		960		900	60	1.7	2.6
Wheat	200		200		248		248	248				
Rice	300	50	200	150	378	50	428	100	200	128	4.2	11.8
Root crops	150			150	180		180		173	7	2.1	2.6
Sugar	150		120	30	195		195	100	50	45	7.6	17.9
Pulses	250			250	310		310		290	20	2.1	3.1
Vegetables	160			160	210		210		190	20	2.5	4.0
Fruits	150		20	130	207	23	230		160	70	3.0	8.5
Meat	30		5	25	44		44	5	30	9	2.6	6.6
Eggs	10			10	14		14		14		4.9	4.9
Fish	30		5	25	41		41	5	30	6	2.6	5.4
Milk products	400		50	350	608		608	100	420	88	2.6	5.5
Oilseeds	40	300		340	54	300	354		390	+36	1.6	0.2
Tea	5	40		45	7	43	50		50		1.5	1.5
Coffee	3	40		43	4	40	44		48	+4	1.6	0.3
Cotton	15	3	13	5	21	3	24	13	8	3	6.9	11.9

the continuation of present trends was expected to result in a surplus, given the absorptive capacity of export markets at present prices.

Plan implementation

Plans are implemented by the creation of incentives that will encourage independent enterprises to act in accordance with the plan. They can also be helped to do this by the removal of obstacles, the strengthening of supporting services and by direct public investment in projects to provide irrigation and piped water; and to clear new land, build roads and the like.

Measures and projects that may be used to implement an agricultural plan are set out in the first column of Table 5.6. The second column shows how long they take to come into effect. Some indication of the investment, current government expenditure and administrative servicing requirements of these measures and projects are given in the subsequent columns. Thus large-scale irri-

gation, provision of fertilisers and mechanisation need most foreign exchange. Domestic investment is almost always needed, though much of this can be provided by farmers and local labour if there is some incentive. Good administrative support is almost always essential.

Many of the measures listed in Table 5.6 help each other and give their best results only when combined. Thus, fertilisers, improved seeds, credit, marketing and extension should also be available to get the most out of an investment in irrigation. This is a strong argument for beginning development on a limited scale and expanding as resources permit.

Taking up too many long-term projects at once can mean a long wait for a return on the capital committed while scarce foreign exchange may have to be used to import food. Projects to meet urgent production requirements would be: extend the use of fertilisers, of improved seeds and of measures to protect crops; set up local irrigation and drainage

Table 5.6 Measures and projects to implement agricultural development plans

Project or measure	Period needed for implementation	Investment requirement			Current government expenditure requirement	Administrative requirement	
		Foreign exchange	Domestic capital	Labour		Organisational network	Skilled personnel
Extend irrigation: large scale	long	high	high	high	low	medium	high (or foreign)
small scale	short	low	medium	low?	low	medium	low
Development of new land: by government	long	medium	high	low	low	medium	medium (or foreign)
by private farmers	short	low	low		low		
Land reform	long				compensation?	high	
Land settlement	long	medium	high	low	high	high	high
Improve feeder roads	short	low or nil	medium	high	medium-low		low
Increase fertiliser use	short	high	medium	low	low subsidies	high (non-government)	low
Increase use of improved seeds	short	nil	low	low	medium	(non-government)	
Strengthen extension services	medium-short	low	medium	low	high	high	high
Improve agricultural education	long	medium	medium	low	high	low	high (or foreign)
Improve marketing systems	short	low	medium	low	low	high (non-government)	medium (non-government)
Improve access to credit	medium		high		medium	high (non-government)	high (non-government)
Stabilisation of farm prices	medium-short		high		medium	high	high

works to make full use of water already available; and improve transport, marketing, storage and processing.

At all stages there must be a clear incentive to the farmer. Input supplies and technical services will not be fully utilised unless farmers consider it profitable to do so and are able to use them at the right time. Lack of attention to this can result in irrigation water running to waste; farm machinery rusting in idleness; or fertilisers lying unused or applied to different crops from those intended.

Not all agricultural planning goals can be reached by financial incentives and voluntary cooperation. Compulsion is necessary for land reform, for the mobilisation of savings through taxation, and establishing a unified system of export quality control,

177

Fig. 5.6 'You have been trained to tell me how to solve this problem.'

for example. Experience in China and elsewhere shows that for most agricultural production and marketing, incentive policies are the most effective.

Planning does not finish with establishing measures and projects. Progress should be monitored continuously and the effects evaluated. This is needed to pinpoint causes of delay and avoid waste. Follow-up action may be needed to hasten implementation.

Project appraisal

We have seen that the establishment and financing of projects is an important means of implementing plans. Such projects must be sound and realistic. They may originate from a resource survey; for example ground water reserves may be discovered that could be tapped by wells and pumps. A project may arise from an evident bottle-neck; in Himachal Pradesh in India, for instance, the widespread planting of apple trees created a need for transport, storage and marketing facilities to deal with their output. In contrast are those projects which are thought up quickly in response to offers of aid and credits, or to attract short-term support to a local politician.

There are three golden rules in formulating a project. The first is to ensure that all the factors necessary for its success are taken into account from the beginning. This means that an irrigation project, for example, should cover not only dams and canals, but also channels to and onto farms, land levelling and drainage, training in irrigated agriculture, and, if necessary, access roads, credit and marketing arrangements. The second is to carry out careful pre-investment studies. The third is to build in flexibility.

When the scope of the project has been determined, five main aspects must then be taken into account.

Technical feasibility Have all alternatives been considered? Is there need for the project at all? For example, could better dry-farming techniques and moisture conservation increase output just as much as irrigation? Are the methods, design and equipment proposed the best for the purpose? Are the cost estimates realistic and can the successive phases of the project be carried out in the time allowed?

Economic viability Does the technical solution chosen offer the highest economic and social returns of all the alternatives that are technically and financially feasible?

Financial Are the necessary funds available? Will the project be able to meet its financial obligations when it is in operation? For example, will farmers have sufficient income to cover repayments and interest on a loan?

Administration Will the administrative structure proposed for the project and its staff be adequate to keep the project on schedule and manage it efficiently? Will inter-departmental rivalries be an obstacle and if so can the coordination machinery proposed ensure an organised flow of decisions and an allocation of responsibility within the chain of command?

Commercial What are the arrangements for buying materials for the project? Where they will come from? How they will be paid for? How will the output of the project be sold?

To formulate a project that is technically sound, has a high, economic return and is within the resources of a developing country to finance and manage, inevitably calls for some compromise.

The following example is taken from the recommendations of the Indian Agricultural Finance Corporation. It is a guide to the formulation of a project to pump water for irrigation from a river.

(a) Describe the source of river water available for the project; the quantity of water available; the periods when it is available and its suitability for irrigation.

(b) Describe and map the fields to be supplied, showing the relevant pump houses.

(c) Indicate the total quantity of water to be lifted, the number of pumping units to be established and the horsepower of the units.

(d) Describe the existing terrain of the fields and work out the cost of levelling and constructing the required main and field channels. There should be irrigation and drainage channels for each field.

(e) Enumerate the individual holdings within the proposed project area, with survey numbers and the area of each holding. Indicate the land which must be acquired for pump houses or channels and the agreements to be made with each farmer according to whether they are owners or tenants.

(f) Enclose a copy of the permission obtained from the appropriate government agency for utilising the river water at the points indicated in the project.

(g) Get agricultural experts to draw up a cropping plan for the area, showing the desirable crop rotations.

(h) Assess the cost of the project. Take into account the cost of the following:
preliminaries
land acquisition
road works
main channel and field channels

pump and other machinery
levelling
cost of power provision
pump house
other items, pipes, etc.
The sum of these will give the total capital outlay.

(i) Estimate running costs per year:
electricity, petrol and oil
staff salaries and allowances
annual maintenance of buildings, machines, channels, etc.
depreciation
interest on borrowed capital
other expenses
The sum of these will give the total running costs.

(j) Assess the time needed for the completion of the project as phased.

(k) Estimate the annual return according to the project cropping plan. For this it is necessary to assess certain values as detailed.

Production per year:

Crop	Quantity produced	Price	Value
Maize	y tonnes	x per tonne	$x \times y$

Cost of production:

Crop	Cost per hectare	Area	Total cost
Maize	m	n ha	$m \times n$

Net return = $\$(xy - mn)$

Average net return per hectare = $\$ \dfrac{(xy - mm)}{n}$

Average net return per hectare before the project = $\$p$

Net additional income per hectare as a result of the

project = $\dfrac{\$(xy - mn)}{n} - p$

(l) Make reports on public works or other government departments concerned with the project to help assess its technical feasibility.

(m) Detail the arrangements proposed for provision of loan funds in order to assess the financial feasibility of the project.

(n) Carry out the following preliminary work:
Obtain demarcation and establishment of the project area.
Obtain farmers' individual consents.

Make arrangements for the acquisition of the land.
Decide on the courses of the channels.
Settle disputes over river rights.

(o) Report on the agency executing the project. Indicate its solvency, ability and local standing.

(p) Organise a method of disbursement to fit the phasing of the programme and arrange for the control of payments.

(q) Organise a method for the repayment of capital, working capital and interest. Detail the amounts of repayments and the time period that they will cover.

(r) Assess the security potential of the land for mortgage purposes, including the value and the possibility of prior commitment from registration offices. Secure the commitment of pumpsets and other machinery as collateral.

(s) Make a note of any other details that must be covered.

Network analysis

The above set of guidelines is one of many available to those responsible for preparing development projects and plans. Nevertheless many projects produce results only slowly. The reasons lie in lack of government commitment, of administrative follow-up and of skilled personnel. Sometimes priorities are wrong; large-scale irrigation projects may be preferred even though they are out of balance with farm practice and market incen-

tives. A common trap is to believe that planning is a solution in itself and to neglect implementation.

Use of network analysis can be helpful. It enables those responsible for project implementation to focus at the right time on stages that must be completed before others can proceed. It reduces the likelihood of delays and the waste of resources. For a particular project element the following questions need to be asked:

(a) What other activities must be finished before this one can begin?

(b) What other activities cannot be started until this one has been finished?

(c) What activities can be carried out at the same time as this one?

The sequential relationship of project activities is illustrated in Fig. 5.7. It represents a situation where work on a pumping station for an irrigation project cannot begin until there is an access road. Irrigation ditches can be dug while the road is being made, but laying pipes depends on the road to bring them in.

The role of an agricultural planning department now seems to be to:

(a) provide a place where representatives of official bodies and of various interest groups can meet to discuss policies and proposals;

(b) help politicians mobilise public support for their programmes;

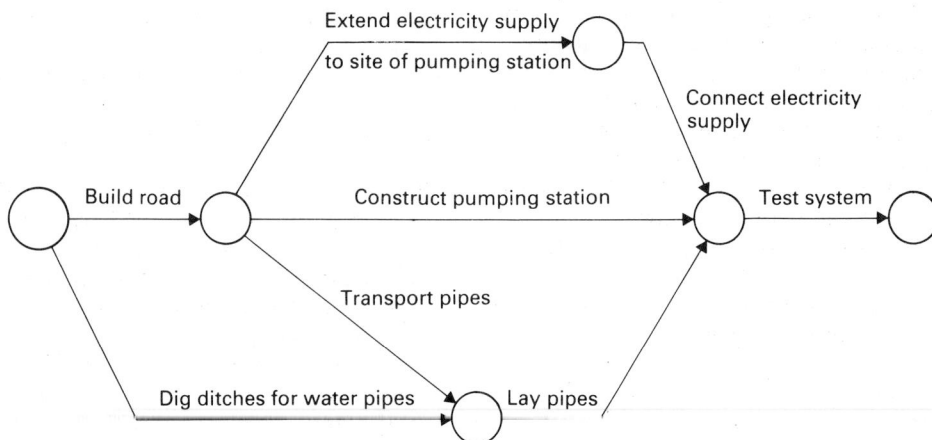

Fig. 5.7 Sequence of activities in an irrigation project

(c) help coordinate budgeting for development programmes and evaluation of their performance.

To do this it must keep up to date on what is happening on the ground, and on ways whereby independent enterprises can be induced to act in accordance with government programmes.

International trade

Through trade, countries can obtain goods that they need but which they do not produce themselves. Most tropical countries have to import a wide range of equipment and machinery needed for economic development. They also want to import cars, clothes, food and other consumption items which raise the level of living and can be obtained at lower cost from other countries.

Production for sale in foreign markets can also be a major source of domestic agricultural income and stimulus for productive enterprises. Table 5.4 (p. 158) shows the share of agricultural products in the total export trade of a fairly representative set of tropical countries. As mentioned previously, agricultural products provide a large proportion of export earnings. It will also be noted that the bulk of these exports are represented by only one or two products.

Should a country expect to grow through continuing to specialise or would it be better to diversify and try new export lines? Though present prices and trade arrangements favour certain agricultural products, can this be relied on in the long term? Does the short-term instability of prices of agricultural exports interfere with development efforts? These are important policy questions which will be discussed in this section.

Overall prospects of increased export earnings from agricultural products are not very favourable for the tropical countries. The main reasons are:

(a) In high income countries which import freely, consumer requirements of established tropical exports, such as tea and bananas, are already met; they would not buy much more even if the price were lower.
(b) In the centrally planned countries such as the USSR, consumption of tropical products is still below what might be expected from the level of personal incomes, but their governments will not allocate foreign exchange for larger imports.
(c) Agricultural raw materials of the tropical countries face competition from synthetic substitutes, particularly fibres such as cotton, jute, sisal and wool, and rubber.
(d) Domestic agriculture in the high income and centrally planned countries frequently benefits from protective and support measures in producing edible oils, sugar, cotton, rice, etc. that could be imported from the tropics.
(e) Processed agricultural products are subject to import duties that tend to rise with the degree of processing, i.e. with the value added. This makes it harder for a tropical country to add to the value of its raw materials by putting its lower-cost labour to work on initial processing.

A major change in agricultural export prospects for tropical countries depends on adjustments in agricultural production and processing in the developed countries. These could come via reduced price support and import protection of products such as rice and sugar and lowering tariffs on vegetable oil and similar processed imports. As a group, the developing countries have pressed for measures to change the terms of trade for their agricultural exports; that is, to raise their value as against that of the manufactured products which must be imported from the developed countries. This resulted in the establishment of the United Nations Conference on Trade and Development (UNCTAD) machinery — but concrete benefits are slow to come. Meanwhile under the Lomé Convention, many tropical countries linked historically to Europe receive EEC import quotas for certain products at preferential rates of duty. Similarly, the USA affords entry privileges to some countries of the Caribbean.

Export promotion

Arguments about the terms of trade and the distribution of gains from technical progress between developed and developing countries, plus 'elasticity pessimism' may have distracted some policy makers from more immediate and practical measures. At any one time, the markets for agricultural products from the developing countries may seem adequately supplied. Even so, opportunities keep opening up.

Over the period 1959–68, Taiwan's export earnings from canned fruit and vegetables rose from $8 million to $88 million.

Rising consumer incomes in Europe have favoured imports of out-of-season vegetables from Kenya and Senegal. Imports from tropical countries of flowers and ornamental plants have also grown rapidly. Cassava chips for livestock feed, unknown until the 1970s, have earned annually more foreign exchange for Thailand than rice.

Individual exporting countries should not hold back from beginning or expanding production of a commodity for export simply because it is currently in surplus on world markets or seems likely to become so. The surplus is likely to include supplies from countries with relatively high absolute or opportunity costs of production. If a particular country believes it can compete from a strong cost position, it may well be fully justified in going for a larger share of the existing market. Restraint of production by any one country to avoid or to reduce apparent surpluses on the world market is not generally in its own long term interest.

The tropical countries may well miss opportunities to increase their export earnings if they do not make a concentrated effort to identify suitable openings and begin to produce and market for them. The following observations by an Israeli delegate to an FAO meeting are very much to the point.

The export business usually begins with the growers producing varieties on the basis of agro-technical aspects and expected yield and returns. When it comes to the harvesting period, the grower may be approached by merchants or he must find one who is willing to accept and pack his produce. The goods are then shipped to the European markets that are usually flooded with fresh and processed merchandise, resulting in a constant pressure on prices. Sometimes the return does not cover the growing costs. In consequence, the unhappy farmers complain to their governments who may approach FAO or one of the other international organisations and finally are invited to a commodity group meeting or to a technical conference. Is this a way to improve the situation or is all this like talking about the weather?

Fig. 5.8 The effect of sales promotion

182

In contrast to focusing mainly on a production system that achieves the optimum yield at lower cost, countries must focus specifically on exporting and apply to it analysis, organisation, control and planning. The following essential steps have been set out.

Generate customers In Europe, for example, there is plenty of basic food available. To promote sales of imported foods a special drive is necessary. This was applied to oranges, bananas and tomatoes and they are now a part of the daily European menu. 'Buyer persuasion' is first priority. Low prices help, but the creation of a 'buying climate' at higher prices is better for the producer.

Reaching the customer In the United Kingdom, for example, there are 300 fruit and vegetable importers, 2 500 wholesalers, 3 000 supermarkets, and more than 40 000 specialised retailers, with street dealers in addition. All are influential links between producer and consumer. So it is essential to know them well. To convince retailers to stock avocado pears, the Israeli export organisation sent agents to shops as customers asking for avocados.

Organising production, with internal and external marketing as one coordinated process For success in competitive exports, research and development, extension, production, marketing, promotion and finance must be coordinated under one management. Whether it is a state marketing board or private export company, it must have full government support. Production planning covers: the varieties required, cultivation methods, plant protection needs, harvesting methods, post-harvest treatment, grading and packing, capital needs and profitability. Pricing calls for a conscious policy with four stages of decision-making: setting the first price of a product for the coming season; changing the price according to demand and supply on the market; responding to the actions of competitors; and considering the relationship with other products in the same sales line. These steps have been outlined for fruits and vegetables; they are equally applicable to other fresh and processed tropical products.

Some initiatives to orient agriculture to export markets have been criticised for depriving lower income rural people of their traditional foods. This can occur, in the short run, during the process of change. However, farmers who acquire new technology to produce for export tend also to become more efficient in growing food crops. Eventually, rising cash incomes provide more employment for those who at first feel disadvantaged.

Stabilisation mechanisms

Much consideration has been given to ways of limiting fluctuations in the prices of tropical export products. Sharp fluctuations can be very upsetting to development plans when earnings from a product have a major role in a country's economy. Only where exports originate from a limited number of countries and there are no close substitutes is there much scope for managing prices by a joint control over sales. Coffee, cocoa, tea and some tropical fruits such as bananas, offer the best prospects. Even here if stabilisation meant a net increase in prices to the consumer, then demand might be diverted to other products. For many other tropical exports such as sisal, rubber and oilseeds, there are synthetic substitutes. A period of high prices can motivate technical innovations that cannot be reversed. Prices will go down, but the markets for the displaced products may not be recovered.

The second condition under which exporters of tropical products can benefit from a low elasticity of demand in their main import markets and 'earn more by selling less' is when they maintain a united front. They must be able to coordinate their price and sales policies, and to meet such competition as may come from current or potential producers outside their own group. Most systems of collaboration to restrict sales eventually break down over some divergence of interest. Some of the participating countries gain more than others. The working of the International Coffee Agreement, has been attributed to the dominant sales position of Brazil with its immense power to retaliate against an exporter which exceeded its quota.

In practice, the problem of unstable prices for major exports may be something of a myth. International agreements are hard to negotiate and operate. This can mean that the prospective benefits are too small to attract the governments concerned. Commodity prices must retain some flexibility if they are to promote an efficient allocation of resources.

Machinery to cushion the effect on producers of short term fluctuations in export prices is easily established by the governments concerned. The use of marketing boards and reserve funds to moderate the effects of fluctuating prices on a domestic economy was discussed in Chapter 3. Export taxes that vary inversely with export market prices can also be used. When shifts in the price of a major export persist to the point that they can no longer be considered temporary, a government may vary the exchange rate for transactions in that commodity. This is a powerful means of stabilising the domestic price while enabling exporters to remain competitive.

The risk with these devices is that export producers will not, over the years, receive as high an average price as if they bore the low prices along with the high. Production may be discouraged and a country's market share decline. This happened to some West African cocoa producers *vis-à-vis* Malaysia during the 1970s, and to West African groundnut growers *vis-à-vis* palm oil and soya.

Loans may be obtained to compensate for a sudden fall in export earnings, though this will increase a country's debt. Food aid can save foreign exchange where a crop failure has led to a need for extra imports. The disposal of surpluses through food aid has also helped to stabilise world markets for products included in such aid.

External aid

The scope, range of sources and value of external aid to the developing countries grew steadily over the decades to 1981. Governments of geopolitical interest had perfected techniques of bargaining for such aid. The richer countries had accepted, on grounds of conscience and their own long term interests, that they should share their wealth with the less well off. A United Nations resolution had set them the goal of 1% of national income per year. The early 1980s saw some shift of attitude. Funds became scarcer in the donor countries. 'Aid fatigue' set in, with increasing scepticism as to the capacity of international bureaucrats to solve other people's problems. It is all the more important, therefore, for the student of agricultural economics

and marketing to know the scope and implications of various forms of aid and how they can be used to the best advantage.

How far is aid effective?
Clearly, the mere transfer of capital to the developing countries is insufficient. The range of factors — organisational, managerial, political, psychological and educational — involved in the development process has already been indicated. Professor P. T. Bauer maintained that:

> If a society cannot develop without external gifts, it will not develop with them. If the required conditions other than capital are present, capital will be generated locally or supplied commercially from abroad, to government or to business, so that aid is unnecessary.

Material progress requires modernisation of the mind; this is inhibited by many institutions and policies in less developed countries. External aid should be directed specifically to the removal of such obstacles. According to this view most multilateral and bilateral aid is far too subservient to the preferences of current governments and influential individuals in the developing countries. These people often support those very attitudes that it is essential to change. Financial assistance should therefore be a lever to secure institutional and policy changes, such as the implementation of land reform or of birth control including free contraceptive pills and abortion services. The argument that these latter measures are intended to keep down the poor is misleading. The countries where population control has been most effective — China, Hungary, Japan and Sweden — are among those where 'the poor' are best off.

After decades in dissent, in the 1980s Professor Bauer received his peerage. His longstanding political opponent, Professor Balogh, with his slogan 'Trade not aid' was — on this issue — in a measure of agreement. It accords with comparative advantage and allowing market forces to lead. The analysis sponsored by the aid donors (*Does aid work?* R. Cassen, 1986, Oxford University Press) agrees that too much aid went to the public sector and was wasted. However, it developed the high-yielding varieties behind the 'Green Revolution' and supported its implementation. It created a rural road network in Malawi and elsewhere; it helped various countries through crises; it trained large numbers of professionals for the future. The most trenchant criticism is of proliferating aid agencies, for example installing 18 different makes of pump in the water system of Kenya, and making 360 visits in one year to government ministries in Burkina Faso.

Considerations in acceptance of aid

For any kind of aid that must eventually be paid back, present benefits must be weighed carefully against future costs. Much of the foreign exchange earnings of tropical countries is now committed to repay past loans. Their governments must wish that earlier borrowings had been pared down to essentials. If not cleared, these loans will remain an obstacle to trading relations and further assistance.

Aid in kind also needs careful consideration. Processing plants, storage, transport and other physical equipment must be adapted to local conditions; high operating costs because of difficulties in raw materials supply and in marketing may involve the government in continuing subsidies. Also to be taken into account are future foreign exchange costs of spare parts and supplies, and whether such aid will increase or reduce employment. Assurance of maintenance and providing spare parts over a 10-year period should be an essential element of such aid agreements.

Foreign experts and fellowships for nationals to study in other countries can help meet immediate needs for qualified personnel. There is much wastage, however, whilst they adjust to local conditions. Practical training under local conditions of a large number of potential technicians and managers can be more useful. They must then learn by on-the-job experience. They will still have to battle against traditional attitudes and established interests. For this, the backing of their own leaders is critical.

Fertiliser, pesticides or other agricultural inputs may be available free or on concessional terms. They can be expected to lead to increases in domestic production far exceeding their cost. A problem to be foreseen is financing continuing imports when farmers have become accustomed to use them, and aid supplies are no longer available. Again, a long term aid perspective is vital.

Food aid   This has developed in response to the complementarity between the surpluses generated by support policies for farmers in Europe and the USA, and continuing food shortages in the developing countries. The concern of traditional food exporting countries like Australia and Canada that food aid should not prejudice their commercial markets was met by agreement on the terms of its use, i.e. for:

(a) emergencies — famine due to exceptional drought, national disasters;
(b) defined development projects — as food for work on the construction of roads, schools, hospitals, tree planting, etc. and for participants in health improvement and training programmes — in countries lacking foreign exchange for commercial imports.

On this basis, grain, milk powder, processed fish, etc. to the value of $3 000 million was provided in food aid through the World Food Programme and bilaterally by the USA, EEC, New Zealand, etc. in 1981. With food surpluses mounting in the donor countries during the 1980s, interpretation of development has widened. Under Operation Flood the WFP provided 126 000 tonnes of dried skim milk and 42 000 tonnes of butter oil for dairy development in India. The proceeds of sale of these products worth $106 million recombined as milk was used to pay for dairy and transport equipment, milk cattle breeding and supplementing of local feed supplies. The project was continued and enlarged by the EEC. Extreme foreign exchange shortage alone has been accepted as grounds for food aid to Bangladesh and Grenada.

Food aid carries the risk that its availability to developing countries will slow down efforts to expand food production domestically. Consumers become accustomed to types of food that cannot be grown in the country; dependence on food imports is perpetuated. Certainly rice growers in West Africa have complained that the prices they obtained fell sharply when supplies imported on concessional terms came onto the market. A private dairy in Bengal which was backed by non-governmental aid was undercut in Culcutta by dairy products leaking from nutritional food aid.

These risks are alleviated where recipient governments can:

(a) Keep the market price of food imported under aid programmes above that of domestic production which it might replace. Cash proceeds from sale of the aid food would be available for development uses.

(b) Confine aid food released free or at token prices for work, nutritional or other special programmes, to types and quantities that truly would be consumed by the intended beneficiaries and their families.

Summary

The theme of this chapter has been the nature of development, the factors which hold it back, and ways in which it can be accelerated. Economic growth is conceived in terms of goods and services or it can be expressed in terms of money. Development includes much more than economic growth: access to education; social and cultural advance; a pleasing environment; and all that goes into the quality of living.

The process of growth and development has stimulated much thought and analysis. Each theory tends to be replaced by another as conditions change. For instance, Malthusians tend to appear during periods when world food production lags behind the rate of increase in population. In the 1980s, with global supplies secure, the focus was on enterprise, growth and the generation of employment.

In most tropical countries, agricultural development is closely linked with the development of their economies as a whole. The most critical needs are for more capital and better management, together with market conditions that favour expansion of production. The political environment is also a determining factor. There must be leadership and drive to change adverse social structures and traditions, and to mobilise human abilities. At the same time it should not shackle initiative or deny expression to new ideas or sound experience.

Finding the best balance between labour and technology for particular sets of production and marketing conditions is important. Long term and indirect benefits of changes should be taken into account as well as the more immediate results. Land reform calls for a similar approach: structures designed to satisfy immediate claims may not be economically viable in the long term. Simple but effective credit institutions that reach the smaller farmers are essential if they are to participate in the modernisation process. Convenience in obtaining loans generally means more to such farmers than a very low interest charge.

Coordination of overall policies for development, current financial management and longer term investment projects is important. Planning units should be oriented to providing up-to-date economic information, promoting initiatives and investments that are complementary, and securing the benefits of potential internal economies. Most effective in policy implementation is a price incentive for the farmers and other enterprises concerned.

The sale of agricultural products on export markets brings cash incomes to farmers and earns valuable foreign exchange for a country. Such markets are likely to remain competitive. They are best won by production and marketing systems that are integrated from planting through final sale. International agreements help stabilise prices for some major tropical products. But they are difficult to achieve and maintain. The prices paid to producers for export products can be stabilised by measures taken by individual governments.

Financial pressures have induced various countries to seek an institutional and policy frame that is more self-sustaining. There is also growing awareness of the need for environmental protection.

Target chasing by international and bilateral aid agencies jealous of their independence has left its mark in overlapping institutions, white elephant processing plants and unproductive debts. Large scale capital assistance is still needed by many tropical countries if they are to maintain a tolerable pace of development. It is important that they use wisely the various forms it may take.

Issues for discussion

1 What are the main indicators of levels of living? How far is access to capital the critical factor for agricultural development in the Tropics?

2 What are the determining factors in the development of good managers? How is your country placed in this regard?

3 How far do recent theories of growth explain the difference in level between one tropical country and another, and between the tropical countries and more developed countries? Is the concept of 'balanced growth' an admission of failure to find a satisfactory explanation of the process?

4 In what order of importance should the various contributions of agriculture to development be ranked?

5 What will be the main development factor for agriculture in your country over the next 20 years?

6 Is it more advantageous for your country to earn additional foreign exchange through agricultural exports or to reduce its foreign exchange outlays by import substitution?

7 How far does agriculture in your country contribute capital to industrial and commercial development? Would it be advantageous for it to contribute more or less? If a change in the balance of contributions seems desirable, by what means would you bring it about?

8 How far in your country does domestic industry provide the things that agricultural people buy? How far does agriculture supply the raw material needs of your industries?

9 Has your country undertaken a 'structural adjustment'? What were the main points? Assess the impact on agriculture.

10 What are the main environmental issues in agricultural development in your country?

11 What changes in agriculture would contribute most to employment in your country? Would these changes be advantageous in the long term?

12 How far do traditional attitudes impede desirable agricultural development in your country? What measures would be most effective in changing these attitudes?

13 In the areas you know well, is social discontent stimulating development or impeding it? What measures would be most conducive to directing such discontent along constructive lines?

14 Is your village keeping up with others in adopting new agricultural methods? What are the factors that hold back its progress?

15 Where do you want to work when you finish your education? In what order do you place the factors that will determine your decision?

16 What strategy of development do you recommend for the rural areas you know best and for what reasons?

17 Is participation in rural decision-making important for the people you know? Would their participation result in decisions more favourable to development?

18 How far do the customary systems of land tenure, in your area, obstruct efficient farming? What changes would you propose?

19 What arrangements would be most instrumental in enabling the livestock owned by nomadic groups in your country to become more productive?

20 Under what conditions is a crop rent tenancy more advantageous than a cash rent tenancy? Under what conditions is a cash rent tenancy more advantageous than a crop rent tenancy? If both are used in your country how do they compare as to productivity of the land and income to the tenant?

21 What kind of land reform would you recommend for your home area? What do you estimate to be the cost per hectare of carrying out such reform? How would this compare with the expected benefits?

22 Do farmers in your area have difficulty in obtaining credit to buy agricultural inputs such as fertiliser, at the time they need it? If so, why? What changes in the credit system would you propose?

23 Assess the relative importance in your country of marketing enterprises, financial institutions and the government in mobilising savings for use in agriculture.

24 Has agricultural planning made a significant contribution to development in your country? What have been its successes and failures? To what factors do you attribute these?

25 Describe a major agricultural project that has been implemented in your country. What has it achieved? What have been the benefits and the cost to date? What changes would you have made to the original plan?

26 What kinds of exports offer the best prospects for your country? If they include agricultural products, what steps would be necessary to fulfil these prospects?

27 What kinds of external aid have been most useful to your country over the last ten years? Has some of this aid had negative effects? If so, why?

28 What kind of aid would be most helpful to your country over the next ten years?

Further reading

Abbott, J. C (1988) *Agricultural processing for development*, Gower Publishing Co., Aldershot.

Bates, R. H. (1981) *Markets and states in tropical Africa: the political basis of agricultural policies*, University of California Press, Berkeley.

Bauer, P. T. (1981) *Equality, the third world and economic delusion*, Weidenfeld and Nicolson, London.

Benjamin, M. P. (1981) *Investment projects in agriculture*, Longman, London.

Cassen, R. and associates (1986) *Does aid work?*, Oxford University Press, Oxford.

Cernia, M. M. (ed.) (1986) *Putting people first*, Oxford University Press, New York.

Cheung, S. W. S. (1969) *Theory of share tenancy*, University of Chicago Press, Chicago.

Clark, C. and **Haswell, M.** (1970) *The economics of subsistence agriculture*, Macmillan, London.

Dorner, P. (1972) *Land reform and economic development*, Penguin Books, Baltimore.

FAO (1985) *The world market for tropical horticultural products*, FAO, Rome.

Hayami, Y. and **Ruttan, V. W.** (1985) *Agricultural development: An international perspective*, Johns Hopkins University Press, Baltimore.

Howell, J. (ed.) (1980) *Borrowers and lenders: rural financial markets and institutions in developing countries*, Overseas Development Institute, London.

Little, I. M. D. (1982) *Development theory, policy and international relations*, Basic Books Inc., New York.

Meier, G. M. and **Seers, D.** (eds.) (1984) *Pioneers in development*, Oxford University Press, New York.

Mellor, J. W., Delgado, C. L. and **Blackie, M. J.** (eds.) (1987) *Accelerating food production in sub-Saharan Africa*, Johns Hopkins University Press, Baltimore.

Mollett, J. K. (1984) *Planning for agricultural development*, Croom Helm, Beckenham.

Price Gittinger, J. (1982) *Economic analysis of agricultural projects*, 2nd ed., Johns Hopkins University Press, Baltimore.

Reynolds, L. G. (1986) *Economic growth in the third world: an introduction*, Yale University Press, New Haven.

Schluter, M. (1984) *Constraints on Kenya's food and beverage exports*, International Food Policy Research Institute, Washington.

Schumpeter, J. (1961) *The theory of economic development*, Oxford University Press, Oxford.

Southworth, H. and **Johnston, B.** (eds.) (1967) *Agricultural development and economic growth*, Cornell University Press, Ithaca.

Timmer, C. P., Falcon, W. P. and **Pearson, S. R.** (1983) *Food policy analysis*, Johns Hopkins University Press, Baltimore.

World Bank (1984) *Toward sustained development in sub-Saharan Africa*, World Bank, Washington.

Appendix 1

Discounting table

Present value of a future lump sum: $PV = \dfrac{A}{(1 + R)^n}$

PV: present value
A: unit amount
R: rate of compound interest per period
n: number of periods

Period				Interest rate, R				
n	4%	5%	6%	8%	10%	12%	14%	15%
1	0.9615	0.9524	0.9434	0.9259	0.9091	0.8929	0.8772	0.8699
2	0.9246	0.9070	0.8900	0.8573	0.8264	0.7977	0.7896	0.7561
3	0.8890	0.8638	0.8396	0.7938	0.7513	0.7118	0.6750	0.6575
4	0.8548	0.8227	0.7921	0.7350	0.6830	0.6535	0.5971	0.5717
5	0.8219	0.7835	0.7473	0.6806	0.6209	0.5674	0.5394	0.4972
6	0.7903	0.7462	0.7050	0.6302	0.5645	0.5966	0.4536	0.4323
7	0.7599	0.7107	0.6651	0.5835	0.5132	0.4323	0.3996	0.3759
8	0.7307	0.6768	0.6274	0.5403	0.4665	0.4039	0.3506	0.3269
9	0.7026	0.6446	0.5919	0.5002	0.4241	0.3606	0.3075	0.2843
10	0.6756	0.6139	0.5584	0.4632	0.3855	0.3220	0.2697	0.2472
11	0.6496	0.5847	0.5268	0.4289	0.3505	0.2875	0.2366	0.2149
12	0.6246	0.5568	0.4970	0.3971	0.3186	0.2367	0.2076	0.1869
13	0.6006	0.5303	0.4688	0.3677	0.2897	0.2292	0.1821	0.1625
14	0.5775	0.5051	0.4423	0.3405	0.2633	0.2046	0.1597	0.1418
15	0.5553	0.4810	0.4173	0.3152	0.2394	0.1827	0.1401	0.1229
16	0.5339	0.4581	0.3936	0.2919	0.2176	0.1631	0.1229	0.1069
17	0.5134	0.4363	0.3714	0.2703	0.1978	0.1456	0.1078	0.0929
18	0.4936	0.4155	0.3503	0.2502	0.1799	0.1300	0.0945	0.0808
19	0.4746	0.3957	0.3305	0.2317	0.1635	0.1161	0.0829	0.0703
20	0.4564	0.3769	0.3118	0.2145	0.1486	0.1037	0.0726	0.0611
21	0.4388	0.3589	0.2942	0.1987	0.1351	0.0926	0.0639	0.0531
22	0.4220	0.3418	0.2775	0.1839	0.1228	0.0826	0.0560	0.0462
23	0.4057	0.3256	0.2618	0.1703	0.1117	0.0738	0.0491	0.0402
24	0.3901	0.3101	0.2470	0.1577	0.1015	0.0659	0.0431	0.0349
25	0.3751	0.2959	0.2330	0.1460	0.0923	0.0588	0.0378	0.0304

Appendix 2

Compound interest table

Growth at compound interest $T = (1 + R)^n$

T: terminal value of one unit of original principal
R: rate of compound interest per period
n: number of periods

Period	Interest rate, R					
n	4%	5%	6%	8%	10%	15%
1	1.0400	1.0500	1.0600	1.0800	1.000	1.1500
2	1.0816	1.1025	1.1236	1.1664	1.2100	1.3225
3	1.1249	1.1576	1.1910	1.2597	1.3310	1.5209
4	1.1699	1.2155	1.2625	1.3605	1.4641	1.7490
5	1.2167	1.2763	1.3382	1.4693	1.6105	2.0114
6	1.2653	1.3401	1.4185	1.5869	1.7716	2.3131
7	1.3159	1.4071	1.5036	1.7138	1.9487	2.6600
8	1.3686	1.4775	1.5938	1.8509	2.1436	3.0590
9	1.4233	1.5513	1.6895	1.9990	2.3579	3.5179
10	1.4802	1.6289	1.7908	2.1589	2.5937	4.0456
11	1.5395	1.7103	1.8983	2.3316	2.8531	4.6524
12	1.6010	1.7959	2.0122	2.5182	3.1384	5.3502
13	1.6651	1.8856	2.1329	2.7196	3.4523	6.1528
14	1.7317	1.9799	2.2609	2.9372	3.7975	7.0757
15	1.8009	2.0798	2.3966	3.1722	4.1772	8.1371
16	1.8730	2.1829	2.5404	3.4259	4.5950	9.3576
17	1.9479	2.3290	2.6928	3.7000	5.0545	10.7613
18	2.0258	2.4066	2.8543	3.9960	5.5599	12.3754
19	2.1068	2.5270	3.0256	4.3157	6.1159	14.2318
20	2.1911	2.6533	3.2071	4.6601	6.7275	16.3665
21	2.2788	2.7860	3.3996	5.0338	7.4002	18.8215
22	2.3699	2.9253	3.6035	5.4365	8.1403	21.6447
23	2.4647	3.0715	3.8197	5.8714	8.9543	24.8915
24	2.5633	3.2251	4.0489	6.3912	9.8497	28.6252
25	2.6658	3.3864	4.2919	6.8485	10.8347	32.9169

Appendix 3

Annuity whose present value is 1: $A = \dfrac{R(1 + R)^n}{(1 + R)^n - 1}$

Annuity A, whose present value is 1 for a term of n periods at a compound rate of interest R per period
A: amount of annuity
R: rate of compound interest per period
n: number of periods

Period	Interest rate, R							
n	4%	5%	6%	8%	10%	12%	14%	15%
1	1.0400	1.0500	1.0600	1.0800	1.1000	1.1200	1.1400	1.1500
2	0.5302	0.5378	0.5454	0.5608	0.5762	0.5917	0.6073	0.6151
3	0.3603	0.3672	0.3741	0.3880	0.4021	0.4163	0.4307	0.4380
4	0.2755	0.2820	0.2886	0.3019	0.3155	0.3292	0.3432	0.3503
5	0.2246	0.2310	0.2374	0.2505	0.2638	0.2774	0.2913	0.2983
6	0.1908	0.1970	0.2034	0.2163	0.2296	0.2432	0.2572	0.2642
7	0.1666	0.1728	0.1791	0.1921	0.2054	0.2191	0.2332	0.2404
8	0.1485	0.1547	0.1610	0.1740	0.1874	0.2013	0.2156	0.2228
9	0.1345	0.1407	0.1470	0.1601	0.1736	0.1877	0.2022	0.2096
10	0.1233	0.1295	0.1359	0.1490	0.1627	0.1770	0.1917	0.1992
11	0.1141	0.1204	0.1268	0.1401	0.1540	0.1684	0.1834	0.1911
12	0.1066	0.1128	0.1193	0.1327	0.1468	0.1614	0.1767	0.1845
13	0.1001	0.1065	0.1130	0.1265	0.1408	0.1557	0.1712	0.1791
14	0.0947	0.1010	0.1076	0.1213	0.1357	0.1509	0.1666	0.1747
15	0.0899	0.0963	0.1030	0.1168	0.1315	0.1468	0.1628	0.1710
16	0.0858	0.0923	0.0990	0.1130	0.1278	0.1434	0.1596	0.1679
17	0.0822	0.0887	0.0954	0.1096	0.1247	0.1405	0.1569	0.1654
18	0.0790	0.0855	0.0924	0.1067	0.1219	0.1379	0.1546	0.1613
19	0.0761	0.0827	0.0896	0.1041	0.1195	0.1358	0.1527	0.1613
20	0.0736	0.0802	0.0872	0.1018	0.1175	0.1339	0.1510	0.1598
21	0.0713	0.0780	0.0850	0.0998	0.1156	0.1322	0.1495	0.1584
22	0.0692	0.0760	0.0830	0.0980	0.1140	0.1308	0.1483	0.1573
23	0.0673	0.0741	0.0813	0.0964	0.1126	0.1296	0.1472	0.1563
24	0.0656	0.0725	0.0797	0.0950	0.1113	0.1285	0.1463	0.1554
25	0.0640	0.0710	0.0782	0.0937	0.1102	0.1275	0.1455	0.1547

Index